CASINO STATE:
LEGALIZED GAMBLING IN CANADA

EDITED BY JAMES F. COSGRAVE AND
THOMAS R. KLASSEN

Casino State:

Legalized Gambling in Canada

UNIVERSITY OF TORONTO PRESS
Toronto Buffalo London

ISBN 978-0-8020-9688-3

Printed on acid-free paper

Library and Archives Canada Cataloguing in Publication

Casino state : legalized gambling in Canada / edited by James F. Cosgrave
and Thomas R. Klassen.

Includes bibliographical references and index.
ISBN 978-0-8020-9688-3

1. Gambling – Canada.   2. Gambling – Government policy – Canada.
3. Gambling – Social aspects – Canada.   I. Cosgrave, James F., 1959–
II. Klassen, Thomas R. (Thomas Richard), 1957–

HV6722.C3C38 2008   363.4'20971   C2008-905674-4

University of Toronto Press acknowledges the financial assistance to its
publishing program of the Canada Council for the Arts and the Ontario
Arts Council.

University of Toronto Press acknowledges the financial support for its
publishing activities of the Government of Canada through the Book
Publishing Industry Development Program (BPIDP).

For all Canadians and their families who haven't been so lucky

Contents

PART THREE: GOVERNMENTS AND GAMBLING POLICY

PART FOUR: GAMBLING AND SOCIAL ISSUES

Contributors

Kerry Badgley is an archivist at Library and Archives Canada and a sessional lecturer in the Department of History at Carleton University. He is the English-language editor of the *Journal of the Canadian Historical Association* and the author of *Ringing in the Common Love of Good: The United Farmers of Ontario, 1914–1926* (2000).

Colin S. Campbell is a criminologist at Douglas College, British Columbia, who has written extensively on Canadian gambling policy. He has previously edited two books: *Gambling in Canada: Golden Goose or Trojan Horse* (1989) and *Gambling in Canada: The Bottom Line* (1994). He is a co-author of a Law Commission report on legalized gambling, *The Legalization of Gambling in Canada* (2005).

James F. Cosgrave teaches in the Department of Sociology at Trent University. He has written on contemporary liberalized gambling as a cultural phenomenon, and on the state's role in gambling legitimation. He is the editor of *The Sociology of Risk and Gambling Reader* (2006).

Jeffrey L. Derevensky is a psychologist at McGill University who has published extensively in the fields of youth and problem gambling. He is a founder and co-director of the International Centre for Youth Gambling Problems and High-Risk Behaviours at McGill University.

Timothy F. Hartnagel is a professor emeritus in the Department of Sociology at the University of Alberta. He is a co-author of a Law Commission report on legalized gambling, *The Legalization of Gambling in Canada* (2005).

Thomas R. Klassen is an associate professor in the Department of Political Science, and the School of Public Policy and Administration, at York University and has written on the state's role in gambling expansion. He is co-author of *Partisanship, Globalization, and Canadian Labour Market Policy* (2006).

Ray MacNeil is a government official with the Nova Scotia provincial government and a gambling policy analyst. He was acting executive director of the Nova Scotia Gaming Foundation at the time he wrote the chapter for this collection.

Jan McMillen is a leading international gambling scholar and editor of *Gambling Cultures: Studies in History and Interpretation* (1996). She is presently researching gambling regulation and comparative policy.

William Ramp is an associate professor in the Department of Sociology at the University of Lethbridge. His publications include articles on Durkheimian sociological theory, and his research interests include the formation of collective identity in early twentieth century agrarian movements.

Garry J. Smith is a gambling research specialist with the Alberta Gaming Research Institute at the University of Alberta. He is a co-author of a Law Commission report on legalized gambling, *The Legalization of Gambling in Canada* (2005).

Harold Wynne operates Wynne Resources, a consulting company focusing on gambling-related issues.

Acknowledgments

In editing this book, we relied on the assistance of numerous colleagues and friends. Most important among these are the authors who have contributed insightful, critical, and current chapters on aspects of gambling in Canada, and beyond. We sincerely thank them for being a part of this collection.

Anna Kim, Ekta Khullar, and Kenneth Pimentel, while graduate students in the Department of Political Science at York University, provided invaluable research and editorial support.

We also thank those who have inspired and supported our interest in studying gambling: Thomas thanks Dan Buchanan and Jim Hart; James thanks Sytze Kingma for his innovative research in gambling studies, Christine Mckay for her valuable insights into gambling in Canada, and Rod Michalko and Tanya Titchkosky for their support along the way.

Trent University and York University contributed research funds and other resources at various times to support the gambling-related research activities of the editors, and the publication of this book.

Lastly, we warmly acknowledge the assistance and guidance of Virgil Duff, Wayne Herrington, and colleagues at the University of Toronto Press, as well as the anonymous readers whose comments served to strengthen the final product.

CASINO STATE:
LEGALIZED GAMBLING IN CANADA

1 Introduction: The Shape of Legalized Gambling in Canada

JAMES F. COSGRAVE AND THOMAS R. KLASSEN

The impetus for *Casino State: Legalized Gambling in Canada* is the pressing need to bring together analysis and foster dialogue regarding the unprecedented growth of legalized gambling. In Canada as of 2007, there were 66 casinos and 28 racinos (racetracks with electronic gambling machines), more than 7,200 electronic gaming machine venues with over 88,000 machines, including slot machines and video lottery terminals, 33,000 lottery ticket outlets, and 256 racetracks and tele-theatres (Alberta Gaming Research Institute 2008; Statistics Canada 2007; CPRG 2007). Between 1992 and 2006, net revenue from government-run lotteries, video lottery terminals, and casinos rose from $2.7 billion to $13.3 billion. In this period, the percentage of GDP growth from the gambling industry outpaced all other industries, and employment in the industry rose from 11,000 to 40,000 (Statistics Canada 2007).

Gambling has become mainstream, no longer regarded as a deviant subcultural activity, but rather promoted by the state as entertainment and a form of leisure. As this book demonstrates, however, legalized gambling, while broadly accepted or at least tolerated, continues to be controversial, raising political, sociological, psychological, and ethical questions. Legalized gambling in Canada is not only an individual choice and consumer activity, but also a public policy instrument and component of state infrastructure. While gambling is marketed as a form of entertainment for its consumers, state-run gambling for the purpose of revenue generation has consequences for citizens and communities. In the consumer society, gambling is a form of experiential consumption that brings with it the risk of addiction (Peele 2003). It is the relationship of the state to citizens that is at the core of this volume.

The proliferation of gambling since the early 1990s has prompted a

number of focused Canadian gambling studies (e.g., Vaillancourt and
Roy 2000; Azmier 2001, 2005; Williams and Wood 2005, 2007), but there
has not yet been a major national study as there has been in other Anglo-
Saxon countries with legalized gambling, such as the United States
(National Gambling Impact Study Commission 1999), Britain (Gambling Review Report 2001), and Australia (Productivity Commission
Report 1999). There have been a number of important recent contributions to the analysis of gambling in Canada from journalistic (Hutchinson 1999; Mandal and Vander Doelen 1999) and scholarly perspectives.
The latter include edited volumes by Campbell and Lowman (1988) and
Campbell (1994), Suzanne Morton's (2003) historical study of gambling
in the twentieth century (covering the years 1919 to 1969), the report to
the Law Commission of Canada, *The Legalization of Gambling in Canada*
(Campbell et al. 2005), and McKenna's (2008) analysis of the politics of
government-owned video lottery terminals in Atlantic Canada. In relation to the global expansion of legalized gambling, there has been com-
paratively little research on state involvement in gambling enterprises
(Della Sala 2004). This volume brings a critical and holistic social science
perspective to the most recent developments in, and debates on, legalized gambling in Canada.

After federal legislation legalizing lotteries and lottery schemes in
1969, provincial lotteries began to flourish starting in the 1970s. During
the 1980s, legalized gambling proliferated in Canada and new forms of
gambling were introduced to the public. However, legal gambling was
largely restricted to bingo, horse-race betting, and lotteries. The early
1990s saw the extraordinary growth of casino gambling so that nearly
all provinces now have casinos. These include: (1) resort casinos designed to attract gamblers from other jurisdictions, (2) rural casinos
located away from population centres, (3) urban casinos located in
major cities, and (4) neighbourhood casino-style gaming, such as gaming devices found in bars.

The 1990s also saw the implementation of video lottery terminals
(VLTs), a particular form of electronic gaming machine, by various provincial governments. VLTs have been a popular, but controversial, form
of gambling in the provinces that have implemented them. Only Ontario and British Columbia do not allow them, although slot machines (a
similar type of electronic gaming) are prevalent in these two provinces.
Also in the 1990s the legalization of sports betting occurred through the
government-run 'Pro-Line' and 'Sports Select' systems. While scratch
tickets have been available since the 1980s, the corner store has now

become a dispensary for a wide variety of legal gaming products: more versions of scratch and win games, instant lotto and keno, all sponsored and marketed by the various provincial and regional government lottery and gaming corporations.

Canada is one of many countries that have legalized gambling, marketed as a form of mass-consumption entertainment, and have utilized it as a form of economic development activity. While Las Vegas and Atlantic City are popularly known as hubs of gambling, particularly casino gambling, the legalization and expansion of gambling in both its privately owned corporate and state-run forms is a global phenomenon (McMillen 1996d, 2003b; Eadington 1997). Aboriginal gambling enterprises (from bingo to slot machines and casinos) continue to grow in the United States and Canada. Revenues from Aboriginal gambling enterprises in the United States are now more than double that from all gambling in the state of Nevada.

The United Kingdom, historically the home of betting shops and smaller restrictive club casinos, has recently relaxed its gaming laws in order to permit larger hotel-resort casinos. The previous gaming laws reflected a moral assumption that additional gambling consumption should not be stimulated. The shift in policy is now based on the assumption that gambling can, and should, be used as a form of economic revitalization for depressed areas, and marks the end of the 'non-stimulatory' model of gambling regulation in Britain (Austrin and West 2004).

Legalized casino gambling enterprises are entrenched in many jurisdictions: in European countries such as Sweden, Denmark, Finland, Switzerland, the Netherlands, as well as the United Kingdom; countries in Asia such as the Philippines; in South Africa, New Zealand, and Australia. The Chinese island of Macau is perhaps now the largest casino gambling locale in the world (York 2005), and rapid gambling growth has occurred in Russia, where lax regulation and licensing rules have allowed slot machines and gambling arcades to flourish with impunity (St Petersburg Times 2008). The spread of electronic gambling is the most notable form of gambling expansion in the last decade. Lotteries, which have a longer history in the twentieth century, exist across the globe, typically, but not exclusively, run as state monopolies.

The availability of, and easy access to, forms of Internet gambling – Internet poker, varieties of sports betting, simulated casino games, etc. – which are presently illegal in Canada, is creating market and political pressures on state regulators. The illegal status has not had a significant effect on the prevalence of these forms of gambling. Internet gambling is a truly global form of gambling enterprise, availing gamblers of the opportunity to participate in gambling activities that may be prohibited by their home jurisdictions, thus contravening national laws and contributing to the growth of a global market. While the United States has effectively prohibited Internet gambling, some jurisdictions, such as Britain and Australia, have legalized some forms. This legalization is a response to market pressures and technological changes in gaming delivery, but is also in keeping with traditions of betting, particularly sports betting, found in these jurisdictions. The British government has proposed legalizing all forms of on-line gambling service, due to the commercial benefits to be derived for British operators (Austrin and West 2004). Gambling legalization and expansion builds regulatory competition between jurisdictions, and gambling globalization through Internet availability – legal or not – will raise the ante as governments consider the revenues lost to Internet-friendly gambling jurisdictions (Della Sala 2004).

Internet gambling is also shaping the technological development and the spatial environments of gambling, not only by offering particular games, such as poker and bingo, structured as on-line forms, but by creating new spaces within which gambling takes place. The availability of poker on the Internet has contributed greatly to its present popularity, along with coverage of poker tournaments on television. Poker represents 'the largest chunk of the on-line gambling market, which had worldwide revenues of $15 billion in 2006 – a figure that may be closer to $20 billion (for 2007)' (The Economist 2007).

The late twentieth century legalization and expansion of gambling in Canada has proceeded along a temporal trajectory not unlike that in other countries. The significant features of the development of legalized gambling are, first, the rapidity with which gambling has become ubiquitous as an accepted form of culture and consumption; and, second, the legalization of increasingly risky forms of gambling (in terms of rates of problem and pathological gambling created by particular forms of gambling). There have been pronounced concerns and concerted citizen actions in relation to the personal and social harms created by VLTs, which provide a significant portion of government revenues for the provinces that have introduced them. In the United States, the state of South Carolina, which at its height had 38,000 video poker machines, completely banned them in 2000 after a long political battle (Rose 2003; Lane 2005). Thus far, it is the only jurisdiction to completely ban VLTs after their implementation. In November 2005, Nova Scotia pulled the plug on 800 VLTs out of the nearly 3,300 in the province. New Brunswick is following suit, with plans to cut the number of VLT sites by 50 per cent (from 625 to 300), and the number of machines by 25 per cent (from 2,650 to 2,000). A moratorium is also being placed on the approval of new VLT sites (Government of New Brunswick 2007).

Costs and Benefits

Gambling regulation in Canada is under the authority of provincial governments, which utilize particular policy and economic strategies such that the shape of legalized gambling varies from province to province. As mentioned, the provinces of British Columbia and Ontario do not allow VLT gambling, while Alberta and Quebec generate large revenues from them. As of 2006, British Columbia and Ontario had 21 and 27 electronic gaming machine (EGM) venues respectively, these being comprised primarily of casinos with slot machines, with Ontario having racinos. By contrast, Alberta and Quebec had 1,099 and 3,125 EGM venues respectively, comprised almost entirely of bars and lounges with VLTs (CPRG 2006). While British Columbia has more casinos than Ontario (20 and 10 respectively), Ontario has several large casino complexes, with its largest (Windsor and Niagara Fallsview) located close to the U.S. border. There are no casinos in the most populous cities of Toronto or Ottawa, although Hull, Quebec, has a casino. However, as analysed in chapter 6, cities such as Toronto do have racinos, which provide some of the same gambling products as casinos. British Columbia has smaller casinos, with some located in the city of Vancouver.

What is interesting about Canadian gambling is the monopolization of gambling opportunities by provincial governments, such that gambling in Canada is part of state infrastructure. While private gaming operators are partners in the development, implementation, and operation of gambling enterprises, especially with respect to casino gambling (see chapters 4, 6, and 7), legalized gambling in Canada is organized as a state monopoly, and in effect Canadian gamblers gamble against – or for – the state. In this situation, while gambling has been liberalized, it is a selective liberalization (Abt 1996).

Consequently, there is not a free market in gambling entertainment where private enterprise gaming corporations can compete to provide offerings; rather, provincial policy makers select the gambling forms and products available to gambling consumers. The attempt in 2006 by

Cirque du Soleil to form a partnership with Loto-Québec for a casino project in Montreal would have permitted a more free-market approach to gambling development. The project failed, however, due to the actions of local citizens' groups opposed to the development of a Las Vegas–style casino.

The arguments for state-controlled gambling include the ability to capitalize on gambling activities as a form of social and economic policy, whereby such activities can be organized to serve the interests in job creation, the stimulation of depressed economies, the creation of tourist areas, etc. However, there is debate about whether other, non-gambling, economic policy levers are better to promote long-run social and economic development (Grinols 2003). In any case, unless gamblers arrive from other jurisdictions, as resort and destination casinos are designed to ensure, gambling by locals merely results in a circulation of money within the economy that would have been spent in other ways, with the exception of some locals who might have travelled to other jurisdictions in order to gamble.

In the growth and development of consumer societies, gambling liberalization provides individuals with opportunities to gamble, without fear of lawbreaking, making legal gambling a social benefit to those individuals who wish to consume these products and experiences (Collins 2003). However, there are costs that arise when legal gambling is introduced into a community. These include crime (apprehension, adjudication, incarceration, and police costs), illness (costs associated with depression, stress-related illness, anxiety, cognitive disorders, chronic or severe headaches, etc.), and suicide (Grinols 2003, 82). Casinos, in particular, alter the economies and infrastructures in the areas in which they are located (Hannigan 1998). The benefits and costs associated with gambling enterprises as economic policy solutions will vary from locale to locale.

From a social perspective, state-controlled gambling enterprises have positive benefits derived from the state's interest in reducing crime and illegitimate gambling, such as illegal electronic gaming machines, fraud, money laundering, and loan sharking, as well as ensuring the integrity of the settings and games, and in the commitment of money to the treatment of problem and pathological gambling. However, a cost of the intensification of gambling is the creation of problem and pathological gamblers that arises when gambling is easily, and legally, accessible and promoted by the state. Experts point to the built-in addictive structure of increasingly sophisticated electronic gaming machines (see chapter 7). The Canada Safety Council estimates that 200 suicides each year are due to compulsive gambling (Canada Safety Council 2005). The incidence is higher in Quebec than the other provinces, due to the availability of VLTs outside of casinos. From the perspective of lawmakers, these problems are solved by the expenditure of a (small) portion of gambling revenues to research, education, prevention, and treatment programs. In Ontario, the amount spent by the provincial government on the prevention and treatment of problem gambling is about 2 per cent of total revenues from 12,000 of its more than 20,000 slot machines, which amounted to $36 million annually. This figure, however, 'represents only 2.6 percent of the 1.41 billion dollars estimated to have been derived from problem gamblers' (Williams and Wood 2007, 383).

The legalization and expansion of gambling has introduced social groups to gambling who had previously been reluctant to pursue the activity on anything more than an occasional and charity-related basis, such as the middle class and youth and, in the case of casino gambling, women and seniors (Fabian 1990). The management of problem gambling also becomes an issue for those groups and individuals who are at risk of developing gambling-related problems. In Canada, as a result of economic expediency and short-sightedness, the implementation of gambling opportunities proceeded far ahead of the establishment of agencies, programs, and treatment centres designed to help problem and pathological gamblers. Increasingly, governments face political pressure to provide money to treat problem gamblers, and reluctantly set up education programs and campaigns to inform individuals of the risks of gambling participation. One such strategy has been the message of 'responsible gambling' (RGCO 2002a, 2002b).

State-funded centres for the study of gambling activities and behaviours were recently created, such as the Ontario Problem Gambling Research Centre, the Alberta Gaming Research Institute, and the Nova Scotia Gaming Foundation, as well as agencies for the dissemination of responsible gambling information, such as the Responsible Gambling Council (Ontario), and government-funded treatment programs. However, problem gamblers continue to be good business. A study of Ontario gambling revenue sources derived from problem gamblers revealed that 4.8 per cent of gamblers contributed 36 per cent of the $4 billion generated from Ontario residents in 2003, amounting to more than $1.4 billion (Williams and Wood 2007). Not surprisingly, government decision makers consider the rates of problem and pathological gambling to be low and the associated problems manageable. Of course, such a conclusion depends upon perspective: 5 per cent of gamblers being problem gamblers in a jurisdiction appears to be a small number, but may represent tens or hundreds of thousands of people who have problems, and it has been thus far difficult to assess the social impacts and costs of these problems. As the authors of the study note, 'Ontario (and other provinces) appear to derive a substantial portion of their revenue from problem gamblers ... Thirty-six percent of revenues from problem gambling would be a problematic figure for private industry, let alone a government-run operation whose purpose is to serve the people, not to exploit the people.' They go on to state that the 'Ontario government is aware of the findings, but has argued that the province has an economic need for gambling revenue' (Williams and Wood 2007, 383). With youth gamblers, rates of problem gambling are much higher than the general population, and the long-term social and personal consequences for this group are not yet understood (see chapter 9).

The most important aspect of state involvement, and the primary reason the state has entered into gambling enterprises, is the generation and use of gambling money as revenues, which, it is argued, will benefit citizens through the funding of social programs and projects, charitable groups, etc. There is much debate about this aspect as well, since gambling moneys are placed into general revenues, with the consequence that governments come to rely heavily on this revenue stream for their budgetary commitments. Gambling is a de facto form of taxation, but one that requires the state to promote gambling in order to maintain voluntary interest in the activity on the part of individuals. As a form of voluntary taxation, it is regressive, with the poor spending a greater percentage of their income on gambling than do the wealthy (Clotfelter and Cook 1989; Nibert 2000; Vaillancourt and Roy 2000).

Markets and Consumers

State involvement in gambling, especially with respect to casino gambling and electronic machine gambling, represents something more than the regulation of activities that have been legalized and through which revenues are captured. This involvement, particularly in a neoliberal political and economic milieu, is a form of state practice, which requires entrepreneurialism and a particular social-political relationship to citizens. In Canada, the state monopoly model, and the interests of the provincial governments in building markets and generating revenues, represents a form of governing *through* markets (Slater and

Tonkiss 2001). The operators of the Fallsview casino in Niagara Falls, for example, have been reprimanded by provincial gaming officials for not generating enough revenues (Donovan 2005). As state institutions, operated through the provincial and regional gambling and lottery corporations, and supported by other gambling-related agencies, gambling enterprises are a vehicle for the enabling of the state (Della Sala 2004; see chapter 3 of this volume).

The selective liberalization of gambling in Canada is enacted through the state monopoly form and produces a limited market. This market requires financial (risk) management by the state as insufficient gambling revenues will impact government expenditures and may require raising income or other taxes. Gambling is also an individualization of taxation that requires market management and the stimulation of gambling activities – through marketing and promotion: the creation of new venues and gaming opportunities, introduction of new products, protection of market share from competing jurisdictions, etc. As governments come to depend on gambling revenues, the rationale for gambling enterprises moves from fund-raising for specific projects to the creation and maintenance of markets that produce revenues (Mun 2002). It is difficult to reverse the trend of the reliance on gambling revenues, and the tendency has been for greater liberalization and market expansion, and therefore greater entrenchment of gambling revenues as part of governmental budgets. As a result, legal gambling has become constituted on the basis of revenue production, which suits the interests of the state, but not necessarily the needs of gamblers, or the larger community.

The fundamental criticism of the organization of legal gambling in Canada is that the state is in a conflict of interest: it is both the regulator and the beneficiary of gambling enterprises (Seelig and Seelig 1998; Campbell et al. 2005). As has been noted, state-operated gambling enterprises, in their search for greater revenues, 'acquire many of the attributes that they would have been expected to acquire if they had been part of the private commercial gambling sector' (Miers 2003, 167). In other words, governments risk being perceived 'as having too close an interest in their citizens' losses' (Miers 2003, 167). This situation raises important questions as to how the state relates to, and governs, its citizens. Citizen action in provinces such as Nova Scotia and New Brunswick, where the injury of VLT play has become a flashpoint, is a response to state policy that is seen as creating harm in its desire to accrue ever more revenues. A central feature of the relationship between citizens and the state concerns the trust that people have in their governments and governing institutions (Giddens 1991; Beck 1992, 2003; chapter 3 of this volume). The recent lottery ticket scandal in Ontario, where allegations of theft of winning tickets by representatives of the provincial gaming corporation in convenience stores have been documented, is an example of this issue of trust (see chapter 6). With the historical associations of gambling with vice and illegality, and public perceptions of social problems produced by gambling expansion, it is crucial that governments promoting gambling demonstrate responsibility, integrity, and accountability.

From a consumer perspective, the state monopolization of gambling limits the free market, as gamblers are forced to consume the various provincial lottery or gaming corporation products. Government-run gambling enterprises also produce market consequences for the existing privately run and operated forms of gambling. The expansion of casino gambling in the 1990s negatively affected both privately owned bingo enterprises and the horse-racing industry. To draw patrons back into racetracks, provincial governments permitted the introduction of government owned and regulated slot machines, turning the tracks into racinos.

In this type of limited gambling market, the gambling consumer is not getting the best gambling value. A free market would no doubt reduce prices, provide more variety, and give gamblers better odds/chances in their games of choice. Because Internet gambling is illegal in Canada, money flows to offshore Internet sites, which provide, in the case of sports gambling, for example, more opportunities, cheaper prices, and better odds. Venerable British gambling operators Ladbrokes and William Hill, both of which are centuries old and at the forefront of Internet gambling, offer a far greater selection and more favourable opportunities for sports betting than the gaming corporations offer in Canada. For example, they allow bettors to bet on single sport matches, in contrast to the structure of sports betting in the Pro-Line and Sports Select systems, which require wagers on a minimum of three matches (parlay wagering) all of which the bettor must get correct for a payout.

Despite the broad acceptance, or tolerance, of gambling, possible in part due to more permissive cultural attitudes arising as a consequence of the decline of Protestant value hegemony in Canada, state involvement has generated controversies and protest. In Quebec, where this hegemony has had weaker cultural significance, attitudes towards gambling have been historically more liberal than those in English Canada. Quebec sought to implement legal lotteries for the funding of public projects before any of the other provinces, but was constrained by the *Criminal Code* and Protestant moral values informing it. After the legalization of lotteries in 1969, Quebec became the first province to implement a state-run lottery, in 1970 (Morton 2003). However, despite more liberal attitudes, the development of gambling in Quebec has not been without controversies, most recently with regard to public response to the harms associated with the presence of electronic gaming machines.

Critics of legalized gambling in Canada challenge the state's role in creating the gambling marketplace and highlight the personal and social harms of problematic forms of gambling. These critics have included groups such as Citizens Against Gambling Expansion and the Multicultural Coalition Against Gambling in British Columbia, the Gambling Watch Network, the campaign for the elimination of VLTs in Nova Scotia (Game Over VLTs), and individuals involved in litigation against lottery corporations (Branswell 2002). Watchdog agencies, such as the Canada Safety Council, the Law Commission of Canada, and professional and lay individuals working, or coping, with the social and personal consequences of gambling addiction, have been vocal in raising concerns.

Comparing state policies on smoking behaviour and gambling is instructive. While smoking has been banned recently in most public places in Canada (although politicians exempted some casinos), no similar protective initiatives have been initiated vis-à-vis gambling, with gambling continuing to be expanded. This divergence reflects the dynamics of Canada's political culture: the collectivist and paternalistic concern with citizens' health existing in tension with the neo-liberal ideology of individualism that locates the source of problems in individuals. As well, the divergence reflects government revenue concerns – while smoking has historically generated large tax revenues, it is also a documented cost to the health-care system. In fact, the provinces have recently been granted the right by the Supreme Court to sue tobacco companies for health-care costs. Gambling revenues, particularly those generated from casino gambling, electronic machines, and sports betting, are a relatively new source for governments, and while the economic and social costs of gambling are still unknown, they are perceived as manageable.

The aim of *Casino State: Legalized Gambling in Canada* is to provide insight into the development of legal gambling in Canada as whole;

although the focus is on English Canada, analyses cover national and provincial developments and issues. The book provides a cross-section of current gambling research and analysis; however, limitations on available scholarly research have not allowed us to address fully some aspects. As alluded to earlier, Internet gambling, while still illegal in Canada, will soon require responses from politicians and communities, which will likely further expand gambling opportunities for Canadians. The rapid pace of technological developments in gambling, both in terms of game features and methods of delivery, calls for more analysis. Aboriginal gambling enterprises continue to grow in both Canada and the United States, and controversies have arisen in both countries over the political significance and legality of some of the enterprises, particularly as they are being utilized to assert Aboriginal sovereignty claims. Conflicts have arisen over legal jurisdiction, and in Canada the *Criminal Code* gives the provinces sole legal rights to conduct on-line gaming. The operation of illegal on-line poker and sports-betting sites by the Mohawks of the Kahnawake reserve in Quebec has prompted the federal government to consider closing down such sites. The controversies also centre on control of gambling markets; the Great Canadian Gaming Corporation, private operators of horse-racing tracks, consider the Mohawks' Internet gambling sites to be poaching from their business (Ivison 2008). Notwithstanding its social, political, constitutional, and economic impacts, Aborginal gambling has received little analysis in the Canadian context, with the exception of Belanger (2006).

The place of gambling in the lives of seniors and the marketing of gambling to this social group is another area that calls for more research in the Canadian context, particularly since low-income seniors have been found to be an especially problematic segment of the gambling market (Preston, Shapiro, and Keene 2007). The relationship of gambling and gender, in particular, what has been referred to as the feminization of gambling, also deserves more research attention in Canada (Volberg 2003; Cosgrave 2006).

Casino State: Legalized Gambling in Canada is composed of four sections. The first part provides the theoretical and historical foundation for the study of contemporary gambling in Canada. In chapter 2, William Ramp and Kerry Badgley, building on original archival and interview sources, examine the moral discourses around the place of chance in everyday life and the ways in which these discourses have changed in the twentieth century. This chapter lays the groundwork for issues raised in subsequent chapters since the civic and moral agenda pursued by organizations associated with 'Social Christianity' shaped gambling views and policies in Canada. James F. Cosgrave, in chapter 3, discusses the implications of the selective liberalization of gambling in Canada, and analyses aspects of the state's relationship to its gambling citizens. He shows that the involvement of the state in the creation of gambling markets is a form of governing through markets, which also entails the management of risky consumption. Taken together, these chapters raise the central question of the volume: What are the implications for citizens, consumers, and the state of the recent legitimation, legalization, and expansion of gambling in Canada?

The second part provides a comparative framework for viewing policy developments in two jurisdictions, Canada and Australia. In chapter 4, Colin S. Campbell skilfully shows how a particular interpretation of the *Criminal Code* has been required to support the legalization of gambling. His chapter considers the broad Canadian context, and critiques the regulatory models that shape legal gambling in Canadian provinces. In chapter 5, Jan McMillen, an Australian gambling scholar and leading expert on global gambling developments, contrasts the political and cultural frameworks of Australian and Canadian gambling. Her analysis suggests that Canadians – both as citizens and consumers – have to date been less concerned, compared to Australians, with seeking to understand and address the implications of intensified levels of legalized gambling. This is partly so because Australia has been less constrained by the kinds of moral dilemmas that we find articulating gambling culture in Canada (analysed in chapter 2), thus allowing for more clear-sighted gambling regulation.

In the third part, the governmental structures, institutions, and policy decisions that underlie the expansion of gambling in Canada are examined. Thomas R. Klassen and James F. Cosgrave, in chapter 6, use the province of Ontario as an example of how the state has eliminated competitors and developed allies in its efforts to secure increased gambling revenues. Their analysis reveals the complexity of relationships that have come to arise in gambling policy and how states remain influential actors even in neo-liberal settings. The chapter is an unsettling analysis of how dependent our governments have become on the revenues from legalized gambling. In chapter 7, Ray MacNeil critically dissects the expansion of electronic gaming machine gambling, using Nova Scotia as a case study. This type of gambling is the defining feature of contemporary gambling and at the core of many of the public policy debates and controversies. MacNeil brings an insider's perspective to his conclusion that electronic gaming machines present a specific and serious danger to users, which governments have failed to fully acknowledge.

The last part of the book focuses on the major implications of widespread legal gambling on, and for, particular groups. Drawing upon current criminology theories, Garry J. Smith, Timothy F. Hartnagel, and Harold Wynne, in chapter 8, provide a case study of the forms of crime that accompany legalized gambling. They mine an impressive array of documents and data, supplemented by interviews with police and security personnel. Their chapter clearly demonstrates the myriad of difficulties in arriving at gambling-related crime statistics that are both reliable and complete. In chapter 9, Jeffrey L. Derevensky conducts a rigorous and well-documented examination of youth gambling in Canada, with a specific focus on youth problem gambling. He explains what we know, and do not know, about treating and preventing problematic gambling in this vulnerable group, which has been exposed to more legal gambling opportunities than any previous generation.

PART ONE

Morality, Markets, and the State

2 'Blood Money': Gambling and the Formation of Civic Morality[1]

WILLIAM RAMP AND KERRY BADGLEY

Stories and anecdotes about gambling are to be found in the lore of many middle-class Canadian families (e.g., Morton 2003, ix). Some celebrate wins, while others communicate reproof, admonition, or caution. They are ways of making moral statements about labour, wealth, weakness, and chance; and ways of orienting to a world in which work, money, and risk condition social success or failure. These anecdotes teach the arts of parsing wisdom from foolishness, legitimate reward from ill-gotten gain, and legitimate wealth production from 'blood money.'

They also reflect elements of a broader moral-reform discourse that dominated the characterization and regulation of gambling in English Canada during much of the twentieth century. This discourse forms part of a 'moral culture': interconnected narratives, ideas, and precepts about virtue and vice, as well as governance, citizenship, economic activity, family life, and collective identity. This moral culture informed and shaped institutional and personal life, including the formal and informal policing of boundaries defining social spaces of legitimate and illegitimate work and leisure; the systematic governance of alcohol production, distribution, and consumption; even the architecture and physical location of venues such as carnivals, racetracks, bingo halls, liquor outlets, and drinking establishments.

For contemporary commentators on gambling, the discourse of moral reform of the twentieth century is mainly a topic of historical interest. In her landmark study *The Age of Chance*, Gerda Reith views moral reform as a form of Puritanism that was ranged against gambling because by 'courting of the chaotic forces of chance' it represented 'a threat to the moral order of society' (Reith 1999, 5). But at least once in her discussion, she draws upon the reformist outlook, when she roundly condemns lotteries as a regressive tax on the poor; a 'brutal exploitation of hope' in which 'entire pay cheques' are sacrificed to a 'chimera' (Reith 1999, 100).

Other contemporary observers have pronounced the morality arguments against legalized gambling dead: the involvement of churches and governments in bingo games, lotteries, and the like has cost gambling opponents their main moral representatives. In the twenty-first century, 'With no one to say what is right or wrong, everything has become a cost-benefit analysis' (Rose 2003, 125). Or, if moralism about gambling is not yet gone, it is now said to be nearly forgotten. This is because the 'generation most vocal in protesting the exploding industry remembers how it used to be and these sensibilities come into play when they debate the good and evil of gambling. It must be remembered that the generation coming of age ... knows nothing of the history of gambling. They have only known a life in which legal wagers can be made at the corner store' (Mandal and Vander Doelen 1999, 184).

In this chapter, we suggest that such generational changes in personal experience are not the whole story. It is also important to recognize the persistence of discourse, of particular ways of formulating statements and judgments[2] even when names change and the specific referents disappear. The formulations on which anti-gambling moral reformers drew still have cultural purchase, and moral reform itself amounted to more than a puritan reaction against forces of disorder and chaos. While there is plenty of evidence – especially with hindsight – of inflammatory rhetoric, this discourse also supported, and still supports, more nuanced responses to different types of gambling (see, e.g., Mandal and Vander Doelen 1999, 129–32). Moral reform in English-speaking Canada constituted, during the nineteenth and early twentieth centuries, a relatively coherent world-view; a set of ideas and a language that shaped a moral terrain for political and civic action and a moral geography of work and leisure, security and danger.

Moral reform articulated a complex metaphorical and emotional universe as well as an intellectual one. In petitions, public statements, letters, and tracts, English-Canadian social reformers of the early twentieth century, through organizations such as the Woman's Christian Temperance Union (WCTU), the United Farm Women, and the Social Service Council of Canada, represented various forms of vice in a distinctive series of highly charged symbols (Valverde 1991, 34–43). The social landscape was organized in terms of evocative examples of respectable, marginal, or dangerous spaces, and people within them

were characterized according to a richly illustrative typology of inno-
cence or culpability, responsibility or irresponsibility: as productive
citizens or wastrels, predators or victims. Some of this symbolism survived the massive transformation in the social, economic, and cultural
place of gambling that occurred in Canada over the past forty years.
The matrix of ideas and statements in which these symbols were conveyed also remains culturally present; no longer as widely accepted nor
as coherent, but still, even in fragments, a resource in contemporary
debates about the social place of gambling in Canada.

Our discussion of this symbolism is organized in terms of the following three questions. First, how were and are individuals, communities,
and governments defined as moral agents with personal and public
obligations in relation to gambling? Second, when, where, and why do
these definitions clash or coincide? Third, what kind of moral space do
they constitute for political and ethical argument, for civic action, and
for the exercise of community and personal responsibility?

We suggest some answers to these questions with reference to two
Canadian examples, one historical and one contemporary, as a contribution to a growing literature on how ideas about, and representations
of, gambling ultimately impact public policy and civic action as well as
personal morality (Cosgrave and Klassen 2001). How do characterizations of gambling, not only by gamblers, but also by those who seek to
regulate it, profit from it, or use its revenue, imply certain claims about
responsibility, reciprocity, freedom, risk, and chance in social life?
When people buy lottery tickets and dream of the big win, for example,
they position themselves by design or default in present and imagined
future situations, in relation to family, friends, and community. They
define themselves, using specific cultural resources, as particular kinds
of citizens and economic agents. When a community group decides to
'do a casino' or to apply for funding derived from lottery money, how
does that act position its members, individually and collectively, as citizens? When a government defines gambling both as a problem and as
a revenue source, how do such definitions reflect or encourage particular views of the state as a public moral agent or of taxation as a public
necessity?

Rather than focusing on problem gambling, we examine particular
constructions of gambling *as* a problem to highlight three ways of representing chance as a moral issue: first, broadly in relation to ideas of
reciprocity, productivity, and economy; second, in relation to specific
moral-reform agendas promoted in early twentieth century English

Canada; and third, in relation to the negotiation of moral stances concerning gambling-derived funding available to community service organizations today. By focusing on ways of representing, we wish to take culture and agency seriously in their own right rather than as mere consequences of some underlying cause (Alexander and Smith 2004; Alexander, Giesen, and Mast 2006). Representations of gambling constituted a particular symbolic performance of subjective agency, as well as an identification and articulation of objects of concern, and those who made them thereby constructed their individual and collective self-identities.

This chapter builds on a somewhat sparse historiography. Until recently, gambling was mentioned tangentially in many historical accounts, usually as a side target of a larger social reform movement – in conjunction with Prohibition, for example. Studies that do focus specifically on the history of gambling often take a narrative approach, highlighting particular legislative and other events in the spread of gambling activities (see, e.g., Mandal and Vander Doelen 1999, ch. 2). Reith's (1999) systematic overview of the intellectual and symbolic place of chance, risk, and gambling in Western culture is a welcome addition to the literature. In the Canadian context, Suzanne Morton's *At Odds: Gambling and Canadians, 1919–1969* (2003), breaks ground in a specific attempt to study how competing social values regarding gambling came to be negotiated and maintained by Canadians. Morton's work is broad in scope and time frame, examining gambling in five provinces, with Alberta a noticeable exclusion. We suggest that the Alberta experience was generally similar to that of other parts of the country, though the province's political culture and its changing social composition (predominantly rural before the oil boom but with instances of rapid urbanization both at the beginning and towards the end of the twentieth century) did make for variation on some aspects of the perceived problem.

While our focus is specifically on English Canada, we use this term with reservation. Morton (2003, 18, 23, 110) identifies different levels of tolerance or condemnation of gambling within English Canada, varying by province, region, and even social status: English-Canadian elites were more tolerant of horse racing, for example, than middle-class social reformers. Public opinion could also vary from official stances taken by heads of reform organizations, churches, service agencies, and governments. A similar diversity existed to a degree in French Canada. Despite a generally more tolerant attitude towards gambling in Quebec, the Roman Catholic hierarchy there was troubled by it and on occasion condemned it in terms reminiscent of statements made by English-Canadian moral reformers, though such condemnation often was not shared by local parishes with limited resources (Morton 2003, 10, 111, 121). Responses to gambling in Montreal, a polyglot city with strong economic and other ties to American cities of the northeastern seaboard, were in some ways quite distinct from those elsewhere in Quebec.

Nonetheless, while moral questions did not divide neatly by ethnicity, region, language, or religion, there was, as Morton suggests, a prominent assumption that they did (2003, 110). She notes that dominant liberal Protestant attitudes towards social virtue and vice, which retained cultural leverage in Ontario into the 1960s, often included a 'not-so-subtle' attack on a perceived lack of individual self-regulation supposedly characteristic of Catholicism (2003, 111). This point introduces a further caution in using terms such as English or French Canada (or even Quebec): for many Canadians in the first part of the twentieth century, it was *religious* divides, rather than ethno-linguistic ones, which most sharply distinguished what we now style as two different Canadas (see Behiels 1985; Morton 2003, 9–10). But while liberal Protestant attitudes to vice represented by English-Canadian social reformers may not have been universally shared, they did strongly impact on public discourse, and they resembled Protestant responses to social questions elsewhere, including the United States and Britain.

Finally, we argue that another dimension needs to be emphasized in the historical analysis of gambling in Canada; namely, rural versus urban. As Keith Walden (1997) has noted, 'In current historiography, gender, ethnicity and class are generally assumed to be the most important constituents of identity ... For many late Victorian Ontarians, however, the basis of difference most frequently highlighted ... involved the rural/urban dichotomy' (p. 214). This distinction may have affected the evaluation and prosecution of different forms of rural gambling (for instance, charitable raffles, local racetrack betting, games of chance at county fairs, back-room card games in small-town business establishments) in contrast to playing dice or poker or buying a lottery ticket in the back of an urban Chinese restaurant. But a larger consideration is why agrarian progressives particularly associated gambling not only with other vices such as alcohol, but also with economic speculation and political corruption, in a broad moral cartography of economic life.[3] And as Valverde (1991, 129–54) notes, rural and urban reformers both characterized the city itself as a moral problem (Woodsworth 1972 [1911], 9–25; Woodsworth n.d., 37).

Considering how pro- and anti-gambling forces incorporated or responded to rural-urban distinctions adds a dimension to the history of gambling important to the historical actors themselves, which shaped their conceptions of the issues they addressed. Though urban gambling and responses to it are better documented (Morton 2003, 18), a sense of the rural dimension can be gained from sources such as the papers of the Attorney General's Office of Alberta and the records of the United Farm Women of various provinces and other reform-oriented groups with a strong rural constituency. A focus on the rural dimension and the agrarian consciousness associated with it can also help explain differences between Canadian and Australian responses to gambling. Jan McMillen, in chapter 5 of this volume, notes the persistence in Australian culture of more tolerant attitudes towards gambling dating back to the convict era, the absence of a Protestant hegemony in moral issues, and a less ambiguous political and legislative framework. We would add that Australia, to a greater extent than Canada, has long been a heavily urbanized society dominated by a few large coastal cities. Australia does have its own agrarian tradition, though marked more by pessimism and perhaps individualism than in the Canadian case (Wear 2000), arguably affecting its political expression. A mobile, skilled working class found employment on vast sheep stations, run by a rural aristocracy, in large tracts of rural Australia. In Canada, small farmer-proprietors formed the backbone of an optimistic and progressivist agrarian consciousness strongly associated in the 1920s with moral reform. Neither family farms nor agrarianism were absent from the Australian scene, but they may not have provided as strong a constituency for anti-gambling activism as in Canada.

Gambling and the Moral Economy

A long anthropological tradition originating in the work of Durkheim and Mauss (see Mauss 1985, 1990, 2001) asserts that personhood is a social category defined and shaped by specific cultural and interactional circumstances, and that personhood and identity are reproduced in acts of recognition, confrontation, cooperation, obligation, and exchange. To be a self, further, involves being in relation to others and to society, learning to see ourselves through others' eyes and in terms of the social whole. Our lives have meaning in terms of a shared language and shared ideas and ideals; we live in a complex web of interaction that engages us in cooperation, contestation, and reciprocity as basic facts of life. Relations of exchange, obligation, and competition, whether in

South Sea island gift ceremonies or Chicago commodity trading, shape the selves which enact them. And as Mauss (1990) noted, symbolic injuries to individual and collective selfhood inflicted by failures to reciprocate or to grant due recognition animate many forms of conflict.[4]

Personhood as a social category, selfhood as the subjective experience of personhood, and agency as the enactment and expression of both, are, in this view, defined by reciprocity and its obligations – to engage in fair exchange, to grant recognition, to cooperate. As we relate to others, so we are. These relations, of course, take different cultural forms, and they are accompanied by other possibilities: of release from obligation, of chance interruptions of the predictable cycles of reciprocity, of actions involving risk, disruption, deceit, competition, or defiance. Tragic heroes, tricksters, or rebels are significant figures precisely because of the test they pose to communal obligation or generalized reciprocity. In this light, games and play reflect a double aspect of human existence (Reith 1999; Caillois 2001), displaying and containing elements of chance, risk, and magic. The challenges are themselves bound and defined by rules and institutionalized forms.

As Reith points out, the idea of pure chance, a matter of mathematical odds only, is relatively recent. Older notions of what we would call chance tend to link it to divine action, divination, or destiny; to risks undertaken in pursuit of a quest. Such risking of self was not necessarily an isolated or isolating act, but a way in which one played a part in a cultural narrative. Mauss's (1990) descriptions of ceremonial extravagance and festive exchange also illustrate how obligation and dare, reciprocity and excess, recognition and confrontation are intertwined.

However, the modern reduction of chance to mathematical probability did not remove it from the sphere of religion, morals, or self-making. Rather, it reconfigured the moral aspects of exchange. The development of the modern economy involved a shift away from the more ceremonial, agonistic, and dramatic aspects of gift-giving and reciprocation towards an institutionalization of exchange as a mundane everyday activity. The sense that exchange involved drama and contained both moral and magical elements gave way to the idea that it was regular, predictable, and rule-bound: the basis of the modern concept of economic life as a distinctive sphere of sustained activity. The idea that there existed something called 'the economy' did not spring into existence fully formed, but itself developed and shifted in meaning over time, and overtly moral valuations even of mundane economic exchange persisted (Polanyi 2001). These were challenged by secular theories that linked economic regularities to natural 'laws,' thus founding the modern science of economics. But paradoxically, such theories also contributed to a new *moral* revaluation of economic life, particularly (though not exclusively) in agrarian and craft-labour circles. Rather than attaching primarily to the quality of particular acts of reciprocation, morality now attached itself to the regularity and rationality of ongoing economic exchange in itself. Regularity and consistency became moral goods: interruptions, crashes, and failures came to be seen popularly not as chance occurrences but as consequences of systematically immoral or unregulated economic action.

Here, chance found a new meaning in a populist moral discourse promoted by agrarian reformers, cooperativists, guild socialists, and others targeting both speculation and gambling as moral evils with economic consequences. In this moral universe, economic regularity was seen to be impaired by three evils: first, hoarding, that is, taking wealth out of circulation, thereby depriving the economy of its lifeblood; second, unrestrained speculation, said to distort the economy, leading (as in the distortion of an organism) to collapse; third, gambling, seen by Protestant reformers as early as the sixteenth century as a sin, and subsequently, in the Enlightenment, as a manifestation of irrationality (Reith 1999, 81–7).

In the universe of moral reform in the nineteenth century, economic irrationality itself thus became a sin. Both gambling (as a 'vice') and more chance-dependent forms of economic activity, such as futures trading (Geisst 2002), came to be seen less as scandalous occurrences than as systemic moral ills, destructive of social productivity, health, and happiness. As Morton notes (2003, 28) and we emphasize, this view of gambling had a strong agrarian-reform constituency in Canada, shared by agrarian progressives in the United States and elsewhere.

Gambling and Moral Reform in Early Twentieth Century Canada

The nineteenth century construction of gambling as a moral and social problem fed the proclamations and actions of an array of early twentieth century social reform movements in Canada (Morton 2003, 9–10, 23–39). This construction was complex but eloquently articulated. It drew from and fed into a number of nineteenth century economic doctrines and moral philosophies, especially a constellation of values that Bryan Palmer terms a 'producer ideology' (Palmer 1979; Palmer and

Kealey 1982; Morton 2003, 25, 28). Besides certain sectors of organized labour, producerism's adherents included many farmers and small urban manufacturers, who in the nineteenth century had formed the backbone of reform-liberal opposition to a Tory patron-client tradition[5] in Ontario and national politics.

While it included what Morton calls a Protestant work ethic (2003, 24–7), producerism also encompassed a range of ideas about social and economic organization, almost exactly parallel to the moral evaluation of economic life outlined above. These included a labour theory of value (of which Marx's version was but one), locating the origin of (genuine) wealth in the work of direct producers, that is, those who laboured with hands and head. A positive moral valuation of thrift and saving, to the extent dictated by prudence, was also part of this range of ideas, as was a fourfold condemnation of irrational or unproductive uses of money. *Unproductive appropriation* kept money from being put to 'work' – its natural function. Money kept for its own sake was as socially and morally valueless as money expended unwisely. The Protestant emphasis on the Gospel parable of the talents illustrates this sentiment. *Arbitrary restrictions on trade* such as tariff protection and monopoly distorted the free and 'cooperative' organization of the market. *Financial, land, and commodity speculation* produced only artificial riches. Making money on money added nothing to natural wealth and perverted the natural order of the economy, leading ultimately to its ruin, and more immediately to inequalities that contradicted natural justice associated with a labour theory of value (Morton 2003, 28–32). Finally, *wasteful expenditure*, like financial speculation, exemplified irrationalities relating to arbitrary movements of money. Gambling was condemned, as it involved unproductive outlays of time and money, and led to loss, inequality, and hardship.

To these ideas, organized farmers and farm women added a particular emphasis on cooperative principles, in vogue among rural and labour organizations worldwide and supported by a vast popular literature (MacPherson 1979). Besides specific cooperative solutions to their own woes, they proposed cooperation as the foundation for a moral and philosophical re-evaluation of the entire basis of economic activity, social organization, education, and political participation, in their more radical moments proposing to eliminate negative individualism, destructive competition, nationalism, and militarism in the bargain.

The specifically moral approach to social and economic issues inherent in these ideas made it easy for those who advocated them to extend moral evaluations and logical or mythic connections to a panoply of other activities and even the locations in which they took place, linking disease, vice, and crime with each other, with economic desperation, and with the urban social space of the slum (e.g., Valverde 1991, 133–4; Woodsworth 1972 [1911], 55–6, 132–7; Morton 2003, 72–4, 82–7). Gambling was associated with the pillars of vice – drink and prostitution – in reference, for example, to 'dens' where liquor was sold and consumed, in which prostitution and drug use often took place, and in which shady characters hung out, taking advantage of the desperate or gullible through loan sharking, extortion, or seduction. These activities were represented both as destructive of families and personal purity and as a moral drain on the economy and society.[6] But stock and commodity exchanges were also characterized as 'pits' in which baser economic motives were concentrated (Geisst 2002, 52). Agrarian reformers promoted a moral critique of aspects of the capitalist economy that resembled gambling, condemning the negative effects of speculation on the provision of land, transportation, and energy resources, credit, health, and social services.[7] If it can be said, with some truth, that 'farmers are the original gamblers' (Mandal and Vander Doelen 1999, 192), one must also consider the long history of grain pools, cooperative stores, cooperative credit agencies, rural telephone cooperatives, and mutual insurance companies by which organized farmers sought to make the necessary risk of their business a community and indeed a civic affair.

In addition, moral reformers, especially agrarian progressive women and members of the WCTU (which had a significant agrarian-feminist[8] constituency), used producerist ideas to condemn production of useless or pernicious goods such as beverage alcohol. The liquor business was characterized not as a productive industry but as a diversion of natural wealth (grain, which was a powerful symbol) to evil ends. Liquor was blamed for family poverty, sexual licence, shiftlessness, mental instability – and also political corruption (Cook 1995). Owners of breweries, and especially distilleries, were put in the same league as speculators and war profiteers,[9] amassing wealth and political connections at the expense of the economy and society as a whole. Consequently, some farmers refused to sell grain to these companies (Drury 1966, 18).

Social service, agrarian, and Protestant mission groups also reinterpreted the moral significance of the family in the development of a new civic discourse. Organized farm women argued that persons had a valid claim to citizenship based not on gender or property ownership but on productive participation in economic, social, and cultural life. Only those dependent on the care of others or the public purse were represented as lacking full citizenship qualifications, either temporarily (children, the ill, the educable) or permanently (the 'mentally defective').[10] The family was to be a central civic site in which children could be brought up in economic and personal safety, and in which they could also learn their first lessons in citizenship – that is, in family democracy and shared responsibility buttressed by 'women's determination and the men's willing help' (UFWO 1922). Especially for farm women, the unfettered right of men to use family finances and family property for their individual ends, and to use them unwisely at the expense of their families, constituted a civic ill and an open door to moral evil. Evaluations of virtue and vice were often gendered, not only in terms of feminine and maternal imagery, but also in competing versions of masculinity: a masculine domestic respectability involving responsibility for home, family, work, and civic life, and a bachelor masculinity involving competitive risk taking, high living, alcohol, and the life of the street (Valverde 1991, 31; Morton 2003, 67–88).[11]

In the new civics that agrarian progressivism contributed to the discourse of moral reform, the idea of mutual aid inherent in visions of the cooperative commonwealth balanced uneasily (at least in retrospect) with an emphasis on the autonomy of individuals, families, and communities. Like protectionism and political patronage, dependency was thought to encourage economic distortion and political corruption. Part of the attack on vice was aimed at its propensity to ruin both perpetrators and victims, necessitating expenditure of time and money by service agencies and police, and draining collective vitality.[12]

What was at issue here was not simply a contest over moral regulation or social order, nor simply class or gender conflict, but also a struggle over state formation and the organization of civic life as cultural projects (Corrigan and Sayer 1985; Valverde 1991, 165–7). Demographic change, the end of the settlement phase, and transformation of the capitalist economy laid the groundwork for a struggle over the cultural and ideological redefinition of state and society. This civic and moral battle was waged variously by labour, socialist, and patriotic groups, but especially by organizations such as the Social Service Council of Canada (SSC), the WCTU, the United Farm Women of various provinces, the Methodist Board of Temperance and Moral Reform, and the Board of Home Missions of the Presbyterian Church in Canada.[13] These latter organizations provided homes for activists (often leaders of Canada's first-wave feminist movement) whose ideas significantly – if incompletely – influenced the social policy agendas of several provincial governments from the early 1920s, of the Co-operative Commonwealth Federation (CCF), and of the Mackenzie King Liberals. Through petitions, letters, and public appeals, they sought to define and position government as a moral agent in relation to gambling and other forms of vice, and to characterize those who profited from them as (im)moral agents in relation to family, community, and nation. This work involved more than simply relaying facts. It was a sort of public symbolic performance (Eyerman 2006; Neville 1994; Turner 1988), in which collective identities, moral agency, and a moralized terrain of action were articulated and given emotional force in certain prescribed ways; in which organizational and other resources were taken up and powers taken in hand; in which specific, symbolically coded appeals directed at particularly designated audiences (Laycock 1990, 142) called on them to embrace a sense of capability and responsibility. Calls for government to 'cooperate' with individuals, churches, and agencies in charitable work (Woodsworth 1972 [1911], 184), for example, would instantly evoke for agrarian progressives a whole set of narratives about cooperative civics, consciously opposed to 'partyism,' patronage, and corruption.

The impact of this social and moral agenda for government – though its roots were not always acknowledged – lasted until the late 1960s. It included banning most forms of gambling in Canada with the contested exceptions of local raffles and bingos, games at seasonal fairs, and horse racing. In its early phase, identification of the moral threat of gambling with particular ethnic groups, such as Chinese men, also led to contestation over enforcement. This moral agenda is well illustrated by two specific instances. One was a movement, following the First World War, urging the Dominion government to make permanent a temporary ban on racetrack betting enacted in 1917 (see also Morton 2003, 42–9). The second can be seen in the manner in which the offices of the attorneys general of the federal government and the provinces (in this case, Alberta) negotiated definitions of gambling, and calls for the prosecution of 'disorderly houses' and other gambling venues, in the 1920s and 1930s.

The racetrack issue involved a concerted campaign waged by the Social Service Council of Canada to have betting on horse racing banned permanently. Members of the council claimed that racetracks (examples of which were primarily drawn from Ontario) were run as commercial enterprises interested in profits from gambling, and were controlled by a wealthy few, including shady American gambling entrepreneurs, and well-connected families associated with Canada's largest liquor producers. They also argued that the tracks were sites of unregulated and clandestine forms of gambling. The Board of Home Missions of the Presbyterian Church in Canada noted that racetracks, as gambling sites, drew men away from familial and civic duties, induced them to spend money unwisely, and exposed them to various sorts of danger. It decried the 'seeming hesitation of the Government to put this vicious business under permanent ban,' claiming that the 'Christian public of Canada' would never consent to the 'financing of a worthy sport by ... a criminal business' or to the 'enriching of privileged public men ... drawing enormous dividends therefrom' (Board of Home Missions 1919).

Similar positions were expressed by those familiar with the local consequences of betting, such as the Rev. John Macartney, a Presbyterian minister from Utterson, Ontario:

> May I draw your attention to the fact that extreme hardship are [*sic*] brought on many families through the bread winner risking his hard earned wages on a bet and losing. That even the winning of the wager at times is only fuel to encourage bigger risks next time. Thus thrift and economy, attention to work and devotion to home are being broken down by such opportunity and sanction being given to our citizens ... One of the essentials to prosperity and maintenance of the state lies in the stability of the home through comfort, diligence and thrift. (Macartney 1924)

The alleged exposure of adults and children to gambling at local agricultural fairs also precipitated pressure on government (see also Morton 2003, 51–2). Fairs constituted liminal occasions on which the boundaries of local communities became permeable, exposing those perceived to be weaker members of such communities to dangers personified by shadowy, foreign characters. The exposure cost them money and taught them vice:

> To-day was Children's Day at our local fair, and the majority of those present were public school children. The Midway has numerous gambling concessions. I saw two operators of wheels entice a group of small boys from nine to twelve years of age by showing seemingly valuable prizes. The boys were induced to play, and they lost their money ... I found a Pro-

vincial Officer, and he was quite sympathetic, but stated that as there was
no age-limit, he could not do anything, so long as money was not the prize
offered ... As soon as the police are out of sight the operators run a wide-
open gambling game with coin-boards. Most of these men come from the
United States, and represent the class from which the gun-men are
recruited. (Hone 1928)

Legislation governing such activities became the focus of a tug-of-
war over interpretation and enforcement. Pressure was put on government by invoking the danger of outside elements, the vulnerability of
local people, and the helplessness or lethargy of local authorities. In the
case of small-town fairs, outsiders were associated with organized and
(by implication) urban vice, and a certain anti-Americanism is evident
in some complaints about non-Canadian carnival operators (see also
Fraser 1988, 142–3). Writing to the federal minister of justice in 1930, C.
Wilmott Maddison, of Lethbridge, Alberta, complained of an 'American organization' displaying a midway in the city, in which, 'perfectly
open to the public eye – adults and juveniles – one concessionist operated a table carrying six metal arrows revolving on an axis, the public
[being] permitted to gamble on numbers one to twelve.' Asking if this
came under the definition of illegal gambling, he noted that 'City
policemen, Provincial policemen and R.C.M. Policemen stood by and
watched ... although they appear to be under the impression – when
asked – that the game is quite illegal in Canada' (Maddison 1930).

As these examples show, concerned individuals and service organizations did not content themselves with general statements but also
waged a vigorous campaign against localized forms of gambling. In a
sense, they served as unofficial surveillance agencies on behalf of government, at the same time chastising government for perceived laxity
on the gambling issue. In the process, inevitable confusion arose about
which level of government had jurisdiction, and what forms of gambling could be prosecuted. The attitude of many complainants was that
the government should not act as a disinterested or impartial arbiter or
regulator, but should be an active moral agent in suppressing gambling, an attitude summed up in comments like 'if there isn't a law,
there ought to be!' At the same time, lawyers defending those involved
in gambling activities, such as J. McKinley Cameron of Calgary, fer-
reted out ambiguities in legislation (for example, in the definition of a
'disorderly house' or a 'game of chance') in order to remove particular
activities, such as Chinese lotteries, from the prosecutorial net (see

Cameron 1936–9). Government itself played an ambiguous role: justice officials might plead helplessness, given the wording of statutes, but they sometimes also enlisted the aid of moral entrepreneurs in seeking tighter legislation, as in the case of the deputy attorney general of Alberta, writing to Rev. Dr Shearer of the Social Service League in 1919:

> A tobacconist has just been in to see me and he quite frankly admits that the [slot] machine which he operates is a gambling one, but says that he has to use it in self-preservation as all the other dealers in tobacco do the same.
>
> I would like to know whether it will be possible to have the Criminal code amended, so as to have the matter beyond doubt, and if you can do anything in this regard it will be very much appreciated by this Department. (Attorney General of Alberta 1919)

The kinds of gambling at issue ranged from games of chance (or mixed skill/chance games) at country fairs, at charity events, or in conjunction with commercial promotions, to slot machines in tobacconists' outlets, and card games in barber shops, restaurants, back rooms of laundries, and grain elevator offices. The Alberta government regularly employed detectives and provincial police officers in the 1920s for surveillance of small-town gambling in response to local complaints.[14] Their reports indicate a lively informal gambling culture, and a spirited debate over what constituted acceptable gaming. For example, informal card games with money stakes taking place in back rooms of commercial premises, attracting local businessmen, municipal officials, and farmers, were seen as innocuous by some and embarrassments by others.[15] One complainant noted that poker was 'getting to a regular curse in these western towns. Every village has its Chinese restaurant, and as a rule they are regular gambling dens' (Linke 1920). In the climate of the times, the Chinese were an easy symbolic target, but the reality was harder to police, especially in small towns. A member of the Alberta Provincial Police noted, in a 1925 report to the provincial attorney general about an 'alleged gambling joint' at Stavely:

> The front room is used as the barber's shop and the rear room for junk & is the place where cards are being played ... The players have been the most prominent business men in the town, ... the Mayor, ... druggist, several well known farmers ... & they claim that during the time they played no rake-off was taken except something taken out of each pot to pay for the

supper they had brought in from the Chinese restaurant ... I saw the town Policeman Const Norcomb & he said I would be a fool to pinch my own bosses, wouldn't I.' (Attorney General of Alberta 1925)

A politics of definition – what was and wasn't prosecutable; what was and wasn't dangerous to morals; what did and didn't constitute gambling – is clearly evident in this correspondence, as are the ambiguities in which gambling was situated by Albertans at that time. In his study of Vulcan, Alberta, Paul Voisey notes some of the contradictions in what constituted acceptable and unacceptable betting behaviour for townsfolk:

Clearly, the 'respectable element' itself could not agree on what constituted proper behaviour. All but the most openly indecent, for example, agreed on the impropriety of playing poker in the back rooms of Chinese restaurants but some thought a quiet game among gentlemen quite acceptable. Others considered poker playing disreputable under any circumstances but saw no harm in a small wager on baseball. A few even carried their condemnation of gambling to the commodity market, but nobody thought it immoral to gamble on real estate. (Voisey 1988, 232)

Nobody, perhaps, except the many farmers who read and subscribed to Henry George's condemnation of land speculation! But there were indeed grey areas, and although some aspects of gambling were clearly viewed with disdain by the majority of a given community, other forms of chance were subject to differences of opinion, even among moral reformers.

Anti-gambling lobbying by reformers brought results, but they were mixed. Most forms of gambling remained illegal, but some were legalized, albeit in a highly regulated environment. Interestingly, some of the relaxation of restrictions came from reform-minded governments. Though it implemented some of the most stringent temperance legislation in Canada, the United Farmer/Independent Labour Party coalition government in Ontario (1919–23) refused to outlaw racetrack betting, merely imposing a tax on winnings and using it to raise revenue for provincial coffers (Badgley 2000, 84). The same government (or more particularly, its crusading attorney general, W.E. Raney) also attempted legislation to curb excess stock market speculation, but it died on the statute book without being proclaimed (Morton 2003, 32). That said, the victories were sufficient to warrant continued lobbying throughout the country, and compromises in legislation or enforcement continued to incite it. But moral-reform crusades had another consequence, popularizing the idea of a civic duty of care owed to vulnerable members of society. Social, medical, and moral improvement as a proper end of public action became enshrined in the social welfare state that was presaged in limited ways by farmer-labour governments in the 1920s, and that came into its own after the Second World War. With that state went a broad consensus about health, education, and welfare that still governs the expectations Canadians have of their governments even after a generation of neo-liberal restructuring. While agrarian progressivism is no longer a significant constituency in Canadian politics, the Social Gospel it promoted retained some purchase in public discourse.

Gambling Revenue and Funding Regimes

Since the 1960s, the moral consensus undergirding this social agenda – a consensus about the legal and moral status of gambling as well as about the moral and social-policy role of government – has been rapidly transformed (Morton 2003, 166–201; Mandal and Vander Doelen 1999, chs. 2 and 8). Further, the spread of electronic gaming machines has made gambling less easy to characterize in terms of rural or urban dimensions, and its ubiquity has erased much of its former status as an episodic or marginal activity. The country fair, the after-hours grain elevator office, the restaurant or laundry back room, the racetrack, have been supplanted by casinos; the Internet brings gaming, albeit still illegal in this form, to any personal computer or cell phone. Cities are still a focus of worry, but less as harbours of vice than as entities that are themselves profoundly shaped by the gambling industry (Miles and Miles 2004; Hannigan 2007).

Pressures for a general relaxation of gambling regulation came not only from a general moral liberalization but also from the circumstances of the modern welfare state (Morton 2003, 189–91). Rising expectations of government services, which increased tax pressures, renewed debates about the place of lotteries and charitable gambling in funding public and community projects: Jean Drapeau's attempt to meet the costs of Expo '67 with a lottery being a striking early example. Governments have since engaged in varying degrees of both economic and moral deregulation, while coming to accept management of various kinds of social, economic, and security risks as inherent to their mandates (Cosgrave and Klassen 2001; chapter 3 of this volume). During the same period, gambling has been revolutionized. While it long had commercial elements, it has become a vast industry that has undergone prodigious expansion and technological revolution. As an increasing number of gambling activities have been legalized (Campbell, Hartnagel, and Smith 2005, 14–21), governments have also become heavily involved in aspects of the gambling industry, and reliant on economic rents from it in troubling ways (Williams and Wood 2007, 383; chapter 6 of this volume). At the same time, both their regulatory role and their revenues are threatened by the globalization of gambling business, and particularly by Internet gambling (Kelley, Todosichuk, and Azmier 2001; McMillen 2003b). In these respects, despite their different histories, there is also marked convergence in the shape of gambling issues facing Canada and countries such as Australia; for example, concerns over cross-jurisdictional leakage of gambling revenue, the dependence of community services and agencies on gambling funding, and problems of electronic and Internet gambling.

The question begged by these developments is, what new conceptions of the role of government in relation to individuals and communities are being prefigured and encouraged, deliberately or by default, by the legalization of gambling, by government intervention into the industry, and, subsequently, by the increasing dependence of governments on gambling revenue? To answer this question adequately, it is important to recognize that this transformation also unsettled a loose but distinctive moral and policy consensus about civic identity – and of specific historical exceptions to it – creating both a need and an opportunity for civic conversation. To stimulate such discussion, the Canada West Foundation published sixteen reports between 1998 and 2001 addressing civic, policy, and public opinion dimensions of gambling (see Azmier 2000, 2005; Azmier, Jepson, and Pickup 1998); however, this initiative subsequently lapsed.

During 2004, one of the authors of this chapter (Ramp) coordinated a series of in-depth qualitative interviews with members of community organizations in southwestern Alberta, involved in a range of activities with different groups and populations. These interviews explored how they referenced ideas about civic responsibility and community relations in forming perceptions and evaluations of gambling, gambling policy, and funding available from gambling revenue. Interviewers sought to understand the moral reasoning (see Skolnick 2003; Collins 2003) that members of these organizations brought to discussions and decisions concerning gambling and the use of gambling revenue.

Community non-profit organizations in Alberta today face a situation in which two decades of declines in funding from all governmental levels have vastly expanded the need for their services while narrowing options both for sources and for uses of funding (McFarlane and Roach 1999). In addition, massive investment in energy extraction has attracted a mobile working population to the province in pursuit of high wages, further taxing housing and social services while providing a market for various leisure industries, including gambling. Significantly more community service funding now comes directly or indirectly from gambling sources. Governments see gambling revenue and non-profit agencies as quick fixes for the costs of meeting social service obligations: the revenue reduces the need for general taxation and the agencies take on front-line responsibility for service delivery and accountability (see Smith 1997). Consequently, non-profits confront unprecedented practical and ethical issues that entail new forms of coping and budgeting, and a new language of justification and accountability (Berdahl 1999; Azmier and Roach 2000; see also Roach 2000; Orr 1999).

Referring to these issues, almost all interview respondents said something to the effect that 'we need to talk about this more.' There was a perceived deficit of opportunity for public discussion, particularly concerning the increased emphasis on gambling money as a primary funding source for community projects. This concern was voiced by respondents opposed to funding from gambling sources, by those who favoured it, and by those who were neutral. However, there were definite divisions of opinion between different community groups, and sometimes within them, over the ethics of accepting funding from gaming revenues. The divergence extended to perceptions of gambling itself; even to what people saw when they entered casinos or bingo halls. Sometimes this had to do with broad philosophical or ideological commitments; for others, it related specifically to the perceived harm (actual or potential) of gambling to the client base of the organization (see Berdahl 1999, 13–16; also Azmier and Roach 2000, for similar findings). Respondents uncomfortable with applying for or accepting funds from gambling revenue, but who nonetheless did so (or acquiesced to decisions to do so), had concerns about how such acceptance might affect the image of the organization, or how it might further the institutionalizing of gambling-related funding. At the same time, particular kinds of moral reasoning were employed to justify acceptance of money from gambling sources. Some pointed to the immediate tangibility and gratification of good work made possible by the funding, compared to more diffuse perceptions of harms caused by gambling. Others noted donor fatigue, and the significant resources needed to engage in other sorts of fund-raising, as factors in their decisions, or also optics:

> It was a difficult decision [to forgo revenue from bingo] ... we got more and more opposed to gambling and when the VLT's came in with a vengeance and there were so many of them around the community, we became very concerned as an agency and as a whole board about the whole dilemma. But the problem was that you had to look at it in light of the larger picture. Because even though we didn't want to do the bingos, we were still in a position where there was a lot of lottery board money that is very lucrative, that as a not-for-profit we needed. So for us to come out publicly and say we think gambling is a terrible thing and we are morally opposed, if we made that statement, we would be very hypocritical, if we were taking any funding from the government that was associated with gambling. (Interview with a member of a southern Alberta community service agency, summer 2004)

While sometimes chafing under restrictions placed on the use of funding from casinos, bingos, and government lotteries,[16] a number of respondents indicated that it was important to them that the gaming industry in Alberta remain strictly regulated, and that the government maintain a disinterested role, fearing that laxity in regulation might lead to graft, corruption, or fraud.

When people were asked to describe the moral reasoning they brought to personal or organizational decisions about accepting gambling revenue, they tended to use ideas, tropes, themes, and illustrations that were assumed to be familiar to the interviewer.[17] Many of these were recognizably part of the old moral-reform consensus (see, e.g., Reith 2003, 17), and appeared in characteristic clusters. Whether or not they agreed with accepting funds from gambling sources, and whether or not they voiced concerns about such funding, or about the social or economic impact of gambling, respondents tended to make arguments or voice observations in terms of these clusters.

Those concerned about reliance on gambling revenue, about gambling itself as a perceived social problem, or about the restructuring of community and social services, had a strong sense of the harm done by gambling, especially to people defined as innocent victims – family members of problem gamblers. They stressed the consequences of addiction (lost jobs, lost money, criminal convictions, poverty, and abuse), representing problem gambling as a drain on the public purse, and gambling revenue as a regressive tax on the poor or vulnerable. They also tended to emphasize a community's responsibility to its weaker members, and the importance of exercising thoughtful stewardship of money to that end; being accountable and responsible to others for the social use of money, not only within community organizations but also in personal and business life. Some linked this to an ethic of civic responsibility in which the activities of those possessing social advantages are properly restrained by a duty of care for the less advantaged or those with an illness, disability, or addiction. Others suggested that gambling might drain funds that might otherwise have been available to other kinds of fund-raising, and that the political autonomy of community organizations might be negatively affected by a narrowing of funding options. The ideal role of government associated with this cluster characteristically included protecting the rights and circumstances of vulnerable members of society, for example, women and children, through economic redistribution or proactive exercises of policy, regulation, and justice.

Respondents more comfortable with gambling as a feature of society and as a source of funding tended to advance a cluster of ideas that one might call a practical neo-liberal philosophy, defining money as individual property to which the holder had a natural right, including a right to free use. They tended to perceive gambling more as a personal recreational choice and responsibility, gambling losses as individual consequences, and gambling revenues as a legitimate alternative to tax funding or other forms of fund-raising, perhaps because they derive from a voluntary leisure activity. These respondents acknowledged that gambling sometimes resulted in personal or familial harm; some noted that agencies existed to help that percentage of the gambling population which got into trouble (see also Azmier, Jepson, and Pickup 1998, 13). Responsibility for the less advantaged was typically phrased in terms of innocent victims (for example, family members of irresponsible gamblers) for whom private or government agencies or services, underwritten perhaps by a public safety or regulatory net, should be in place. Those who were socially advantaged were seen to have such advantages as a moral right of labour (they worked for it), as a consequence of character, as a result of good fortune, or some mixture of the three. Financial accountability and responsibility were related to appropriate use of money within family or business, or to proper stewardship of 'other peoples' money' – donated funds and tax dollars. The civic ethic most strongly associated with this cluster emphasized individual rights to participate in the political process or to express opinion, and a personal moral duty to volunteer or give back to the community. Ranging farther afield, these views were sometimes linked to ideas about complementary 'weak' and 'strong' roles for government in relation to gambling. The weak role positions government as protector of last resort offering specialized services to addicts and innocent victims, the goal being their restoration to self-sufficiency and family responsibility. The strong role defines government as a vigilant regulator of gambling industries to keep corruption, fraud, and organized crime at bay (local communities and groups being seen as unable or perhaps in some cases unwilling to provide proper self-policing).

These ideological clusters were relatively loose. Individual respondents did not always stay within their boundaries or adopt them entirely. They are best read as tendencies rather than fully articulated philosophies or ideological stances. Nonetheless, they exist as potentialities in the sense that articulate opinion leaders could easily develop positions to activate such latent connections in their hearers. Such latency, we suggest, indicates a discursive and cultural past as well as a future political potential. It would be easy to spin these two clusters of ideas and judgments as examples of 'nanny-state' civics on one hand, and of heartless (or freedom-loving) neo-liberalism on the other. Yet what stands out, on closer examination, is the extent to which older moral-reform ideas and judgments appear still to inform *both* clusters, even if different elements of the old moral consensus are selected, and put to different uses. For example, the emphasis placed on personal autonomy and responsibility by respondents who saw gambling as a matter of individual choice echoes the emphasis early twentieth century moral-reform advocates placed on the autonomy and self-sufficiency that vice undermined. There continues to be a concern, variously expressed, for the damage done to families, and especially to women and children, by problem gambling, along with worry about a new population of the vulnerable: the elderly. One significant shift is the replacement of older references to vice with addictions language, part of a broader medicalization of moral issues (Reith 2003, 20–1). 'Addiction' and 'problem gambling' are now tropes of choice among professionals. But their apparent neutrality sometimes disguises allusions with a long history: contemporary charges that governments are 'addicted' to gambling revenue retain something of the rhetorical flavour of an older language in which it might have been said that governments had 'fallen prey to vice' in their enforcement approach to racetrack betting or alcohol consumption.

However, certain aspects of the old language are being consistently set aside in some circles. Moral reform, for all its faults, was part of a larger discourse about practical civics. But in current policy debates about gambling, references to organized publics, civic education, and collective responsibility are often displaced by the language of polling, referenda, and aggregate individual opinion on one hand, or of personal rights and responsibilities on the other. Talk of democratic institutions and civic participation is replaced by references to 'science-based' policy or to 'stakeholder' consultation, as noted in discussions of the Reno Model for responsible gambling (Blaszczynski, Ladouceur, and Shaffer 2004; and chapter 7 of this volume). Talk of moral purpose is eclipsed by that of stakeholder protection, industry sustainability, and quality of life improvements (e.g., Verlik 2005).[18] A recent commentary on the state of opinion on the public place of gambling in Canada describes it as 'uniformly grey' (Mandal and Vander Doelen 1999, 193).[19] Continuing concerns about the personal and social costs of gambling are moderated by its growing acceptance as a familiar and established feature of everyday life, signalled by the use of the term 'gaming' to distinguish recreational gambling as a harmless indulgence from 'problem gambling' as something attached to a pathologized minority. A similar moderation of concern is accomplished by discussions of trade-offs and a search for balance in their evaluation (see Azmier 2000; Azmier, Kelley, and Todosichuk 2001, 18–19; Eadington 2003b).

This grey moderation is still sometimes interrupted by a 'fickleness' (Eadington 2003b, 46) that can result in dramatic shifts in public opinion and sharp critiques of the language of science, management, sustainability, and balance (Shellinck and Schrans 2005; Borrell 2005; Yealland 2005; Azmier 2000, 31). Efforts to articulate a measured acceptance of gambling in contemporary discussions mask an ambivalence deriving from an ongoing struggle – both personal and civic – that occasionally surfaces, as in Morton's (2003) reflection on her own research:

> I have been guilty of making easy jokes at the expense of those whom I imagine to be the humourless men and women who formed the temperance movement, but the issue of gambling is not so clear to me. I am enough of a late-twentieth-century / turn-of-the-millennium libertarian (and moral relativist) to recognize the failure of prohibitive laws and to

accept diverse ethics, yet I retain profound unease around the role of government in promoting and operating gambling for its citizens. I reject the classism and racism of many of those who opposed gambling, and I find distasteful their righteousness and sanctimoniousness. However, in an age dominated by pragmatic utilitarianism, I also find their idealism appealing. Despite the anti-gamblers' tendency to make exaggerated claims concerning gambling's destructive potential, I also agree that excessive gambling has destroyed and continues to destroy real individuals and families. (pp. ix–x)

Concerns about the role of government in the gambling business, and about government reliance on gambling revenue, reflect another latent tendency in present-day discussions, one with a similar legacy from earlier times: the tendency of specific questions about gambling to incite larger questions about economic and public commitments. The moral-reform concern that vice led to dependency, and dependency to a drain on social vitality, is today reconfigured as a concern about a drain on the public purse and about the individual rights of taxpayers. Slumbering in concerns about government use of gambling revenue are fundamental and powerful questions about the definition, purpose, and ethics of taxation and public money. If licensing fees constitute a hidden tax, or if gambling revenue is a sucker tax on the willing, do they allow deferral of hard and perhaps unpopular decisions about taxation in a climate in which the legitimacy of government claims on 'our' tax dollars are begrudged? By extension, these are concerns about the legitimacy of government and of public action, and about what J.S. Woodsworth (1972 [1911], 211) called 'the responsibilities of citizenship.' They reference ideas about property rights, personal rights, and collective rights; about individual and collective responsibilities; about economic agency; about families and of communities. They evoke a suspended discussion about the ethical and practical exercise of citizenship beyond voting, polling, and stakeholding, and about that sphere which agrarian reformers of old were pleased to term a 'commonwealth.'

Through these concerns, the language of what Durkheim called 'civic morals' reappears. Gambling and responses to it, past and present, allow a glimpse into struggles over what new versions of governance, the social compact, and citizenship – as cultural and moral projects, as administrative and consumerist strategies, as frames of identity, or as a mixture of the three – will emerge in an era in which globalized, electronic commerce, rapid social transformation, and the normalization of risk form the everyday matrix of postmodern social experience.

NOTES

1 The authors thank the Alberta Gaming Research Institute, which funded research out of which this chapter was written, research assistants Viola Cassis, Jennifer Green, Tim Patterson, and Tyson Will, and several anonymous reviewers. Ideas in this article were initially presented at the conference 'Gambling Theory,' Centre for the Study of Theory and Criticism, University of Western Ontario, London, Ontario, 15 October 2004, and at the conference 'Social and Economic Costs and Benefits of Gambling,' Alberta Gaming Research Institute, Banff, Alberta, 22 April 2006.

2 Also the development of characteristic terms, definitions, allusions, tropes, and rhetorical strategies.

3 Woodsworth (n.d., 55–6) associated vice with economic struggle, and labelled excessive self-reliance a vice.

4 The idea that reciprocity is basic to social life and personal identity (Sahlins 1972) has also informed literature on social policy (Titmuss 1970).

5 On this tradition, see Noel (1990).

6 On 'purity' as a central theme of moral reform, see Valverde (1991), ch. 3.

7 As Geisst (2002) notes, agrarian opposition to financial and commodity speculation, and to gambling, was also a feature of the American political scene during this period. Like Hofstadter (1960, 1966), Geisst associates this with an unsophisticated anti-Semitism; a somewhat tendentious caricature of the Progressive movement.

8 See Halpern (2001, 8–17) for useful discussion of the interplay of 'social' and 'agrarian' feminism at the time.

9 Many Canadian social reformers (in particular, organized rural women) advocated a pacifist internationalism popular in cooperative circles (see Thompson 1982; McClung n.d.[1914?]), representing their support for the 1914–18 war effort as a fight against 'Kaiserism' in all forms, including excessive militarism among leaders on their own side. The fact that backers of racetrack betting included prominent businessmen, among them owners of breweries and distilleries, who represented horse racing as a class-appropriate sport that also served military and imperial interests in the provision of cavalry (Morton 2003, 11–12) cannot have eased hostility between its supporters and opponents.

10 See Woodsworth (1972 [1911], 169–70) for an interesting table of such dependencies.

11 For agrarian and social feminists, this latter form of masculinity tended to be associated with militarism as well as vice. On the politicization of masculinity in moral reform, see Valverde (1991, 31, 59); McLaren (1997); also Henry (2001).

12 On another front, the perceived threat of dependency led moral reformers such as Irene Parlby of the United Farm Women of Alberta, and Nellie McClung, to see eugenics as a self-evidently 'progressive' answer to mental and moral 'degeneration.'

13 It is no accident that some of these organizations were explicitly religious, nor that most were heavily populated by (Protestant) church members. In English-speaking Canada, the Social Gospel became a popular phenomenon, especially among agrarian progressives (Allen 1971, 1976). It was rooted in the social consciousness of nineteenth century evangelicalism; in particular, international evangelical movements in the Presbyterian, Methodist, and Anglican churches (see Bebbington 2005, 215–16, 246–51, 257). Another significant influence was the Danish churchman Nikolaj Frederik Severin Grundtvig, who inspired widely emulated cooperative and popular-education initiatives.

14 Complaints could cut both ways, however. A 1927 form letter prepared for the deputy attorney general of Alberta, to be sent to mayors of cities or larger towns in the province, noted that 'complaints have been made ... that the provisions of the Criminal Code against lotteries and games of chance ... are not being enforced in the larger centres of the Province, but that in the rural districts and smaller centres, owing to the activities of the Alberta Provincial Police there is strict enforcement of the law in this regard.' The letter urged 'a rigorous enforcement of the law' so that 'in future there may be no ground of complaint' (Attorney General of Alberta 1927).

15 Anecdotal evidence suggests that this sort of gambling, with a unique culture and strict rules, survived in Alberta for many decades.

16 Several noted that the drastic expansion of state-sanctioned gambling in the past three decades has changed the nature both of gambling and of community funding. Bingo was seen as a declining source of revenue, whereas hosted casinos provided a much better payback. The strict regulation of community-group hosting of casinos (including restrictions on use of funding so generated) and the long wait-time for available casino-hosting time slots were also noted.

17 A tendency perhaps encouraged when interviewers illustrated questions with examples from their own or others' experiences.

18 However, Morton notes (2003, 201), 'Pragmatic utilitarianism's attempt to discount moral stances is no more ideologically neutral than past versions of uncompromising Protestant morality.'

19 It is a sign of the times that Mandal and Vander Doelen's carefully nuanced study was published by the United Church Publishing House, an arm of a denomination associated historically with the Social Gospel and a strong anti-gambling stance.

3 Governing the Gambling Citizen: The State, Consumption, and Risk

JAMES F. COSGRAVE

The cultural liberalization of gambling that has occurred in North America in the late twentieth century reflects the overturning of particular social values, grounded in Protestant world-views, which framed gambling as problematic for the social and economic order. After the Second World War, Canadian attitudes towards non-commercial gambling 'coincided with new perspectives on moral issues as diverse as alcohol, extramarital sex, and Sunday observance' (Morton 2003, 169). In this climate of permissiveness the traditional power of Protestant churches to enforce their moral standards declined. Moving into the twenty-first century, many forms of gambling have been legalized and commercialized, and liberalization is occurring in relation to activities that would have been unthinkable in the 1940s and 1950s; pornography has become mainstream in a fragmented North American media environment, recreational drug use is acknowledged, same-sex relationships are undergoing destigmatization, and, relatedly, same-sex marriages are being championed.

In this chapter, the liberalization and legalization of gambling in Canada is analysed through a framework of risk, particularly as it relates to the state's active involvement in the shaping of gambling markets and consumption. The notion of risky consumption is developed as a theme that cuts across the areas of individual choice and responsibility, the state's role in developing and maintaining gambling markets, and the state's moral obligations in terms of this involvement. A distinction can be made between risky consumption and the consumption of risks. The latter refers to forms of consumption whereby risks are integral to the consumption experience, and provide the desired experience, for example, skydiving, forms of drug taking, and gambling (Lyng 2005; Reith

2005; Goffman 1967). The risk is not avoided but is actively consumed.

The risks involved in gambling vary from game to game; it is difficult to speak of the risks involved in playing the lottery where there is little consequentiality, unless one wins a large jackpot (Goffman 1967); the odds are long and the price of a ticket is typically low, as is the intensity of the experience. There is much more risk in high-stakes poker games. It might be objected that there is no real risk with many commercialized gambling games, as the probabilities and other forms of house edge built into the games will ensure player losses with sustained play over time.[1] Nevertheless, the discursive construction of gambling activity as a form of entertainment, leisure, or excitement presents gambling as the consumption of 'safe' risk (Gephart 2001), and this is the way gambling is mass-marketed, whether by states or private enterprises. Gamblers in commercial gambling environments are motivated by, or drawn to, the consumption of risk in gambling.

Risky consumption, by contrast, is consumption whereby risk may be entailed, but as an unwanted feature. As an example, the pain-relief drugs 'Vioxx' and 'Celebrex' have been discovered to produce significant risks of stroke and heart attack. This discovery, however, has occurred only after a significant period of consumption such that initially the consumer knew of no risks. Here the consumption, while originally thought to be safe, has turned out to be a risk.[2] Consumers who continue to take the drugs are orienting to the positives that arise from consumption, rather than the risks that are now known to be a possible consequence of prolonged use. It is the risky consumption of gambling that, to date, has not been represented to consumers: the fun of gambling (itself a feature of the social construction of gambling) is advertised but the risks – problem gambling and related issues, family conflict, debt, bankruptcy, etc. – are under-represented. The representation of gambling as consumption of risk is then a feature of the socially constructed symbolic representation of gambling by those 'stakeholders' who have market (revenue) interests in the gambling field.

As mentioned, the liberalization and legalization of gambling represents an overturning of Protestant values, such as the emphasis on the equation that work equals reward, and the notion that relying on chance is irreligious. In relation to the overturning of these values and the 'producerist' attitudes to work and money discussed by Ramp and Badgley in the previous chapter, gambling has nevertheless been put to work, and is now economically productive for the state, as a form of productive leisure or consumption (Cosgrave and Klassen 2001). It is now well noted by gambling researchers and commentators that gambling has moved from 'sin to vice to disease' in its historical-moral career; gambling has been transformed from a stigmatized activity into social policy (Rose 1988; Dombrink 1996; Will 1999; Campbell and Smith 2003). It should be pointed out, however, that while each of these characterizations of gambling is framed within particular moral discourses, in the 'disease' formulation it is only particular orientations to gambling that are viewed as problematic and not gambling activity per se.

The current 'disease' formulation, representing the negative construction of gambling through such categories as pathological gambling, exists alongside the entertainment characterization – the latter representing the socially positive representation of gambling under particular social, economic, and political circumstances. These formulations exist under the umbrella of an economic phase, where gambling is conducted as legitimate business for both state revenues and private profit, depending on jurisdiction. The former cultural suppression of gambling with its negative moral corollaries has been overcome by its potential for economic productivity.[3] In Canada this manifests itself as a feature of the way in which the state (through provincial governments' regulation of gambling enterprises) conducts itself in relation to citizens. The economically productive aspect of gambling is further reinforced in the distinction between gambling for fund-raising purposes and gambling for revenue purposes: each requires a distinctive rationale and forms of organization and governance (Mun 2002). The significance of these constructs is developed in this chapter; the continuum from entertainment to disease thus raises the issue of gambling as a form of risky consumption, which calls forth responses from the state and its gambling-related agencies, from health-care providers, as well as from gambling consumer-citizens.

Gambling Markets, the State, and Risk Management

As a framework for understanding the development of gambling markets, formulations of the 'risk society,' developed in the work of Ulrich Beck and others (Beck 1992; Beck, Giddens, and Lash 1994; Giddens 1991), draw attention to the societal dynamics generated from attempts to formulate strategies and implement practices of risk management on the one hand, and the uncertainties and unintended consequences of actions on the other. The concept of uncertainty raised in these works concerns both the epistemological and everyday life realms; but also how individuals, as well as institutions (such as the state), orient and respond to uncertainty. With respect to the relationship between gambling implementation and the orientation to risk, gambling scholar Sytze Kingma notes:

> In this new social condition of the risk society, gambling organizations have come to depend on the scientific analyses of the external effects of their games. Gambling practices have to be accounted for constantly in terms of possible consequences. This is how governments and gambling enterprises legitimate their proposals for expansion (or curtailment) of the market. (Kingma 2004, 64)

From a macro-perspective, the orientation of states entering into the field of gambling enterprises is a form of economic risk management. Indeed, within neo-liberal political and economic contexts, the economic rationale for state actions in relation to markets becomes paramount. A dominant feature of these contexts is the way in which the governing of social relations is framed as taking place *through* markets (Slater and Tonkiss 2001). The spread of legalized gambling in Canada (and elsewhere) since the 1960s and 1970s, initially in the form of state lotteries, was instigated by governments as an economic policy solution to the problem of revenue generation, where traditional methods, such as raising income and corporate taxes, are not viewed as feasible. In Canada, the state's entry into the gambling field has less to do with capturing revenues from an activity that individuals are going to do anyway (since the state has been the primary maker of gambling markets), and more to do with creating and sustaining gambling markets that provide economic benefits for the state. The intensification of gambling involvement by the state has become more apparent with the introduction and expansion of casinos and electronic gambling forms in a number of provinces since the 1990s. With the move into these forms of gambling, the state has not only legalized riskier forms of gambling (as several of the chapters here reiterate with respect to video lottery terminals, for example), but also must manage the risks of the entry into, and the constitution of, this field. The gambling field is now global, where states and corporations are the dominant actors (Wacquant 1989; Bourdieu 1991; McMillen 1996, 2003). The move into casinos, video lottery terminals, and sports betting is a response to developments and competition where ongoing liberalization creates market pressures, and where jurisdictions are in competition for gambling dollars. For those types of gambling where there is little chance that gamblers will seek out cross-border gambling experiences (whether through travel or Internet technology), governments nevertheless orient to developments in other jurisdictions, drawing upon data and forms of knowledge produced in these jurisdictions, to shape their own gambling offerings (Pierce and Miller 2007).

In Canada, along with the objective of raising revenues, gambling as a form of state practice is used to stimulate economic growth in depressed towns, to create jobs, and to attract tourists. But the provincial (regulatory) contexts in which this is occurring – where provincial governments have had legal jurisdiction over gambling enterprises since 1985 – cannot be analysed without reference to the national context, and by extension a globalized context where national economies are increasingly intertwined and implicated. The colonization and creation of gambling forms by states is a form of nationalization (Neary and Taylor 1998). This is evident in the large state-run lotteries such as Powerball in the United States, the National Lottery in Britain, El Gordo in Spain, Super 7 and Lotto 6/49 in Canada. It is also evident in the indigenous regulatory forms that shape gambling enterprises in particular jurisdictions (Austrin and West 2004).

But as gambling expansion is occurring globally, regulation remains a state-centred jurisdictional response to economic and governance risks, where local and national cultural dynamics come into play, producing forms of 'glocalization' (Bourdieu 1991; Austrin and West 2004). Commercial gambling enterprises, whether state sanctioned and operated or privately operated, exert pressure on national boundaries (McMillen 2003b). This is evident in the Canadian context with the location of casinos close to the national borders to attract gamblers from the United States: in Ontario, with the Niagara Falls casinos and the Thousand Islands Charity Casino (near Kingston) across from New York State and its casinos, and the Windsor casino across from Detroit. Globalizing pressure is also evident with the increasing popularity of forms of Internet gambling, including sports betting, poker, and simulated casino games, where due to laws prohibiting such gambling within national boundaries (as in Canada), gamblers seek other – and often more economical – opportunities to gamble through the Internet sites located in jurisdictions that permit such gambling. Gambling competition has the consequence of producing more gambling opportunities, putting particular kinds of pressure on gambling markets, where the outcomes of such developments – positive and negative – have a reflexive impact on the legal gambling environment and regulatory agencies, the social organization of gambling, and the culture more broadly.

Beck (1992, 1994) has argued that the risk society concerns the management of 'bads' generated by industrial modernity, rather than the production of goods, and that this management also has reflexive impacts on modernization processes. This framework is applicable to gambling expansion, where the consequences of expansion were/ are not known in advance (Kingma 2004). Gambling 'bads' have manifested themselves in the form of social problems such as gambling-related crime (chapter 8) and the production of problem and pathological gamblers (chapter 9). In his analysis of gambling liberalization in the Netherlands, Kingma (2004) has noted that it was not apparent to government officials that problem gambling would be a consequence of liberalization and expansion (see also chapter 7). This is also true of the legalization and expansion of gambling in Canada; gambling enterprises expanded far ahead of the implementation of programs to deal with the problematic aspects of gambling and their aftermath. The lag with respect to concerns with personal harm and social costs is attributable to the cultural and political habituses of the government officials responsible for the implementation of gambling enterprises, reflecting an ignorance (or limited knowledge) of gambling cultures and the potential negative consequences of gambling participation. More seriously, it can also reflect political expediency and cynicism in the desire to generate the revenues from gambling without due consideration of the possible negative consequences of gambling promotion (Borrell 2007; McKenna 2008). Potential or possible negative consequences would in any case have to register as risks and be present in the discourses and forms of knowledge of those responsible for the policies.

There have been other unintended and unforeseen consequences of gambling legalization in Canada – one such present issue being the demands by addicted gamblers for state liability for its contribution to their addiction (Branswell 2002; also chapter 4). For example, in 2008, a class action lawsuit was lodged against the Ontario Lottery and Gaming Corporation. The claim was that the Corporation's 'self-exclusion' program was not working, allowing these gamblers to get back into casinos. The lawsuit is for $3.5 billion (Canadian Broadcasting Corporation 2008). Another unintended consequence centres on the issue of declining public trust in governments and political institutions (Campbell et al. 2005). One high-profile instance of public concern over government-run gambling occurred in 2007 in the province of Ontario, with the documenting and airing of fraud cases linked to the theft of winning lottery and scratch tickets by official lottery retailers (see chapter 6).

The negative outcomes of gambling expansion, such as the extent and significance of problem and pathological gambling and the potential for litigation, represent risk controversies and call for their management and representation to the public (Leiss 2001). Internet gambling will call for risk management if it is to be legalized in Canada. Certain jurisdictions, such as the United Kingdom and Australia, already permit certain forms of Internet gambling, such as sports betting on-line. However, with gambling expansion, there is the potential for a 'legitimation crisis [which] refers to a situation in which politics are giving in to market demands without convincing and conclusive (legal) legitimations' (Kingma 2004, 50). The spread of gambling has produced unintended consequences, and particularly with state-owned gambling, the 'bads' have had to be managed.

In terms of how the risks related to gambling are constructed, a governmentality perspective provides a framework for distinguishing between the regulation of activities and the governing of actions: regulation concerns behaviours that require control and management, while governmentality analyses how objects and actions are produced and made governable, thereby moving beyond the relationship of regulation and suppression (Foucault 1991; Collins 1996; Rose 1996; Dean 2001; Mun 2002). For example, and in relation to this distinction, the state must regulate the gambling industry, it must regulate itself (a problem since it is both the gambling regulator in Canada, but also a promoter and major beneficiary of gambling), and it must regulate its gambling consumer-citizens. However, institutions (including the state) must learn to govern themselves in relation to the gambling practices that relate to them (e.g., gambling knowledge producers, problem gambling agencies and counsellors, charities and recipients of gambling money, etc.), and individuals must come to learn to govern themselves in relation to their own gambling proclivities and behaviours. In terms of the latter, various kinds of knowledge are disseminated by institutions to produce and inculcate practices of self-governing by individuals. Gambling legalization and liberalization is to be understood, then, not only in terms of the requirements of regulation, but through the ways in which behaviours and markets are produced and shaped.

In Canada, since gambling legalization and market development take place as state practice(s) and as a component of state infrastructure, the notion of the citizen must be considered in relation to the place of gambling in Canadian society. Individual consumers of the state's gambling products, who orient to gambling activity as a form of leisure or entertainment, are gambling citizens. Insofar as the activity is legitimized for its potential economic contribution to the public good (Campbell 1997), the consumer is the citizen, but the citizen becomes the consumer. Legalized gambling activities are thus practices that demonstrate a particular way in which the state and citizenship are performed. The state's incursion into gambling enterprises represents a form of practice, a contemporary method of conducting and performing the neo-liberal state. This will be developed further in the last section of the chapter.

Reflexive Liberalization

The ongoing liberalization of the activities mentioned at the beginning of this chapter is linked to the development of the consumer society and the particular ethos of individualism that underlies it; if enough individuals tolerate, accept, or participate in a particular activity, whether gambling, recreational drug use, etc., then this may become the basis for collective action, and calls for the legalization of an activity and changes in laws. Individual taste is shaped as a source of profit in capitalistic consumer societies, and the social and legal restrictions to this individualism occur when one's consumer taste infringes upon and harms others. When it comes to individuals' tastes, desires, and pleasures in such societies, the utilitarian notion of the greatest happiness of the greatest number is upheld in an ideal sense, but concretely, the manifestation of the pursuit of desires occurs within an environment of social conflicts concerning values, beliefs, world-views, rights, harms, etc., and raises social and political concerns with risk (Leiss 2001). As such, liberalizations may have retrograde aspects (Eadington 1996), as is the case presently with cigarette smoking, which is banned in public places. Unhealthy food is also presently under attack for its contribution to obesity, which is being constructed as a public health problem. Interestingly, the liberalization of activities must contend with current orientations to, and emphasis on, individual and public health, which are examples of forms of the governing of citizens in neo-liberal societies (Foucault 1991; Lupton 1995, 1997, 1999; Rose 2001, 2006). Health concerns are conceived not only in terms of how the individual is enjoined to orient to him/herself, but are also used as methods of governing the practices of populations (e.g., the smoking ban, etc.). Gambling is not viewed as a health threat to others, but as a (potential) threat to one's own health, as in the case of gambling addiction and suicide. Gambling suicides have increased in Ontario, and the Canada Safety Council, an independent health watchdog, wants gambling-related suicide to be considered a public health issue (Canada Safety Council 2005). Gambling problems in North America, however, are constructed largely within an individualistic and medicalizing framework (Castellani 2000). This may be contrasted with the Australian approach to problem gambling as discussed by McMillen in chapter 5.

While gambling markets are being exploited, the risks have to be managed, thus producing particular discursive constructions of social relations and responsibilities. One form of this management is the dissemination of data on gambling behaviours, such as rates of problem gambling generated by prevalence studies. A question that arises here is: What are acceptable rates of problem and pathological gamblers (see also chapter 7)? Also, at what point does the communication of information about gambling-related social problems open up a risk controversy for governments? Beck suggests that one source of the political explosiveness of risk statements 'is tied to the attribution of dangers to the producers and guarantors of the social order (business, politics, law, science), that is to the suspicion that those who endanger the public well-being and those charged with its protection may well be identical' (Beck 2004, 215).

Liberalization itself should be viewed as a social process. The freedom to engage in an activity must be supported by laws. Discussions of liberalization, however, must also take into account the forms of regulation and governing practices that are implemented to organize and shape individuals' behaviours in relation to the activities. This also leads to the question: How do the processes of liberalization, and the social risks associated with them, affect those institutions that have traditionally sought to regulate the actions of citizens, such as the state? As such, liberalization pertains not only to the cultural acceptance of particular activities and individuals' choices to engage in them, but also to how social institutions are altered in the process. While liberalization is thought in common-sense ways to assume or represent a more laissez-faire attitude and approach to activities, since the activities in question no longer have to be policed due to illegality, these activities may in fact require more state involvement and regulation, and new forms of governing. In other words, as gambling markets move from a restrictive to a permissive phase, gambling as a cultural activity is submitted to state control. Kingma's (1996) study of the liberalization of gambling in the Netherlands notes that while the cultural definition of gambling had changed, 'the liberalization of gambling presupposed a stronger state, not a weaker one' (p. 218). This has proven to be true in the Canadian context as well. Liberalization of activities and behaviours demonstrates reflexive relations between culture and the state: on the one hand, liberalization and legalization of activities presupposes a positive, or at least broadly tolerant, orientation to the activities in the culture; on the other, the liberalization of activities requires the adjustment of regulatory and governing forms as behaviours are made visible.

With respect to the development of gambling in Canada, we are witnessing the development of an interesting type of consumer market: Canadian gamblers have no legal choice but to consume the offerings presented by the provincial (state) monopolies; the liberalization of gambling itself is a selective liberalization, suiting the needs of the state, since gambling enterprises are part of its mode of conduct (Abt 1996). The primary objective is the generation of revenue, rather than meeting the needs of gamblers; not only does this entail the extraction of as much as possible from existing gamblers, but it also means the interest in creating new gamblers. The interest is stimulatory and the market is artificially created (Mun 2002). In this type of market, gambling becomes an object of governmental and social-scientific knowledge through the state's interest, not only in generating revenue, but in regulating and governing both (gambling) citizens and itself. In Canada, regulation is enacted through the various provincial and regional lottery and gambling corporations, and in the creation of institutions to provide governments with knowledge regarding the impacts of gambling activities on citizens, the community, and society at large (such as the Ontario Problem Gambling Research Centre, the Alberta Gaming Research Institute, and the Nova Scotia Gaming Foundation). It is also found in the relationship to those agencies that deal directly with the negative outcomes of these impacts (the 'bads'), such as addiction centres and other problem-gambling related institutions. In terms of the particular forms of the governing of consumer-citizens, gambling knowledge provides the basis for the influencing of behaviours, and orientations such as 'responsible gambling' are advocated.

Gambling as Risky Consumption

Gambling in Western societies has been understood and represented as a culturally ambivalent activity (Downes 1976; Reith 2002). It has existed as a popular cultural activity while being officially prohibited; it has been indulged in by the working class despite the dominance of the Protestant work ethic (Morton 2003); it has allowed disenfranchised economic and social groups to blow off steam in the face of mobility obstacles (Devereux 1949); it has allowed the capitalist stock market to legitimize speculative orientations, while disavowing irrational and unproductive gambling (Fabian 1990). The ambivalence around gambling continues, however, despite its broad acceptance and legalization (chapter 2). As a recently destigmatized legal activity, gambling is promoted both by corporations and by states. And at the level of popular culture, we find the celebration of various types of gambling activities: the popularity of large-scale state-run lotteries with their large jackpots, legal and illegal sports gambling, televised and Internet poker tournaments, and the representation of gambling in television genres, whether reality series ('Casino') or dramas ('Las Vegas'). But there are also parallel concerns about the creation of problem gamblers and gambling-related suicides, the social-ecological conditions being fostered in Canada by gambling-friendly provincial governments (Branswell 2002; Campbell and Smith 2003; Canada Safety Council 2005; Williams and Wood 2004, 2007). Gambling legislation and policy development in the Canadian context has taken place largely without the input of the public into decision making (Azmier 2001; Smith and Wynne 2004; McKenna 2008), this being evidence of particular characteristics of Canadian political culture, namely bureaucratic statism.

Canadian provincial governments are developers of gambling markets and the largest beneficiaries of gambling revenues (Campbell and Smith 2003). The legalization and expansion of gambling, however, with the consequent greater ease of access to gambling opportunities, is producing gambling behaviours, notably 'the increased incidence and visibility of problem gambling in Canadian communities' (Campbell and Smith 2003, 131). But it is also producing 'normal' gambling behaviours as well – in other words, with the creation of gambling markets, a variety of consumer behaviours are exhibited, and the non-problematic behaviours are of just as much importance as objects of knowledge and governance for the legitimation of market activity and the stabilization and expansion of markets. 'Normal' gambling orientations provide the behavioural and attitudinal material for the shaping of knowledge to be deployed to manage the risks of undesirable gambling behaviours, and for the marketing of socially acceptable orientations to gambling. The concerns with problem gambling, and the money now being spent on dealing with it (a percentage of gambling revenues generated by the provincial lottery and gambling corporations), as well as the development of knowledge-generating agencies (also funded by governments through gambling revenues), have been, however, after the fact, both in temporal and ideological terms. The state has created and stimulated a market, and the unintended consequence of state legalization and promotion of gambling has been the production of problematic forms of gambling consumption, or risky consumption.

While there are a variety of possible orientations to gambling and reasons for engaging in the activity, gambling is marketed and sold as entertainment.[4] Indeed, the state now has a direct and vested interest in the entertainment industry. However, while responsible gambling guidelines enjoin individuals to govern themselves by not treating gambling as a way to make money (RGCO 2002), this is clearly not the case for states, where, in a monopolistic market situation, the statehouse will always win because there is no competition from privately run gambling enterprises.[5] Also, the recommendation to not orient to making money is belied by the advertising and the environmental aspects of gambling where winning money is the lure and the objective (Mun 2002). Images of winning are pervasive in gambling advertising, and images of money are ubiquitous in casinos (e.g., displays of slot-machine jackpots, etc.) and in lottery advertising.

Entertainment is not only a socially constructed representation of gambling activity, but the Canadian market for such entertainment is not a free market, although new gamblers are sought and new forms of gambling are created to sustain gamblers' interest. States that support and operate gambling, such as we find in Canada, are actually a form of professional gambler, which make money from setting up the games themselves (Fabian 1990). Professional gamblers, committed rational gamblers, however, know not to gamble against the house edge. Since gambling is culturally destigmatized, it is intriguing to think about why gambling is not (re)presented as a possible social commitment, since it is after all a revenue-generating commitment of the state. An entertainment orientation to gambling, however, is advocated, where one wins money rather than makes money. But in a monopolistic situation, gamblers will not be getting the most for their entertainment dollars. This is quite obvious in the state-run sports gambling systems such as Pro-Line and Sports Select, which provide poor odds and payouts compared to sports gambling Internet sites based in other jurisdictions. While state-sanctioned and other commercial forms of gambling are viewed as a consumer activity and a form of entertainment, gambling enterprises in monopolistic situations may represent poor consumer value, and more – and perhaps better – entertainment could be provided if a free market were actually allowed to develop. McMillen (1996c) suggests that 'underlying [the] common negative perception of gambling is a particular view of the relationship between gambling, society and the state; namely, the belief that the state provides the only viable or legitimate means for mediating between people and gambling operations' (p. 15). We might also ask, however, what the risks are to the state if a free market is permitted. The deployment of gambling by states is an active form of risk management (e.g., economically, in relation to taxation and tax bases, the interest in the generation of revenues, and the provision and dispensation of budgets; morally and legally, in relation to the regulation of health and the management and control of crime – on the latter see chapter 8). However, with free-market gambling, what could be at risk is the state's interest in certain forms of conduct and governing, its conceptualization of the citizenry, and the question of its own self-definition and authority.

Despite the liberalization of gambling in Canada, the state monopoly model suggests the continuance of the negative perception of gambling. The state's role in the definition of gambling activities, however, must also be situated in relation to broader cultural values, whereby the state expresses, represents, and responds to such values as a condition of legitimacy.

Kingma (2004, 49) distinguishes two models for understanding gambling liberalization: the first refers to what he terms the alibi model; the second, the risk model. While, as the discussion in this chapter has emphasized, a focus on risk helps to understand the development of gambling markets in Canada, the state monopoly structure also suggests the alibi model:

> In that model, gambling is still intrinsically controversial. Gambling can be legalized to avoid illegal markets; the exploitation of gambling [in the Netherlands] was severely restricted by discouraging the private pursuit of profit; and gambling revenues were allocated to social interests, in terms of welfare, sports and other 'just causes.' With restrictive policies and the central role of the government in organizing gambling markets, the alibi model closely concurs with the principles of the welfare state. (Kingma 2004, 57)

While the social organization of gambling within the economic phase represents gambling activity as no longer morally problematic, the Canadian monopoly situation suggests that it is still intrinsically controversial. Gambling must be linked to societal interests, as defined by provincial governments, and more broadly to the management of the welfare state. Private-enterprise gambling then, at present at least, runs counter to Canadian cultural values as these are filtered through political culture and the understanding of the role of the state in relation to such values.

The idea that gambling should contribute to good causes, a feature of the way in which gambling has been framed historically in Canada (Campbell 1997; Campbell and Smith 1998, 2003), persists in relation to its present-day role as contributor to revenues. The selective liberalization again demonstrates how the state and its relationship to citizens are performed and appears to confirm the notion of the alibi model.[6] The liberalization of gambling, partial or selective, reveals something then about how the state is imagined and culturally constructed. While gambling is no longer stigmatized from a broad cultural perspective, the state nevertheless has the symbolic power to continue to affirm its position and define aspects of Canadian culture. The Canadian state continues its paternalistic orientation to legal gambling activity.

Governing the Gambling Citizen

In an analysis of the development of the British state, Neary and Taylor (1998) argue that the reintroduction of the British National Lottery in 1994 illustrates the inability of the Keynesian social-welfare state to respond to increasingly incalculable economic circumstances. The implementation of the lottery represents a shift in the historical manifestation and development of the state, which has moved from the 'law of insurance' to the 'law of lottery' (Neary and Taylor 1998). In effect, this means that the state can no longer govern citizens using the insurance model, within which events and risks can be calculated according to actuarial principles, but is now orienting to this new lottery principle. For Neary and Taylor, this is evidence not only of the way in which states are coming to generate revenues but of a new form of state practice and governing.

It is also symptomatic of neo-liberal social and economic environments that individuals must manage themselves in relationship to risks. The concept of responsible gambling, advocated by government gambling corporations and agencies, is itself a form of neo-liberal individualism (see also the discussion of responsible gambling in Australia in chapter 5). Here we see the linkage between the role gambling plays on a macro-level as mode of policy intervention and enabler of state conduct (through revenue generation), and its problematic status as a potentially risky consumption activity where individuals must be enjoined to govern their gambling proclivities.

Advocating responsible gambling through prevention, awareness, and education programs, as well as therapeutic interventions, is required in the neo-liberal environments of gambling legalization, legitimation, and expansion. As Campbell and Smith (2003) point out, however, the discourse of responsible gambling 'runs counter to the medical model's precept that problem gambling is a disease, that implies that afflicted individuals are not responsible for their condition' (p. 14). It is not only that the medical model deflects questions of individual responsibility (2003, 14), but rather that 'responsible gambling' constructs a discourse of individuals' choices and behaviours, and suggests that anyone is at risk of gambling irresponsibly. As such, responsible gambling is a form of risk management taught to individuals, for individuals, but it is also a method of risk management for states that need to legitimize their role in gambling enterprises (Cosgrave and Klassen 2001). It is disseminated as a desired moral orientation to consumption practices, in particular as a way of being a gambling citizen in neo-liberal societies where various types of behaviour are liberalized or deregulated (Foucault 1991; Rose 1999; Mun 2002).

Within neo-liberal social orders, where social relations are framed primarily as economic relations, responsible gambling must be viewed in terms of its political import: 'the responsible gambling paradigm transposes social problems affiliated with excessive gambling into individual problems and depoliticizes them' (Campbell and Smith 2003, 143). With such depoliticizing, the social structural, economic, and political factors that produce excessive gambling and the social and economic rationale for (more) gambling are not problematized. Responsible gambling then is a legitimation strategy for states and stakeholders, a strategy that seeks to normalize gambling, build a stable gambling market, and govern citizens' gambling behaviours. We thus find a depoliticizing of addictions insofar as they are viewed as individual and not social problems (Castellani 2000; Campbell and Smith 2003; Borrell 2007).

In relation to problem gambling, responsible gambling, and the risk management of gambling markets, the social production of gambling knowledge(s) has followed the incursion of state-sponsored gambling into culture, aimed at the normalization of gambling behaviours. Alan Collins (1996), in his analysis of the category of pathological gambler, reflects on its late emergence: 'Until the late 20th century the means of assessing the extent of gambling were not in place: its illegality made much of it hidden, the informal and secretive nature of many gambling forums made them extremely difficult to assess, there were the thorny issues of defining gambling, and perhaps most importantly of all, there was the technical problem of distinguishing money new to the gambling market from money being recycled within the market' (p. 93). Problem-gambling researcher Howard Shaffer has remarked: 'By the end of the twentieth century, almost 50% of gambling studies journal articles had been published during the 1990s ... almost 33% of gambling studies journal articles have been published between 1999 and 2003' (Shaffer 2004). There is also the ongoing production of knowledge from consumer and market research perspectives by private industry and state gambling corporations and agencies with stakes in maintaining and expanding gambling markets.[7] This includes the tracking of individual gambler play by casinos through player loyalty cards used to monitor amounts of time and money spent on particular gambling games – particularly useful in the case of EGM gambling.

It is possible to distinguish between the production of front-end and back-end gambling knowledge. These refer respectively to knowledge that seeks to liberate gambling behaviour, and knowledge that aims to regulate such behaviour, particularly the negative manifestations. Both contribute to the governing of gambling behaviours in the sense being used in this chapter. Front-end knowledge relates to the revenue (or profit) imperative and the stimulation of gambling behaviour in relation to this: gambling marketing and advertising, casino construction (its external construction, and more importantly its internal environment), the design of games and their technological appeal, physical access to gambling – all forms of knowledge that contribute to the generation of revenues. Back-end knowledge refers to the forms of knowledge related to the management of gambling behaviour and any negative consequences: problem gambling knowledge used by counsellors and treatment centres, criminal enforcement knowledge (chapter 8), strategies produced to appease gambling expansion or opposition, etc. Gambling expansion is producing behaviours, both problematic and non-problematic, and the generation of front-end and back-end knowledge is central to a risk-management orientation:

> Rather than being a programmatic failure or a source of resistance to be overcome, risk represents an opportunity for governmental expansion, refinement and modification. Concrete indicators of risk such as revenue audits and rates of pathological gambling ... allow the state to judge the level of activity of these economic and social risks, which subsequently empowers it to improve upon its performance of casino provision. (Mun 2002, 229–30)

Gambling promotion emphasizes the emotional, if not the irrational, appeal of gambling, and casinos are liminal spaces where rational orientations are discouraged (Mun 2002). As such, gambling is marketed as entertainment, as a vehicle for the possibility of winning and spending money, but not as a way to make money. So, gambling should be risk-free, and yet gambling populations have to be enjoined to treat it this way, which requires self-regulation and responsibilization (Ewald 2002; Rose 1996). The desired orientation to gambling as a form of entertainment is an ideal, because other orientations are possible, including risky orientations. The risks, however, arise from precisely the orientations through which gambling is made desirable and appealing to the public, for example, as a method of generating excitement, and where one should not attempt to make money doing it.

Here again, it is not just a question of the preferences and orientations of consumers, but of the desires of citizens, whose actions (and not only spent money) should contribute to the public good. The public good is to be thought, therefore, not only in terms of the societal contributions of gambling revenues – the 'alibi' conception – but also through the self-governance of individuals, who will not be harmful to themselves or others, nor be a social cost. The liberalization and destigmatization of gambling does not mean, then, that there are no moral risks for the gambler.

Responsible gambling is thus communicated and advocated, but not rational gambling (Mun 2002).[8] The programs and policies generated from individuals' orientation to risk, directed at gambling behaviours (such as responsible gambling and voluntary casino self-exclusion programs), relate to and serve both front-end and back-end forms of knowledge. In other words, they serve the building of legal gambling markets, where 'the commoditization of consumer preferences may generate new forms of visibility of the attitudes, aspirations and desires of citizens ... [in order] to construct relays and relations between the predilections and passions of the individual and the attributes and image of the product' (Rose 1999, 245).

To date, the risky consumption related to gambling activities is not getting the same attention as the depiction of the pleasures derived from the consumption of gambling risks from the official gambling agencies, but coverage of gambling in the media provides no shortage of stories related to the negative consequences of the activity. Indeed, it has also become a cliché to say that governments are addicted to gambling revenues.[9] It is significant here that where gambling is marketed as entertainment by the state, the state itself has moved into the gambling field out of economic necessity. The state may pursue gambling as a way to generate revenues, but the gambling citizen should not think about it in these terms. The issue then is not only one of communicating the risks (problem gambling, financial problems, etc.) and providing equal time, but of responsible government. One version of irresponsibility points to the state's conflict of interest in its role as both regulator and beneficiary of gambling activities. A related issue here is the governments' interpretation and use of criminal law in relation to gambling expansion, as discussed by Colin Campbell in the next chapter. A problematic manifestation of state involvement in gambling markets, raised in the chapters by Campbell and MacNeil, concerns the level of consumer protection with respect to EGM gambling, regarded to be the riskiest form of gambling from an addiction perspective.

These issues ask us to consider the self-understanding of the gambling-friendly state as a moral entity, prompting critical reflection on the forms of moral regulation directed at citizens through the state's desire to exploit gambling markets.

Conclusions

In this chapter the social organization of legalized gambling in Canada has been considered in relation to three intersecting forces: (1) the individual as citizen and consumer, (2) the state's position in the gambling market and its orientation to risk, and (3) the particular manifestation of gambling enterprises within Canadian culture. The gambling market is a restricted market due to the state monopoly of legal gambling enterprises and opportunities. Nevertheless, the state's involvement in such enterprises places it in a risk domain. The social construction of gambling in its 'disease' form is related to its construction as entertainment, such that the state has a vested economic interest in the entertainment industry, and must manage the risks of the entry into the gambling field. As a particular form of consumption, gambling activities are marketed as the consumption of risks, but which may entail risky consumption.

The entrepreneurializing of the state that is demonstrated through the entry into and exploitation of gambling markets is a response to the pressures placed upon states by economic globalization generally; the expansion of global gambling markets and the various jurisdictional regulatory responses are thus a particular expression of these pressures and dynamics.

The social organization of legal gambling in Canada represents an ongoing response to the increasingly global market in gambling, but it is also, despite provincial variation, a particular political-cultural response. This organization manifests, and is an alibi for, statist interests, and the monopoly form is framed within particular Canadian cultural values, such as collectivism and paternalism (as well as regionalism), which, with respect to the creation and development of gambling markets, exist in tension with neo-liberal values such as individualism and marketization. Within neo-liberalism, the state's involvement in gambling enterprises is a way in which the state and its relationship to citizens is conducted and performed. The risk-managing responsible gambler is constructed and advocated in this context. Nevertheless, the Canadian state symbolically reaffirms itself through its ability to organize and represent gambling enterprises and activities in particular ways. Between alibis and risks, gambling is mobilized in Canada as a political-economic vehicle, and the citizen and consumer are merged.

NOTES

1 As Kingma (1997) notes, players will account for their participation (and losses) in terms of a process of 'negating instrumentality.' The latter is also a feature of the way states involved in gambling enterprises legitimize their participation.
2 The Merck & Co. Corporation, the creator of Vioxx, has been in court in the United States for charges that it withheld information related to the risks of heart attack and stroke arising from consumption of the drug, thus contributing to a number of deaths. The most recent federal case ended in a mistrial (Tesoriero and Martinez 2005). Aside from the potential health risks related to the consumption of unsafe products, cases that involve claims of corporate

fraud or deception produce another level of risk for both the corporation and the consumer; i.e., the risk of (mis)trust related to the transparency (or not) of corporate-consumer relations. The potential cost to the corporations of taking illegal risks is also a factor since, in some cases, the penalty for illegality (fines) may be worth the risk of withholding information.

3 The development of commercialized gambling and its marketization can be linked to the broader development of modern economies, which, as Ramp and Badgley point out in chapter 2, undergo rationalization, and which strive to be 'regular, predictable, and rule-bound.'

4 Certainly, cultural permissiveness towards gambling is a condition for it to be organized as a commercial enterprise, and marketed as a form of entertainment. However, the configuration of gambling as entertainment, expressed in its commercialized forms (primarily in its casino manifestations), is also a legitimation strategy and a form of risk management, where the suggested orientation to gambling as entertainment can be considered a form of governing. To not orient to gambling in this way becomes a risk to the individual, risky consumption (RGCO 2002). As entertainment, the risks of gambling are deconsequentialized. The entertainment construct is symbolically and spatially reinforced in larger casinos that also offer the opportunities to shop and attend concerts. This framing of gambling has been referred to as a form of 'Vegasification' (Gottdenier et al. 2000).

5 In Canada, the competition faced by provincial casinos is not between provinces so much as it with American cities such as Las Vegas and Atlantic City, and with those states with casinos located close to the Canadian border. Provincial gambling enterprises also have to contend with market pressures from presently illegal forms of Internet gambling and with other technological developments affecting global markets.

6 The work of anthropologist Mary Douglas, and her sociocultural approach to risk, has pertinence for this discussion. For Douglas, understandings and perceptions of risk are shaped by cultures, and thus their social-symbolic constitution must be considered (Douglas 1966, 1992; Douglas and Wildavsky 1982). In terms of this discussion, the development of a gambling market monopolized by the state is expressive of Canadian cultural values whereby certain political or economic behaviours are understood as risking such values. While the contours of gambling markets can vary from province to province, the state-run model of gambling suggests the idea of Canadian risk.

7 Eadington (2003b) notes: 'Until casinos spread beyond Nevada and Atlantic City in the United States, there was little institutionally funded research on gambling. Similar circumstances prevailed in other countries. Since the

1990's, a number of major national studies have been undertaken in various countries, including the National Gambling Impact Study Commission, *Final Report* (Washington, D.C.: Government Printing Office 1999); Britain's *Gambling Review Report* (London: Stationery Office 2001); and Australia's *Productivity Commission Report* (Canberra 1999)' (p. 47). There has yet to be a major national study conducted in Canada (Campbell et al. 2005).

8 These orientations to gambling may appear on the surface to be the same: the responsible is the rational. However, responsible gambling literature typically educates the gambler to treat gambling as entertainment, to not treat it as a way to make money, etc. Rational gamblers, by contrast, take gambling seriously, often as a way to make money (such as professional poker players), and will avoid games with built-in disadvantage or a house edge. They would seek out better gambling value. One can be a 'responsible' VLT player; in some respects the responsible gambler can be an irrational gambler.

9 The *Toronto Star* had a four-part series on gambling in Ontario, titled 'Bad Bets,' focusing on such things as problem gambling, gambling suicides, gambling in ethnic groups, and how governments are making gambling easier (19–22 December 2004). The first line of an editorial was 'Ontario is hooked on gambling, and like many addicts, it is in denial.'

PART TWO

Comparative Gambling Policy Frameworks

4 Canadian Gambling Policies

COLIN S. CAMPBELL

Gambling is a big business in Canada. It employs a sizeable number of people; provides a significant source of revenue for provincial governments and for community-based, non-profit charitable organizations; and offers social and recreational opportunities for those who are motivated to participate in its diverse formats.

There are currently over 145,000 venues and/or opportunities to gamble legally in Canada (Azmier 2005). Government-run gambling (bingo, EGMs, table games, and lotteries) generated a gross profit of $13 billion in 2005 (Statistics Canada 2007). After paying costs associated with generating gambling revenues, government-run gambling produced a net profit of $7.1 billion (Statistics Canada 2007).[1] In other words, net profits and the costs associated with conducting government gambling result in an almost 50/50 split of the gross profit between provincial governments and gaming service providers. In addition to government-run gambling, other gambling formats licensed by provincial governments (charitable bingos, raffles, casinos; horse racing; and several First Nation venues) together generate another nearly $2 billion in gross profits.

As a proportion of provincial government revenue, gambling constituted 3.8 per cent of all revenue raised by government and ranged from a low of 2.9 per cent in British Columbia to a high of 5.5 per cent in Manitoba (Azmier 2005, 7). This percentage is higher if only provincial revenues are considered, so that in 2005, 5.5 per cent of all provincial revenue came from gambling (Statistics Canada 2007). While provincial governments are the single largest beneficiary of gambling revenues, it is to be noted that other levels of government also garner a share of gambling revenues, albeit much smaller. More specifically, under the terms of the agreement that resulted in the 1985 amendment to the *Criminal Code*, an amount is paid annually (adjusted according to the Consumer Price Index) to the federal government. Each province contributes a share calculated proportionally to its lottery sales. In 2003, the amount contributed by the provinces under this agreement amounted to approximately $60 million and represented about 0.93 per cent of net profits (Canada 2004, Proceedings of the Standing Senate Committee on Legal and Constitutional Affairs, 1–2 December; Canadian Partnership for Responsible Gambling 2004). In British Columbia, Alberta, Manitoba, and Ontario, revenue-sharing agreements have been negotiated with some municipalities. Under these relatively recent agreements, municipal governments receive approximately 2.6 per cent of net profits (Canadian Partnership for Responsible Gambling 2004). It is thus clear that all levels of government in Canada are now reliant to some extent on revenues derived from gambling sources.

With the growth of the volume of dollars involved in legal gambling in Canada, employment in the gambling industry has also risen dramatically. In 1993, 14,000 people were employed in the gambling industry, but a decade later this had risen to over 40,000 (Marshall 2004).

In Canada, one of the key features of gambling's expansion is the distinct nature of the legal 'gaming industry' that has developed – a diverse multi-billion-dollar sector that provides a wide variety of gambling formats and that increasingly generates its revenues from sophisticated modern electronic gaming technologies such as video lottery terminals (VLTs), slot machines, and electronic bingo – generically referred to as electronic gaming machines or EGMs. This industry is now comprised of a diverse set of increasingly competitive stakeholders that include provincial and municipal governments; Crown corporations; non-profit community-based organizations; fairs and exhibitions; private sector gaming operators and suppliers; and hospitality-tourism interests. All of these gaming stakeholders seek to maintain or increase their share of the gambling marketplace. Of course, beyond charitable non-profit organizations, the largest beneficiaries of liberalized public attitudes towards gambling have been Canadian provincial governments (Campbell 2000, 2; Azmier and Smith 1998).

Canadian *Criminal Code* Gambling Provisions[2]

The type and extent of gambling permitted in Canada was dramatically transformed as a result of two landmark amendments to the *Criminal*

Code of Canada in 1969 and 1985. The 1969 amendment granted provincial governments the authority 'to manage and conduct' gambling games such as lotteries alone or in partnership with other governments. Under the amendment, provinces were also allowed to permit community-based non-profit organizations to conduct 'lottery schemes' under provincial licence. Provincial governments have interpreted the meaning of 'lottery scheme' liberally and under this provision have licensed the operation of casino-style games of chance such as blackjack and roulette.

The 1985 amendment subsequently gave exclusive control of lotteries and lottery schemes to provincial governments. Importantly, this amendment permitted computer, video, and slot devices – prohibited in Canada since 1924 – to be managed and conducted exclusively by provincial authorities (Campbell 1997).

Taken together these changes to the *Criminal Code* reflect four major trends in Canadian gambling: (1) a clear transition from criminal prohibition to legalization; (2) a consistent pattern of greater provincial authority over gambling and a corresponding decline in federal responsibility; (3) a continuing escalation of new gambling products, particularly electronic gaming machines (EGMs); and (4) legal gambling expansion being driven by vested interest groups (Campbell, Hartnagel, and Smith 2005; Campbell and Smith 2003, 1998).

The discussion below reviews the provisions of the *Criminal Code* that selectively legalize certain types of gambling and describes the regulatory and operational regimes that have emerged to manage and conduct legal gambling. These regimes vary dramatically in nature and scope from province to province. The variation is attributable to the different interpretations of the provisions contained in section 207 of the *Criminal Code*.

As noted above, gambling in Canada is a multi-billion-dollar legal business. However, in a strictly legal sense, gambling in Canada is prohibited – except for the exemptions spelled out in Part VII of the *Criminal Code*. Exemptions to the prohibition have been granted for parimutuel wagering on horse racing conducted under the jurisdiction of the minister of agriculture; private bets between individuals not engaged in the business of betting; governments of a province alone or in conjunction with other provinces to conduct and manage a lottery scheme; a charitable or religious organization pursuant to a licence issued by a province to conduct and manage a lottery scheme for the purpose of raising proceeds for a religious or charitable object or purpose; and for a board of a fair or an exhibition to conduct and manage a lottery scheme pursuant to a provincial licence.

Section 204 of the *Criminal Code*, which in addition to exempting private betting between individuals, since 1920 has also permitted betting on horse racing via a pari-mutuel system. Indeed, it was this provision that enabled racetracks and the horse-racing interests to hold a virtual monopoly over legal gambling through most of the twentieth century.

It is under section 207 titled *Permitted Lotteries* that the transformation and expansion of gambling in Canada over the last thirty-five years has occurred. Section 207 legalizes the creation and operation of lotteries run by any of the bodies specified in section 207(1)(a) to (d). As well, it provides for the regulation of such schemes under provincial laws and under terms and conditions of licences that may be granted pursuant to provincial authority. In other words, section 207(1) permits lotteries to be created and operated by a province, or under licence by charitable or religious organizations, by a board of a fair or exhibition, or by any other person to whom a licence has been issued if the ticket cost does not exceed two dollars and the prize does not exceed $500 (*Martin's Annual Criminal Code* 2005, 397). It is under these *Criminal Code* provisions that provinces have acquired legal authority to operate and/or license particular forms of gambling. As a consequence, all Canadian provinces and territories conduct or permit gambling to some extent.

With the amendment in 1969 and with the consolidation of provincial authority over almost all forms of legal gambling as a result of the 1985 amendment, Canadian provincial governments have significantly increased the extent and availability of gambling in Canada. The two formats that now dominate Canadian gambling are: (1) electronic gaming machines (EGMs) such as video lottery terminals (VLTs) and slot machines; and (2) casino gambling, which in addition to the traditional green-felt table games now offers a variety of electronic gaming devices such as slot machines. Lotteries – once the primary source of government gambling revenues – have been eclipsed by revenues derived from electronic gaming machines and casinos. For example, in 2005 total government revenue from EGMs amounted to approximately $8.9 billion while ticket lottery revenues amounted to $3.2 billion (Canadian Partnership for Responsible Gambling 2007).

Canadian Operational-Regulatory Models

It is evident, despite the otherwise uniform application of the *Criminal*

Figure 4.1: Permitted gambling under the *Criminal Code*

s. 204(1)	s. 207(1)(a)	s. 207(1)(b)	s. 207(1)(c)	s. 207(1)(d)
Pari-mutuel betting on horse races	Provincial lottery schemes	Licensed charitable or religious lottery schemes	Licensed fairs and exhibition lottery schemes	Licensed 'minor' lottery schemes
	s. 207(4)(c) Provincial computer, video device, slot machine, dice games			

Code and its provisions, that provincial operational and regulatory structures in regard to gambling differ dramatically across the country. These differences are attributable to varying interpretations of the language of the *Criminal Code*. More specifically, Canadian provinces differ in their interpretations of two particular phrases contained in the gambling provisions of the *Criminal Code*.

The first phrase, 'lottery scheme,' was inserted into the *Criminal Code* in 1906 and has since become a significant phrase in Canadian gambling law, particularly after 1969. It has been broadly construed by provinces to encompass not only 'true lotteries' but other games of chance such as bingo, sports betting, and casino-style card games such as blackjack and poker. More recently, with developments in electronic technology, slot machines, video devices, and games operated on or through computers have, since 1985, been incorporated within the *Criminal Code*'s definition of permitted lottery schemes, if managed and conducted by the government of a province alone or in conjunction with other provinces.

The second phrase, 'manage and conduct,' has also been interpreted in different ways by Canadian provincial governments. Stemming from the varying provincial understandings of the *Criminal Code* gambling provisions, four models of managing and conducting gambling have emerged.

1. The Crown Corporation Model

Manitoba, Quebec, and Saskatchewan have interpreted 'manage and conduct' such that major gambling formats such as casinos and lotteries within their jurisdiction are directly owned and operated under the auspices of Crown corporations.

With regard to Crown corporations, it is important to understand their role in the delivery and regulation of legal gambling operations. Provincial Crown corporations are government-owned corporations that are, ostensibly, at arm's length from government control. They are usually formed to pursue economic and social objectives that generate revenue by selling goods and/or services on the open market (Canadian Tax Foundation 2004). In Canada, Crown corporations are the favoured policy instruments used by provinces to manage and conduct legal gambling businesses.

The province that historically was the most ardent supporter of legalized state lotteries was also the first to inaugurate a provincially owned and operated lottery corporation following the landmark 1969 amendment to the federal *Criminal Code* (Labrosse 1985; Campbell 1994; Morton 2003). Operational since 1 January 1970, Quebec's Crown corporation, Loto-Québec, was created as the province's vehicle for managing and conducting state lotteries for three explicit reasons: (1) compliance with the federal *Criminal Code*; (2) maximization of the economic and social benefits for the residents of Quebec; and (3) minimization of opportunities for the involvement of organized crime interests. Thus, in contrast to other provinces, particularly those that have developed hybrid operational models discussed below, Loto-Québec has tended to restrict the involvement of private sector corporate partners in its operations. Nevertheless, Loto-Québec has from its outset demonstrated a relatively aggressive entrepreneurial style.

From its earliest days, Loto-Québec, realizing the potential financial windfalls that lay within the newly created space for legal gambling, was one the first provincial agencies to contemplate seriously the introduction of casino gambling (Labrosse 1995). As well, Loto-Québec quickly gained considerable domestic marketing and management experience with lotteries and sought to further capitalize by providing consultative services to other jurisdictions contemplating the establishment of state lotteries. Loto-Québec International, a subsidiary, was created with a mandate to provide lottery management consulting services to countries such as Colombia, Morocco, Zaire, and Senegal (Labrosse 1985, 204).

In the intervening years, Loto-Québec's operations have expanded to include the creation and ownership of the Société des casinos du Québec (SCQ), a subsidiary corporation, to finance, manage, and operate three major casinos (located in Montreal, Hull, and Pointe-au-Pic) and their related restaurant and hotel services. Loto-Québec has also established another subsidiary corporation, the Société des loteries vidéo du Quebéc (SLVQ), to operate a provincial video lottery network, and recently, in cooperation with community-based non-profit organizations, Loto-Québec has implemented an electronic bingo network under the auspices of its subsidiary, the Société des bingos du Québec (SBQ) (Loto-Québec 2006).

Loto-Québec's entrepreneurship in the modern international gambling marketplace also continues. For example, in 2005, Loto-Québec invested $87 million to acquire an interest in Moliflor Loisirs, the third largest casino operator in France. And, through yet another wholly-owned subsidiary corporation, Ingenio, established for the purposes of research and development of innovative gambling software and hardware products, Loto-Québec has sought to provide gaming products and services to lottery operators worldwide. Towards this end, Ingenio has awarded a licence for the use of its patents to GTECH, an American multinational corporation that is a dominant supplier of gaming products in the global marketplace (Loto-Québec 2006).

Despite its domestic and international financial successes, Loto-Québec has not been without controversy. For example, in 2001 Loto-Québec and its subsidiary SLVQ were named as defendants in a much-publicized class-action lawsuit. In 2001, Quebec City lawyer Jean Brochu initiated a class-action lawsuit against Loto-Québec, claiming it failed to warn players about the potential dangers of the 15,000 video lottery terminals that SLVQ operated in over 4,000 bars in the province.

The genesis of the legal action stemmed from Brochu's battle with his gambling addiction. As a result of his out-of-control VLT play, Brochu lost his car and home and was disbarred from practising law because he stole $50,000 to cover his gambling debts. In an ongoing action, Brochu is suing on behalf of 119,000 Quebecers (a figure derived from a Quebec problem gambling prevalence survey) and asking for $700 million in damages and an admission of liability from Loto-Québec and the VLT manufacturers who provided the machines (Thorne 2002; Campbell, Hartnagel, and Smith 2005). Irrespective of the outcome, this will be a watershed case. A decision that favours the plaintiffs likely will lead to a spate of similar lawsuits in Canada and elsewhere.

Coinciding with the class-action lawsuit, Loto-Québec and the SLVQ have been the focus of further controversy regarding both the location and operation of the VLT network in the province of Quebec. More specifically, a series of articles in the Montreal *Gazette* in 2002 alleged that

Loto-Québec has been complicit in the establishment of a loose licensing system that has allowed a handful of businessmen with questionable pasts (including connections to organized crime) to dominate the province's VLT retail operations (Norris 2002a, A1).

To the chagrin of the Crown corporation, it has also been demonstrated that there has been a disproportionate number of licences granted and a correspondingly disproportionate number of VLT machines situated in low-income neighbourhoods. This finding has raised the spectre that Loto-Québec, in partnership with ruthless holders of VLT licences, is shamelessly exploiting those least able to afford gambling losses (Norris 2002b, A15).

In response, Loto-Québec and the SLVQ have been forced to reconsider both the number and availability of VLTs throughout the province. As of 2005, Loto-Québec was moving to reduce the overall number of machines in the province as well as trying to restrict the number of machines per venue (Loto-Québec 2006).

2. The Hybrid Model

The hybrid model is a joint venture partnership arrangement in which provincial governments contract with private sector companies to provide gambling facilities and oversee gambling operations. For example, when Ontario implemented casino gambling in the early 1990s, the province adopted a hybrid ownership, management, and operation model. Under this arrangement, casinos are owned and controlled by the Ontario government. However, daily operations are overseen by private sector operators acting as agents of government (Alfieri 1994).

The Ontario Lottery and Gaming Corporation (OLGC) was created in 2000 by merging two existing Crown corporations: the Ontario Casino Corporation and the Ontario Lottery Corporation. The OLGC is responsible for four business divisions: lottery products, charity and Aboriginal casinos, commercial casinos, and slot machines at racetracks. In these business divisions, private sector companies are retained under contract to provide a range of gambling services and products directly to the public. For example, Casino Windsor is operated and managed on a day-to-day basis by Windsor Casino Limited (WCL). WCL is a privately owned consortium consisting of major corporations such as Park Place Entertainment and Hilton Hotels. WCL provides its operational services to the OGLC on the basis of a contractual arrangement.

Nova Scotia also employs a hybrid model. A provincial Crown corporation, the Nova Scotia Gaming Corporation (NSGC), is responsible to a board of directors appointed by the provincial government. It is governed by the provincial *Gaming Control Act* and is responsible for ticket lottery, video lottery, and casino gambling in Nova Scotia. Day-to-day operation of these gambling formats is carried out under the jurisdiction of the Atlantic Lottery Corporation (ALC) and Casino Nova Scotia.

The Atlantic Lottery Corporation, the regional Crown corporation created to oversee lottery schemes in the Atlantic provinces, functions under the umbrella of the Nova Scotia Gaming Corporation. The ALC is mandated with the task of overseeing the operation of ticket lotteries and video lottery terminals within Nova Scotia. Casino Nova Scotia, a private company, is a subsidiary of American-based Caesar's Entertainment. Under its contractual agreement with NSGC, Casino Nova Scotia operates casinos in Halifax and Sydney.

A further variation of the hybrid model exists in British Columbia, whereby private sector gambling service providers own casino facilities and supply personnel to operate the games. However, the gambling equipment, such as blackjack tables, roulette tables, and slot machines, is owned and maintained by the provincial Crown corporation, the British Columbia Lottery Corporation (BCLC). Under contractual agreements with BCLC, private sector operators derive a percentage of the casino winnings as remuneration for their operational services.

3. The Charity Model

The *Criminal Code* has long allowed lottery schemes to be conducted and managed by charitable and religious groups under a licence issued by a provincial authority, if the proceeds are used for charitable or religious purposes. All provinces license some form of charity gambling (mostly bingo, raffles, sports pools, and break-open tickets), but Alberta is the leading exponent of this gaming model because casinos also fit under the charitable umbrella. In Alberta, private casino companies provide the facility, personnel, and gambling services for the delivery of gambling activities.

It is common practice for charities to provide volunteers to help run gambling events and to spend considerable time on waiting lists to host an event due to the high demand for the privilege (Berdahl 1999). A major consequence of charity or 'worthy cause' gambling has been to legitimize what was once seen as a vice or a sinful activity (Campbell 2000).

4. First Nations

Some Canadian First Nation communities have gained access to gambling revenues through agreements with provincial authorities. The approval of gambling on Native lands has been driven by the rationale that gambling proceeds are a vehicle for financial autonomy that will improve social and economic conditions on reservations. Existing Canadian First Nation gambling ventures are regulated in one of three ways (Kiedrowski 2001): (1) a First Nation community applies for a licence similar to other charitable organizations; (2) a First Nation enters into an agreement with the province to operate a casino (depending on the province this may be on or off reserve); or (3) a licence to conduct gambling events is obtained from a provincially approved First Nation licensing body.

The amount and type of gambling allowed on First Nation lands varies considerably from province to province. For example, in Saskatchewan four of the five full-time casinos are on Native reservations, and Aboriginals hold over 70 per cent of the jobs in the 1,100 person workforce.

Both Alberta and Manitoba have a First Nations Gaming Policy, which allow for on-reserve casinos. In Alberta one First Nation casino has been approved and several are at various stages of the application process. Five First Nation casino proposals have been recommended in Manitoba; one is operational and the others are working their way through an implementation process. Casino Rama in Orillia, Ontario, is a mega First Nation gambling resort featuring a hotel, over 2,000 slot machines, 120 gaming tables, and high-profile entertainers.

Provinces such as Nova Scotia, Quebec, New Brunswick, and Manitoba have agreements with First Nation groups allowing them to operate bingo, sell lottery tickets, and have VLTs on reserve, while the British Columbia, Newfoundland and Labrador, and Prince Edward Island governments have no special gaming arrangements with their First Nation communities (Kiedrowski 2001).

Irrespective of the operational or regulatory model that has been adopted, provincial governments have exclusive authority over the type and extent of legal gambling operated within their borders. The gambling provisions of the modern *Criminal Code* and the operation and regulatory regimes that have been embraced are directed less at preventing participation in a harmful activity and more towards securing and justifying provincial monopolization of gambling as a revenue source.

Policy Objectives Underpinning Gambling's Legalization

The history of legal gambling since the 1969 amendment, however, illustrates that policy formulation in respect to gambling has been in many respects ad hoc, reactive, and incrementalist (Campbell and Ponting 1984; Campbell 2000) and controlled and developed by executive levels of government for political and economic advantage. Nowhere is this more evident than in the machinations that led to the 1985 amendment in which provincial governments negotiated criminal law revisions that gave them exclusive authority over lotteries and lottery schemes and legalized electronic gambling formats. A contractual agreement, brokered by federal and provincial ministers responsible for amateur sport, fitness, and culture, saw the 1985 criminal law revisions enacted in exchange for a $100 million payment from the provinces to the federal government. The $100 million payment was, in turn, contributed by the federal government to the Calgary Olympics (Osborne and Campbell 1988; Campbell, Hartnagel, and Smith 2005). In other words, an agreement to amend the criminal law provisions with regard to gambling was negotiated by officials who normally have little or no direct involvement with criminal law or with justice policies. Yet, the agreement was approved by the minister of justice and subsequently rubber-stamped by Parliament with very little public debate.[3] Indeed, it can be noted that the last genuine public debate on gambling law revisions occurred in the 1950s when a special committee of the House of Commons and Senate examined the issues of lotteries (Campbell and Smith 1998; Campbell, Hartnagel, and Smith 2005).

Typically since the 1969 and 1985 amendments, provincial cabinets, usually on the advice of policy elites of senior bureaucrats, have tended to control the formation and implementation of gambling policies, often without resort to legislative bodies. Western Canadian provinces, the first provinces to dramatically increase the level and extent of permitted gambling, opted to expand, license, and otherwise regulate gambling by passing orders-in-council rather than enacting legislation that would have required the passage of bills through provincial legislatures. For example, the province of British Columbia did not enact legislation to control and regulate gambling until 2002, which by then was nevertheless generating annual gross profits in excess of $1.6 billion via lotteries, bingos, and 18 casino operations (B.C. Lottery Corporation 2002).

While rational and open policy processes have not always been evident in the lead-up to the expansion of legal gambling in Canada, the legalization and expansion of gambling has nevertheless not been without broad objectives. These broad objectives have simultaneously served as rationalizations or justifications for the selective removal of criminal prohibitions and for expansion of gambling industries.

American economist and noted gambling expert William Eadington (1994) has observed that Canadian jurisdictions have legalized gambling for the purposes of funding non-profit community-based charitable organizations; generating government revenue; stimulating economic growth (including tourism, urban revitalization, job creation); apprehending revenue leakage to jurisdictions where gambling is legally available; preventing illegal gambling (such as 'grey machines') and preventing organized crime and disreputable persons from penetrating legal gambling operations; and modernizing outdated or unworkable laws. As is evident in the review of the extent of gambling presented earlier, the obvious objectives that have been sought in Canada through the legalization of gambling have been the generation of revenues for provincial governments and for non-profit community-based organizations. However, the above goals have all played a role to some extent in the decisions to permit or to expand particular forms of gambling in Canadian communities and are considered below. As the discussion suggests, the goals and objectives to be achieved through gambling are not nearly as neat and clear-cut as proponents of gambling would advocate.

Policy Paradoxes

In the wake of the expansion of legal gambling growth in Canada, unexpected and unanticipated consequences have occurred. Perhaps the most disconcerting unexpected and unanticipated consequence of the expanded availability of legal gambling revolves around the issue of problem gambling. Not one province in Canada had the foresight to anticipate the emergence of problems associated with persons unable to limit their gambling expenditures. Furthermore, as provincial governments have developed policies on gambling that are predicated on the goal of revenue generation, the legal monopoly granted to provinces over electronic gambling formats has contributed to a significant expansion of the gambling formats generally agreed to be most problematic in terms of social impact. More specifically, technological developments in electronic gaming machines in consort with provincial willingness to expand the availability of legal gambling for the sake of revenue generation have facilitated the expansion of a type of gambling that is widely believed to be addictively potent (see chapter 7).

Studies conducted in Canada using the Canadian Problem Gambling Index (CPGI)[4] indicate that, nationally, one in 15 adult gamblers (6.3 per cent) exhibits either problem gambling or at-risk behaviours associated with gambling (Azmier 2005, 11). This amounts to approximately 1.2 million Canadians who show some indication that their gambling is problematic to themselves, their associates, or their communities. Provincially, Manitoba has exhibited the highest level (9.4 per cent) of problem gamblers in the general population and Quebec the lowest (4.6 per cent) (Azmier 2005, 11).

With specific regard to the relationship between electronic gaming formats and problem gambling, Smith and Wynne (2004) concluded: 'The academic literature on electronic machine gambling is, with few exceptions, faultfinding. While there is unanimity about the superior revenue generating capacity of electronic gambling machines for both the state and gambling venue proprietors, there is also concurrence on the distress these machines can visit on the public' (p. 54). In affirmation, Williams and Wood have estimated that 35 per cent of gaming revenues in Ontario and 39 per cent in Alberta derive from moderate and severe problem gamblers. They conjecture that such estimates, however, may be low and that there are sound reasons for believing that problem gamblers may account for as much as 60 per cent of all government gambling revenues (Williams and Wood 2005).

It is apparent in the history of gambling in Canada that local, nonprofit community-based organizations have enjoyed a historical exemption from prohibitions contained in the criminal law. Good causes that have been underwritten by gambling funds have played a discernible role in legitimizing gambling in the minds of Canadians. However, with the veritable explosion of electronic formats, non-profit community-based organizations that have paved the way for the widespread public acceptance of gambling are now inadvertently being squeezed from the gambling marketplace by competition from provincial governments (Campbell 2000).

As Morton (2003) has demonstrated, gambling in Canada has been a crucial component of Canadian life throughout the entire twentieth century despite considerable ambivalence towards it. With continued secularization of Canadian society, and with the close alliance that was forged in Canada in the wake of the 1969 amendment between gambling, community-based charities, and the expanding welfare state, Canadians have become openly tolerant of a wide variety of legal gambling formats. Indeed, the Canadian public's expectations of government services – alongside a corresponding disdain for increased taxes – have made lotteries and other forms of gambling an attractive alternative form of government revenue.

It is undeniable that gambling in Canada is a crucial component of contemporary popular culture – as a recreational pastime, as a means of raising funds for governments and community organizations, and as an increasingly global entertainment industry. Unlike other mass popular culture entertainment media, such as professional sports or motion pictures, as McMillen (2003) has observed, gambling is intensely participatory.[5] People are gambling more than ever before on an increasingly wider range of electronic gambling formats (McMillen 2003, 49). Furthermore, while 'gambling in the past was shaped by the cultural values of localized communities, contemporary gambling is increasingly commercialized, standardized, and global. It has become big business, central to the activities, values and commercial imperatives of national and transnational organizations' (McMillen 2003, 50).

As a consequence of these developments, Canadians, like others elsewhere, are now 'less likely to play games instilled with local meanings and practices' (McMillen 2003, 49). Indeed, horse racing, which in Canada has enjoyed a long and vibrant history and, along with charitable organizations, has also enjoyed special exemption from the general prohibition of gambling through much of the twentieth century, has been transformed. No longer able to compete successfully with new electronic gaming formats and with the proliferation of urban casinos, many racetracks, for example, those in Ontario, Alberta, and British Columbia, have been transformed into 'racinos.' That is, horse-racing interests have successfully persuaded provincial legislatures that their continued viability lies in being able to offer electronic gaming machines as an adjunct to their regular repertoire of pari-mutuel betting. In British Columbia, traditional forms of racetrack wagering have lost meaning and appeal for traditional racetrack gamblers. As a result, local agricultural economies that are dependent on racetrack gambling revenues have been threatened. Similarly, with the amendments to the *Criminal Code* that have specified that electronic games must be 'managed and conducted' by provincial governments, local racetrack gambling practices and the local cultures that grew out of them are being transformed. Participants no longer frequent the track out of an undying love for the 'sport of kings.' Rather, they are drawn now by the appeal of EGMs.

Charitable gambling has been an important feature of the modern Canadian gambling landscape. This, too, however, has been transformed by the availability of new gambling technologies, by the laws that govern gambling, and by provincial government policies that seek to appropriate even larger shares of gambling revenues.

With the commercial appeal and success of casino-style gambling and with the broad appeal of slot machines to the gambling public, gambling venues and games of chance have become homogenized and standardized. Casinos in Canada are virtually identical to casinos operated anywhere else in the world. That is, casinos and electronic gaming machines are not the logical evolution of local cultural preferences. Instead, they are gambling formats that have been promoted primarily by transnational American gaming operators who export their games and supporting technologies throughout the world. Electronic gaming machines are in no small measure the product of global, commercial entrepreneurs who have successfully promoted gambling as a mass entertainment to the extent that it has become the world's most rapidly expanding consumer activity (McMillen 2003).

Globalization of gaming as a consumer activity has also meant globalization and standardization of games of chance. Every modern casino in the world now offers the same familiar inventory of primarily American games – blackjack, craps, and, of course, slot machines. Las Vegas casinos have become paradigmatic of the global casino gaming experience. The marketing rituals used to promote gambling and the social rituals surrounding 'play' at such games are virtually identical anywhere in the world (McMillen 2003). In short, casino gambling and the games they offer now permit the global gaming industry to rival the Golden Arches' global dining experience.

As electronic games of chance have appeared in the gaming marketplace, private sector interests, governments, and other stakeholders have come rapidly to appreciate their revenue potential. This is particularly evident in Canada – as it is in other jurisdictions throughout the world.

The Canadian *Criminal Code* specifies who can and cannot operate gaming in Canada. Under this legal regime, Canadian provinces have become the single-largest beneficiaries of legal gambling operations in Canada. The new and immensely profitable gambling technologies such as slot machines are only legal in Canada if they are 'managed and conducted' by governments or by designated 'agents of the Crown' such as provincial lottery corporations. As a result, as these new and profitable devices came into the Canadian gambling marketplace, they could only be managed and conducted by governments. As a consequence, older, more traditional gambling formats such as charity casino table games and traditional community-based bingos have not been able to compete. Consequently many community organizations have lost market share to the onslaught of competition from an array of government-monopolized electronic gaming machines in provincially run casinos.

As a 2000 review of gaming policies in British Columbia noted, 'the introduction of slot machines in British Columbia has had a profound, and to some extent, disturbing effect on the gaming sector' (Meekison 2000, 17). As correct as Meekison's observation may be, there is no single factor that directly accounts for the reconfiguration of policies that now financially favour the provincial governments at the expense of local, non-profit, community-based organizations. Rather, the gaming laws, policies, and operational practices that characterize provincially operated gambling are in part driven by the global technological changes that have transformed gaming formats (i.e., the popularity and profitability of electronic games), in part by Canadian criminal law (i.e., the federal *Criminal Code*, which specifies who may legally conduct particular games of chance), and, lastly, given the context of these factors, by provincial governments that yearn for new revenue to augment their budgets. It is only in the context of these developments that one can begin to understand the transformations with regard to legal gambling policies and operations in Canada and their overall effects.

Regulatory Issues

To date, regulatory policies have focused on integrity and probity issues regarding both individuals and public and private organizations that are involved in providing legal gambling activities and services. Given the historical legacy that has attended gambling, particularly in the United States (Skolnick 1979), measures to address organized crime, graft, and corruption have been prominent in Canadian regulatory policies. All provinces have built relatively sophisticated structures to license and regulate legal gaming in order to ensure its ongoing integrity. The primary concern of provincial gaming authorities has been the registration and licensing of private sector corporations and personnel seeking active involvement in gaming operations. Extensive and intrusive background checks are conducted to ensure the probity of both individuals and corporations before licensing and regulatory approval is granted. Similarly, extensive testing and ongoing monitoring is undertaken to ensure that the sophisticated hardware and software platforms through which electronic gaming is conducted are impervious to fraud or other forms of deceit and dishonesty.

In a 2005 review of gaming regulation in British Columbia, the provincial auditor general sought to examine the adequacy of the processes used to ensure that error, criminal exploitation, and employee dishonesty are minimized. It is noteworthy that the auditor general identified three potentially major consequences that may arise if government fails to ensure that strict integrity is maintained, particularly in provincially operated casinos. First, unsavoury elements such as organized crime and dishonest individuals may become involved in the industry and thus compromise patrons and their confidence in the industry. Second, and in turn, this may lead to a drop in government revenues. Third, and consequently, government may not receive all the revenues to which it is entitled (Auditor General 2005). Representative of the regulatory priorities in other provinces, the conception of integrity in British Columbia is narrowly and instrumentally conceived as something essential to enhancing government profits. What is conspicuously absent in both the auditor general's focus and more generally in British Columbia's overall regulatory priorities is the issue of consumer protection. A review of standard formal regulatory policies and concerns across the country reveals little formal concern with the fairness of games offered to consumers.

While all provinces have embarked to some degree on a range of initiatives to prevent, reduce, or treat the consequences of problem gambling (see Campbell and Smith 2003), there are few initiatives that seek to address the fundamental fairness of proffered games such as the odds or rates of return paid by EGMs, which are overwhelmingly advantageous to the gaming operator. Likewise, other measures that could easily be instituted in the interest of protecting consumers remain conspicuously unaddressed in regulatory policies: eliminating credit and the availability of ATMs from gaming premises, both of which are known to facilitate excessive gambling losses by players.

Certainly, other aspects of the culture of commercial casinos facilitate patently illogical player beliefs and encourage misconceived gambling practices, but nevertheless remain outside both regulatory policies and the prevailing gaming industry conception of what constitutes integrity. For example, as a courtesy to customers, casinos routinely display illuminated signs at roulette tables that track the sequence of winning numbers. Casinos also provide complimentary cards on which players can track winning roulette numbers. However, given that every number that occurs in the course of roulette play is entirely random, facilitating and encouraging the tracking of numbers by players is a deceitful marketing ploy that encourages a false belief that certain numbers may reoccur more frequently (i.e., be luckier) than others. Such false beliefs work to the player's financial disadvantage and could easily be ended by stringent policy measures.

It is thus questionable why provincial governments that manage and conduct gambling venues do not assertively work to minimize both the prevalence of problem gambling and the amounts of money derived from problem gamblers.

Economic Benefits

While it is undeniable that gambling makes enormous amounts of money for provincial governments, non-profit community-based organizations, and private corporations, it is not clear that expanded gambling within Canada has produced a net economic gain. Claims that gambling can be a catalyst for increased tourism expenditures or a mechanism by which local economies can be revitalized are frequently overstated and remain empirically undemonstrated. With the rare exception of such communities as Windsor and Niagara Falls, which are distinct in their geographic proximity to large populations of potential American gamblers, there is little convincing evidence to demonstrate that gambling ventures facilitate an influx of new capital to a community. Indeed, in most communities in Canada that have instituted commercial gambling ventures, expenditures most typically derive from local residents, not tourists. Similarly, it is increasingly suspect that rather than apprehending 'revenue leakage' to nearby jurisdictions that permit legal gambling, the availability of local gambling, particularly in the form of urban casinos, may actually encourage an outflow of money from the local community. As more and more people are introduced to slot machine gambling located in casinos in their own communities, interest in travelling to more appealing jurisdictions may increase. For example, persons who find local gambling entertaining are increasingly likely to travel to other gambling destinations such as Las Vegas that offer enhanced entertainment opportunities that cater to adjunctive patrons – those who are seeking gambling entertainment alongside a combination of other entertainment opportunities such as fine dining, live entertainment, and outdoor recreational activities available in warm-weather climates.

Controlling Illegal Gambling

Dating back to the 1950s and particularly salient leading up to the 1969 amendment to the *Criminal Code*, calls for legalization of gambling have frequently argued that legalization and strict regulation will suffice to remove gambling activity from the hands of organized criminal interests who pay no taxes and who use their profits to fund other criminal activities. In more recent times, similar arguments have been offered to justify legalization of EGMs. In provinces such as Quebec and British Columbia through the 1990s, mounting concerns about the widespread availability of 'grey machines'[6] spurred calls for government operation and control so that revenues could be directed to government coffers and, in turn, put towards public good.

Coupled to these concerns have been problems identified by law enforcement officials who have argued that criminal prohibitions against gambling often have been ambiguous, problematic, and unworkable (Campbell 1994). For example, lotteries and bingos were carried out by community-based groups extensively in Canada prior to 1969 despite their formal prohibition under the *Criminal Code*. Attempts by police to enforce unpopular laws often put them in difficult situations, especially with so many ordinary citizens apparently willing to flout the law.

Today very similar concerns are apparent in regard to Internet gambling. The *Criminal Code* clearly specifies that only provinces in Canada can operate computer-based lottery schemes. However, given the relative openness of the Internet, gambling games are offered free of charge to anyone who has a computer and Internet access. To wager for money, however, players must register and establish an account, typically using a deposit drawn on a credit card. Given the private and solitary nature of computer betting on the Internet in tandem with the universality of access to the Internet, on-line gambling is extremely difficult to police. While the *Criminal Code* may prohibit Canadians from participating in gambling on a website located in another country, there is no mechanism to effectively enforce the prohibition (Kelly, Todosichuk, and Azmier 2001).

It is to be noted that the Quebec-based Kahnawake Mohawk First Nation has operated extensive on-line gambling sites since the late 1990s. Located on the outskirts of Montreal, the Kahnawake Mohawks assert that they are a sovereign nation and entitled to grant gaming licences for lottery schemes. The Kahnawake Mohawks themselves do not operate Internet sites but have established the Kahnawake Gaming Commission (KGC) to license and regulate some 30 gambling websites operated through Internet servers physically located on their tribal lands (Lipton 2003; Kelly, Todosichuk, and Azmier 2001).

Although the Kahnawake Mohawks are allegedly violating the *Criminal Code*, and although the Quebec and federal governments, together with the provincial police, have investigated their Internet gambling activities, no action has been taken to halt the operations. Even though Internet gambling is not yet a popular activity for Canadians, policy and law enforcement dilemmas are posed for Canadian authorities (Kelly, Todosichuk, and Azmier 2001). Of course, as provincial governments expand their repertoire of gaming products through on-line media, it is likely that Canadian provinces will assert their legal monopoly in this domain as well.

According to a report prepared by the Canada West Foundation on Internet gambling, it is a breach of the *Criminal Code* for private, commercial, Canadian-based gambling sites to accept bets from Canadian citizens. However, the fact remains that Canadians have the ability to gamble at offshore Internet sites with relative impunity (Lipton 2003). However, conflict has already been evident between provincial lottery corporations and the Canadian Football League (CFL), which had accepted relatively lucrative sponsorship contracts from a for-profit Internet gambling operator, Bowmans.com. Canadian lottery operators, also sponsors of CFL activities, demanded that the league sever its ties to Bowmans.com. At present, Bowmans.com no longer sponsors the league, but does sponsor individual teams. While Canadian policing authorities are aware of Bowmans.com and that it allows gamblers to place bets on the outcome of CFL games, including the Grey Cup, it is uncertain if or how they can move to enforce the Canadian *Criminal Code* against a company whose operations are conducted in Mauritius, an island off the coast of Africa (Westhead 2005).

Conclusions

Given the current provisions of the *Criminal Code*, it is apparent that modern criminal law in Canada has not functioned to restrict or prevent either the operation of or participation in gambling activities. Rather, existing provisions have facilitated a widespread expansion of a variety of gambling activities provided they are conducted and managed under provincial jurisdiction.

With specific regard to gambling, Brodeur and Ouellet have argued that 'the creation of a state monopoly has led to such an overwhelming expansion of gambling that it is possible to speak of an *expansionist monopoly*' (2004, 27; emphasis in original). Indeed, somewhat ironically, Canadian criminal law and policies developed pursuant to it have been used to consolidate provincial authority over gambling as a revenue-raising instrument and to expand its availability rather than restrict it in any meaningful sense. As Campbell, Hartnagel, and Smith (2005) have pondered, is this is an appropriate use of the criminal law function in a democratic society?

NOTES

1 'Gross profit' includes government share of gambling revenues plus the expenses associated with its delivery. 'Net profit' represents the amount of gambling revenue that accrues to government after expenses have been deducted. See Azmier (2005, 2). Some gambling observers refer to 'gross profit' as the 'win' or the amount equal to that lost by gamblers.

2 Condensed from Campbell, Hartnagel, and Smith (2005).

3 For greater details, see Osborne and Campbell (1988) and Campbell, Hartnagel, and Smith (2005).

4 The Canadian Problem Gambling Index (CPGI), developed in 1999 by Canadian researchers, is a survey instrument that accurately identifies and classifies non-problem, at-risk, and problem gamblers in the general population. It has been used widely in Canada and elsewhere in telephone surveys to determine the prevalence of problem gambling in the general population. See Ferris, Wynne, and Single (1999).

5 Although with the current surge in the number of televised Texas-Holdem poker tournaments in North America, it is apparent that vicarious involvement in gambling has an appeal to a growing number of viewers, including

many below legal age. Of course, televised poker tournaments often carry subtle and not so subtle encouragements for viewers to participate in Internet poker.

6 A grey machine is an EGM that may be used for mere amusement but may also be used for gambling purposes. In the former, the activity is quite legal. However, in the latter, it is illegal. Since both legal and illegal activities can be conducted, the machine is neither black nor white. Hence the term 'grey' is used to describe its dual but dubious nature.

5 Gambling Policy and Regulation in Australia

JAN MCMILLEN

Preceding chapters have focused attention on the historical context of gambling policy in Canada. This chapter amplifies those contributions to offer a reflective overview of gambling regulation in Australia. Given their shared Anglo-European heritage and the hegemonic influence of American-style casinos and electronic gaming machines on contemporary gambling, it is instructive to consider the historical events and themes that have contributed to national gambling development in both nations.

Particular attention is given to the role of governments and industry in the policy-making process and to the notion of public interest. This focus raises questions about democratic policy formation and gambling regulation: why and how it occurs, and who participates in these processes. It concentrates on the implication of democratic inclusion, outcomes, and accountability implied in policy development and regulatory practice, and offers explanations for national differences.

Historical Origins

An understanding of the historical forces and resolutions behind the development of gambling policy is an important starting point for any explanation of contemporary gambling. There are many and diverse contextual factors that influence the particular character of gambling: the way it fits into each society, shapes government policies, and impacts upon different communities. The four key contextual factors are sociocultural values, economic conditions, political structures, and technology. Social values and community attitudes, including religious beliefs and traditions, frame national debates over public morality, cultural practices, and preferences of gambling, ultimately shaping the class and regional differences that come to exist, as demonstrated in chapter 2. Economic conditions and trends, such as economic booms and slumps, market competition, periods of economic restructuring, and the revenue needs of government, also determine the manner and extent to which gambling is legalized. Political structures and processes including public policy objectives, political conflicts, and power relations further impact the specific decisions that politicians and regulators will make. Finally, technological development and innovation have the potential to alter the gambling landscape.

Gambling policies in Canada and Australia share a common political-legal heritage and a historical nexus between legalized gambling and welfare funding. Yet neither can be simply viewed in an Anglo-European colonial tradition. Each country has approached gambling policy in a particular and idiosyncratic way.

Historically, Australian governments have not viewed gambling as either vice or inherently immoral, in contrast to Anglo-Protestant countries such as Canada (Campbell and Smith 1998, 2003; Campbell, Smith, and Hartnagel 2005; Morton 2003), the United Kingdom (Munting 1996; Miers 2003), and the United States (Mason and Nelson 2001; Pierce and Miller 2004). Morton (2003) stressed the ambiguity of Canada's gambling history, with middle-class Protestant morality ensuring prohibition of most forms of gambling on one hand, and a growing acceptance of gambling in post-war years on the other (see also chapters 2 and 3).

Gambling in Australia has taken a distinctively different path. From the early days of white settlement, Australian governments have accepted that gambling is a popular recreational activity among all social groups (McMillen and Eadington 1986; McMillen et al. 1999; O'Hara 1988). Gambling among convicts and emancipists was initially perceived as a social problem by early administrators and free settlers convinced of their social and moral superiority. However, early governors were more concerned with stamping out the thriving trade in illicit alcohol than with punishing gamblers, and widespread gambling became an enduring feature of the colony's social life. As gambling became more popular, authorities preferred to regulate rather than prohibit. This premise continues to guide Australian policies to the present.

In Australia, the general thrust of legal and moral arguments has been not so much about whether gambling should be permitted or not (as it has been in Canada and the United States) but which forms of gambling should be permitted and which should be restricted. Rationales for legalization have included control of illegal gambling to remove criminal influence and corruption, and strategies to maximize public revenue. Debates have focused on whether legalization would induce gambling by social groups that otherwise might not gamble, and practical issues such as provision of rational and well-ordered public access to approved forms of popular gambling.

To some extent this liberal approach reflects official tolerance of the cultural practices and values of Irish-Catholic convicts who settled the colony, reinforced by Chinese migration to the goldfields in the nineteenth century and by southern European migration in the 1960s. Protestantism and anti-gambling sentiment have always been in the minority in Australia. This contrasts with the moral and cultural frameworks for understanding the place of gambling in the Canadian context, as discussed in the previous chapters. In contrast to the ambivalence of many Canadian provinces, the common Australian policy response to widespread gambling (e.g., the persistent growth in illegal off-course bookmaking during the 1950s) has been to legalize and deprive illegal operators of their market.

Legalization has been less contentious than in most other countries (McMillen and Eadington 1986). One fundamental reason for this has been the close institutionalized association between legal gambling, community values, and social purposes. Most legal forms of Australian gambling were community-based and controlled (horse and greyhound racing, charitable gambling, community clubs) or were introduced to specifically raise revenues for public services and infrastructure. State lotteries, for example, were introduced early in the twentieth century to finance much-needed health systems and, later on, other public projects.[1] This positive social initiative was vindicated by economic evidence of racing as a vital and growing industry, providing employment and generating economic activity and revenue. In this regard, Australian governments were remarkably successful in ensuring a fit between community values and gambling.

Consequently, across the nation different forms of gambling were legalized at different times, while others were restricted. Gambling laws, regulations, and institutions have varied from state to state – in organizational characteristics, in the considerations that determine policy, and in their long-term capacity to regulate market trends. For example, during the 1930s to 1950s, states adopted different policies to off-course betting, ranging from legalized betting shops to sustained at-

Figure 5.1: Real total gambling expenditure in Australia, 1978–9 to 2003–4

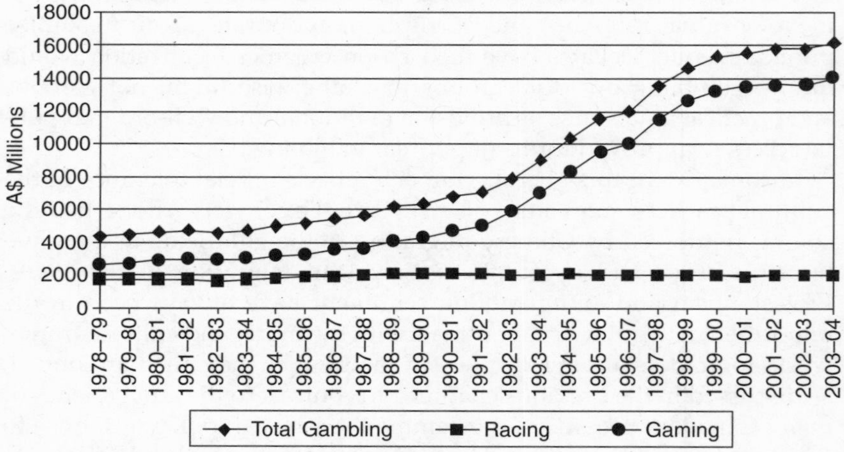

Note: 'Real' expenditure is adjusted for the effects of inflation over time. Per capita expenditure refers to people over 18 years. The amount gambled by individual gamblers is likely to be higher because not every adult over the age of 18 gambles. However, this bias is to some extent ameliorated by the way gambling expenditure data are collected, with no distinction made between gambling revenue accumulated from gamblers resident outside Australia.
Source: Queensland Government Treasury 2008.

tempts at suppression; lotteries and lotto evolved in an uneven way; and the introduction of casinos produced a variety of outcomes.

Even so, during the twentieth century Australia developed the most liberal gambling environment in the world. A large variety of legal gambling options has long been accessible to adult Australians on a daily basis. The legitimacy and popularity of gambling is reflected in the high participation rate (82 per cent of adults in 1999; Productivity Commission 1999) and relatively high levels of gambling expenditure (Figure 5.1).

Australian state governments generally also have avoided the ambiguity and inconsistency that have characterized Canadian and U.S. gambling policies (Morton 2003). The Australian Commonwealth government has had no direct legal authority over gambling like Canada's *Criminal Code*. The Australian Constitution is silent on gambling; hence, gambling regulation is a residual power of states and territories.[2]

Nor has Australia experienced the persistent regional differences that have been a feature of Canadian gambling policy. Concentration of a large French-Catholic population in Quebec has produced a markedly different gambling environment to other Canadian provinces, for example. In contrast, despite Australia's federal structure and the parochial interests of stakeholders, policies in all states and territories have been relatively consistent (McMillen et al. 1999). A process of policy learning has occurred as Australian governments have observed the experience of other jurisdictions and adjusted policies to suit their own particular needs, aspirations, and contexts.

In the past, one of the most distinctive historical features of Australian gambling policy was condemnation of gambling for private profit. Until the 1970s the most popular forms of gambling (lotteries and off-course betting totalizators [TABs]) were operated by government monopolies.[3] Other popular forms of gambling (horse and greyhound racing, raffles, bingo) were administered by community clubs or charities. Another feature was the uniform prohibition of Asian games and casino gambling. Notwithstanding the generally liberal attitude to gambling, Asian gambling and casinos were seen as particularly difficult to control and potentially a disruptive social influence.

Another important distinction between Australian and Canadian gambling policy (and to lesser extent, the United States) is the relative absence of plebiscites or referenda to inform important policy change. Only two gambling-related referenda have occurred: to authorize lotteries in South Australia (passed by a majority of three to one) and to approve the proposal for Australia's first casino in Tasmania in 1972. As previously noted, casinos had been singled out as inappropriate for Australian society (McMillen 1993; McMillen et al. 1999), yet the Tasmanian community narrowly endorsed the proposal, persuaded by promise of economic rewards and the state's reputation for effective regulation. Moral protests were dismissed as a conservative residue of outmoded religious attitudes.

The main aberration to this national uniformity has been state policies on gaming machines (called 'pokies' or poker machines), first legalized in 1956 for community clubs in New South Wales (NSW), the most populous state. Because registered clubs are run on a non-profit basis, they are expected to use gaming revenues to improve club facilities for members and to subsidize community programs. By the 1970s poker machines had become a distinctive feature of NSW social life. Financed by gaming machine revenue, some clubs in NSW had developed into large multifaceted complexes providing a wide range of recreational activities, entertainment, and quality restaurants. The significant in-come-earning capacity of gaming machines had also enabled many reg-istered clubs to assume several of the functions of local government, for example, undertaking the construction and maintenance of public facil-ities such as sporting complexes and convention facilities (Caldwell et al. 1985). In return for these community benefits, clubs negotiated low tax rates on gaming turnover. Even so, the NSW government had become heavily reliant on poker machine revenue.

But persistent criticisms of improper conduct in the NSW club sector, along with more general accusations of gambling-related corruption, prompted a number of royal commissions (McMillen 1993). Those inquiries found evidence of criminal involvement, hidden ownership, and money laundering in the NSW club industry, as well as large-scale illegal casino gaming operating openly at several inner-Sydney clubs. Criminals involved in the management of NSW clubs were found to have connections with known criminals operating in the gaming indus-try in the United States. Faced with this evidence, and despite persis-tent industry lobbying, other Australian states resisted the introduction of gaming machines for decades.

By the 1980s, however, a combination of factors gave impetus for a period of rapid national legalization and privatization, including pri-vately owned casinos and the introduction of electronic gaming machines (EGMs) to clubs and hotels beyond NSW.[4] First, public accep-tance of expanded legal gambling opportunities was achieved around a twofold state interest – to control illegal gambling and to boost govern-ment revenues (McMillen 1996a; Smith 1998). Second, state economies experienced declining incomes and revenue pressures during the lin-gering global recession of the 1970s and 1980s. The economic crisis was exacerbated by significant cutbacks in Commonwealth funding to state and territory governments. Third, while state governments were strug-gling to maintain a stable revenue base, changes to federal financial arrangements also shifted administrative responsibilities in health care, education, and provision of infrastructure to the states. Fourth, in-terstate competition increased as governments attempted to counteract cross-border leakage of poker machine revenues to NSW (McMillen 1997a). Fifth, post-war economic developments (e.g., affluence, leisure, tourism, computerization) created new opportunities for commercial investment in gambling and market expansion. Lastly, Australian gov-ernments were caught up in the general philosophical shift towards neo-liberal economics, including lower taxes, privatization, and free-market policies more receptive to commercial gambling providers (McMillen 1997b). Government monopolies were either privatized (TABs) or corporatized (state lotteries) to encourage a more commercial approach. By the 1980s, commercial gambling had become a legitimate and integral part of Australian society.

In two decades of unprecedented growth, between the 1970s and the 1990s, privately owned casinos were introduced to every major Australian city; and electronic gaming machines (EGMs) were introduced to clubs and hotels in every jurisdiction except Western Australia (McMillen et al. 1999) (Table 5.1). In the process, Australian governments negotiated a careful path between liberalization and regulated markets, thus encouraging public demand for legal gambling without opening the door to unconstrained market forces and increased risk of social disorder.

The steady expansion of legalized gambling is reflected in the growing expenditure (the amount spent or lost) by Australians on gambling activities (Figure 5.1). Only Alberta has levels of gambling spending comparable to Australian states (Azmier 2001). Australian gambling expenditure has increased dramatically since the 1970s. Growth was mainly in the gaming sector, with EGMs accounting for an increasing share of gambling activity. Between 1991–2 and 2000–1, real per capita expenditure on gambling increased from AUD$509.39 to AUD$988.90. This represented an average rate of annual growth of 7.75 per cent during that period. The rapid growth rate was directly linked to the introduction of gaming machines in many jurisdictions during that period and an increase in the number of casinos.

Gaming machine policies during the 1980s to 1990s were developed incrementally and were increasingly characterized by inconsistency within and between states. Hence, the contemporary pattern of development exhibits significant regional variations. For example, the situation in NSW (which in 2000 had 104,000 EGMs in hotels and clubs) contrasts sharply with the prohibition of EGMs in Western Australian clubs and hotels.[5] Consequently gambling expenditure varies across jurisdictions, reflecting the availability and spending on EGMs. In 2000–1 spending was highest in NSW (AUD$1,196 per adult, 3.87 per cent of Household Discretionary Income [HDI]) and lowest in Western Australia (AUD$464 per adult, 1.67 per cent of HDI).

Similarly, industry profits also had soared during that period. The net takings by Australian gambling industries increased by 41 per cent between 1994–5 and 2003–4, a growth rate of 12 per cent per annum.[6]

Table 5.1

Availability of casino and machine gaming, per capita expenditure, prevalence of gambling problems and harm: by Australian states and territories

	Casinos	*No. EGMs in casinos	*No. EGMs in clubs & hotels 2004–5	Gambling expenditure per adult $ 2005–6	SOGS 5+ % 1999	HARM % 1999	***CPGI % High risk	***CPGI % Moderate risk
NSW	1	1,500	98,808	1,336.22	2.55	1.96	0.80	1.60
VIC	1	2,500	27,124	1,133.88	2.14	2.05	0.97	0.91
NT	2	714	985	1,918.38**	1.89	1.24	0.64	N/A
QLD	4	3,473	39,484	1,003.64	1.88	1.79	0.83	2.70
WA	1	1,318	0	520.73	0.70	1.50	0.55	1.97
SA	1	850	14,062	922.37	a	1.44	N/A	N/A
TAS	2	1,158	2,289	814.45**	0.44	0.12	1.20	0.40
ACT	1	0	5,144	998.18	2.06	1.32	N/A	N/A
Australia	13	11,513	187,896	1,097.47	2.07	1.80	N/A	N/A

* Note that racing, sports betting, lotteries, keno, football pools, interactive gambling, and charitable gambling are also available in all jurisdictions.

** NT expenditure figures are inflated by on-line expenditure by overseas gamblers; Tasmanian figures are incomplete.

*** The CPGI has been used in Australia since 2001; however, only Queensland has used the CPGI in two surveys (2001 and 2003–4). Prevalence findings may not be directly comparable due to different survey years, the wide variety of types and availability of gambling, the effect of different times and context, etc.

Source: Australian Gaming Council 2007; Productivity Commission 1999; Queensland Government Treasury 2008.

Extrapolation of this growth trend would have seen gambling rapidly become Australia's largest industry (Productivity Commission 1999).

Despite different origins and values, however, contemporary gambling in Canada and Australia has many common features. The legalization of contemporary gambling in both countries has been the outcome of several interrelated global forces. Increased institutionalization and commercialization have stimulated the growth of legal gambling, and the influence of the U.S. industry and its marketing philosophy has been embraced by gambling interests in both countries. Social values and public opinion have vied with commercial investors to shape government responses. The extent and types of legal gambling have been circumscribed by state governments to accommodate local concerns and expectations as well as entrenched industry preferences.

Furthermore, the fiscal interests of government have played an important role in rationalizing and separating legalized gambling from the moral and cultural values that typify disputes over it. Provincial and state governments' fundamental task of maintaining law and order and social harmony has been central to their authority over gambling; the process of policy learning encouraged a degree of homogeneity and standardization between jurisdictions. Demographic and economic factors have also affected both the level and type of gambling. The age and ethnic composition of the population, cultural practices, urbanization, changes in the structure of the economy, increasing affluence and leisure, women's economic independence, and technological developments have all shaped the extent and form of gambling in both countries.

As has occurred in Canada, much of the rationale for the expansion of Australian legalized gambling during the 1980s and 1990s assumed that gambling (especially casinos and gaming machines) would stimulate economic development, and thus generate net social benefits. The combined rhetoric of community benefits and government regulation in the public interest garnered public support and legitimacy for rapid expansion of commercial gambling.

Regulation

In Australia since the 1980s, in marked contrast to earlier preference for public ownership, the preferred model for all forms of gambling except lotteries has been private industry ownership with a comprehensive system of government regulation often administered by an independent, non-political control authority.

Australian regulations over gambling industry practices, venue design and location, rules of the games, and return to players have been more restrictive than those in most other countries. When considering the legalization of casino gambling, for instance, all Australian governments concluded that the U.S. casino regulation model was deficient in many respects and did not meet Australian community standards of commercial probity, conduct, and accountability. A program of proactive regulation and policy development has effectively prevented serious problems from occurring. For example, purposeful collaboration between regulators and casino licensees in Australia and New Zealand has prevented the crime and corruption problems associated with casinos elsewhere (McMillen 1993, 1998, 2000a).

Australian governments have also extracted high 'rents' and other benefits as price for the monopoly casino licences. The prescribed requirements and competitive tendering process for casino licences have resulted in construction of major public facilities and regeneration of rundown city areas. The exclusivity attached to these licences was a critical factor in attracting high bids from investors on the one hand, and minimizing adverse impacts from overdevelopment on the other (McMillen 2000a). Contrary to theories of market economists, this Australian model of restricted casino development has been effective in terms of achieving both high regulatory standards and community benefit.

Regulatory regimes over casinos and EGMs in clubs and hotels typically include an independent statutory 'watchdog' authority, appointed with specific functions to safeguard the public interest, to license and monitor venues and key industry participants, and to mediate relationships between the community, government, and industry. Models for these authorities vary from state to state (McMillen 2000b). In Queensland, for example, the independent Gaming Commission regulates only EGMs in clubs and hotels; in NSW the statutory authority controls only the Sydney casino. In other states the powers of independent authorities have progressively been extended to cover all gambling sectors.

Australian gambling regulation has avoided accusations of corruption by government officials comparable to the highly publicized scandals in British Columbia and Manitoba (McMillen 1996c; Smith and Wynne 2000, 35). In most states, legislation prevents Australian senior regulators from accepting positions in the gaming industry without a 'cooling off' period. Nor have there been allegations of political appointments to statutory commissions charged with regulating the industry, as occurred in Alberta (Smith and Wynne 1999).

In establishing the gaming machine industry, for example, the Queensland government adhered to a number of specific principles with regard to probity issues. These principles included government responsibility for many of the key functions (e.g., the ownership of gaming machines, centralized monitoring, and auditing of operations); ensuring the separation of key responsibilities to minimize the potential for 'kickbacks' and anti-competitive practices; and adoption of a vigorous licensing system to ensure that persons and employees involved in the industry are honest and of good repute. Queensland's casino regulations became the template for subsequent casino controls in other states.

Regulation of Australian gambling has established an international reputation for integrity and effectiveness. Regulation has achieved stable markets for gambling operators and a generally accepted level of consumer protection. Issues of legitimacy, respectability, and market stability have been key factors in market growth and the public acceptance of gambling as a legitimate recreational activity. The regulatory regimes for Australian gambling have also provided operators with comparative advantage at the global level.

Yet experience has shown that Australian gambling regulations are deficient in important respects (McMillen 2006). While independent authorities have to some extent shielded regulatory outcomes from direct political or commercial influence, their restricted powers and resources limit the extent to which they can query political decisions. The integrity and democratic objectives of Australian gambling policy processes also have been compromised in other ways. Regulatory arrangements and decisions have been shaped by local circumstances and political priorities, rather than uniform regulatory principles and national objectives (McMillen and Wright 2008). Contextual factors as well as contradictory policy objectives have challenged state capacity (McMillen 1997, 2000a; Productivity Commission 1999, 12.14).

Government policies and reforms inevitably have been shaped by parochialism and relationships with industry operators. Political patronage, the lobbying power of industry, and the influence of ministers over regulatory decisions continue to compromise regulation in some states. The most blatant offence occurred when a former NSW minister for gaming and racing was fined regarding a consultancy that advised the gambling industry while he still held public office. In recent years the NSW gaming sector also has mobilized effectively to defeat several reform proposals that conflicted with its economic interests (McMillen and Wright 2008).

Other more subtle forms of political leverage are more common. Since the 1970s commercial forms of gambling have been strongly influenced by American commercial practices. Whereas many forms of early Australian gambling were community based with a pronounced British and European influence, the most rapidly growing forms of contemporary gambling involve large private corporations and transnational games.

Private gambling providers tend to operate by different principles and with different objectives to charitable and public organizations. The privatization of gambling in Australia since the 1980s (casinos, hotel and club gaming, TABs, corporatization of state lotteries) has introduced the profit imperative, which arguably has come to dominate public interest objectives.

In an increasingly competitive gambling environment, market changes have outpaced regulation and the original intentions of lawmakers. During the growth period (1980s to 1990s) gambling policies lacked explicit policy rationale or coordination (McMillen 1993, 1996a; Productivity Commission 1999, xiv). Policy decisions typically were not based on independent advice, objective information, or research. Community consultation, even on those rare occasions when it did occur, has been deficient.

Interstate rivalry and competition for a share of the gambling market also increasingly determined policy decisions. The introduction of large casinos to Sydney and Melbourne and the legalization of gaming machines by Queensland, Victorian, and South Australian governments were motivated primarily to stop cross-border leakage of gambling revenues as more residents travelled interstate to gamble.

As in Canada, many forms of Australian gambling have been supply-driven rather than demand-driven. Technology and the collective commercial power of the industry have become the principal drivers of market supply. New technological forms of gambling such as Internet and interactive betting have emerged as major areas of potential growth. Race betting, lottery sales, casino games, and sports betting are all provided by Australian Internet services. Aggressive marketing and promotion of EGMs (e.g., loyalty programs, note acceptors, linked jackpots) and development of more profitable games have encouraged increased gambling expenditure.

During the 1990s, in the absence of a clearly defined and legislated social objective, Australian regulators reacted to fiscal pressures and market forces, resulting in social problems and regulatory difficulties, rather than taking a proactive approach to maximize public benefit. Ad hoc decisions by policy makers, slanted by their shared goal with industry to maintain or increase revenues, allowed the market to expand beyond community expectations. During the 1980s to 1990s, Australian gambling policies progressively shifted emphasis from community benefit and crime control to economic imperatives – giving priority to tax revenues and economic growth. While this policy shift facilitated industry expansion, subsequent research has demonstrated that the anticipated national economic benefits of this period of industry growth, such as tourism and job creation, have been illusory (Productivity Commission 1999). All industry sectors, particularly those with an entrenched power base, have also been able to negotiate lower taxation rates and other concessions that reduce the public benefit from gambling.

Social Costs and Problem Gambling

At the first national gambling conference in 1985, welfare agencies and a small group of Australian researchers drew attention to the potential adverse effects of the gambling boom (Caldwell 1986; McMillen 2005a), but their warnings had little impact. At the time, there was no rigorous evidence linking gambling and possible damaging effects on gamblers and the community. Industry and governments, intent on protecting market share, typically were prepared to wait for scientific proof (e.g., based on a statistically significant proportion of the population) that linked gambling and social problems before taking remedial action.

Conclusive epidemiological evidence was slow in coming. Only Queensland and Victorian governments, through their regulatory agencies, had invested in research programs to monitor the impacts of gambling. During the 1990s, a growing number of small regional studies showed that social problems were increasing. Research consistently found that gaming machines in particular, and to a lesser extent casino games and wagering, are associated with unacceptably high levels of problem gambling (Victorian Casino and Gaming Authority 1996–2000; Victorian Local Governance Association 2002).

Consumer protection has always been a central principle of Australian gambling policy. However, it was not until 1999 that the harmful effects of gambling received serious national consideration. The rapid expansion of gaming machines during the 1990s and their daily accessibility for most Australians created growing community alarm about adverse social impacts. Unlike debates over religious morality in Australia's early gambling history, churches and community groups in the late 1990s were no longer concerned to prohibit gambling as such. Rather, their protests focused on the social impacts on vulnerable groups in the community.

Mounting evidence of an apparent partnership between the gambling industry and governments precipitated a strong public backlash. As state governments continued to delay protective action, a sustained media campaign and organized community protests provoked Commonwealth intervention.[7] In August 1998, the Australian government commissioned the first national inquiry into Australia's gambling industries and impacts.

Public concern was reflected in the adverse findings contained in the report of the Productivity Commission's inquiry, particularly in relation to EGM gambling (Productivity Commission 1999). The commission's findings highlighted the contradictory tendencies associated with rapid industry growth and commercialization, and the social costs experienced by individuals and the community. Problem gambling was identified by the commission as the most significant social cost; over 2 per cent of the adult Australian population were estimated to have gambling problems. The commission found that problem gamblers comprised 15 per cent of regular (non-lottery) gamblers and accounted for one-third of the gambling industries' market. Overall, the perceived benefits of gambling as a pleasurable activity and economic industry were outweighed by the perceived social costs; 75 per cent of Australians surveyed by the Productivity Commission believed that gambling does more harm than good. Subsequent state surveys have found even higher levels of community concern (McMillen et al. 2004b; S.A. Department of Health 2007).

When considered in the context of consistently high rates of gambling participation in Australia, these findings highlight the current ambivalence that exists in Australian attitudes towards contemporary gambling. As a form of leisure and entertainment, gambling has retained its popularity, a popularity that has its roots in colonial history. However, the appeal of gambling as leisure and entertainment in Australia is now coloured by a high level of public concern about adverse social impacts, which are perceived to flow from the commercial character of gambling.

Importantly, the Productivity Commission argued that gambling is not 'just another industry,' and that it required an independent and transparent regulatory system to improve regulatory governance and reduce community harm. This finding was more notable given the commission's general reputation for supporting free markets and reduction of the regulatory burden on industry. The commission concluded:

> The 'questionable' nature of the gambling industries reflects their ability simultaneously to provide entertainment that is harmless to many people, while being a source of great distress – and even of financial ruin – to a significant minority. The imbalances between the consequences for each group can be very marked, a feature not found in other entertainment industries.
>
> Furthermore, the benefits which may derive from gambling – to the extent that they include occasional winnings – are in part derived from the financial losses of others, and the consequent suffering of some. This too sets the activity apart. (Productivity Commission 1999, xxii)

The convergence of factors that prompted a social backlash in Australia and the establishment of the Productivity Commission's national inquiry were also experienced in North America. However, concerns in Canada and the United States continue to have a religious-moral foundation. Nor have those countries had the advantage of authoritative national research to identify the nature and extent of gambling-related social costs. The national study of U.S. gambling (National Gambling Impact Study Commission [NGISC] 1999) relied mainly on a review of 'admittedly weak research' (Smith and Wynne 2000, 17). It thus did not produce a definitive analysis of gambling and its impacts comparable to Australia's national inquiry. As noted in chapter 1, while there has been an increase in research at the provincial level, the Canadian federal government still has not undertaken a similar national study of the impacts of gambling in Canadian society.

Regulatory Reform and Re-regulation

The Productivity Commission report was an important watershed in the political history of Australian gambling. In addition to a range of consumer protection measures, the commission concluded that there was a case for stronger, explicit government regulation. Governments and industry were caught off guard by the commission's findings, but could not ignore them. It was clear that a more restricted and regulated market was required to achieve the social and integrity objectives of gambling policy.

A new regulatory paradigm has begun to emerge in response to social issues (problem gambling, adverse social impacts) and to public demands for more democratic and accountable gambling regulation. Responses to the national inquiry have shaped a new stage in the development of gambling policy in Australia, characterized by regulatory reform and acceptance of harm minimization as a central regulatory principle.

Importantly, in Australia, problem gambling is no longer viewed from a medicalized perspective as an individual addiction or mental disorder (see, for example, Allcock 2003; Blaszczynski 1985; McMillen 2005b; McMillen and Wenzel 2006; Walker 1996; Wenzel, McMillen, et al. 2004). Research has consistently found that problem gambling can affect any gambler; there are no apparent psychological or psychiatric predictors. Moreover, gambling problems are often episodic and can occur periodically anywhere along a continuum from low to extreme severity. Significantly, in Australia the definition of problem gambling also has been extended beyond individual gamblers to include 'at-risk' families and vulnerable communities.

Rather than an individual's psychology or behaviour, all states have accepted a national definition of problem gambling conceived more broadly in terms of harm experienced by gamblers, families, or communities (Neal et al. 2005). In effect, problem gambling is seen as a complex public health issue requiring a multifaceted, epidemiological approach that emphasizes prevention (Figure 5.2).

This comprehensive redefinition of the problem has meant a reconsideration of policy solutions. While gamblers are held to be responsible for their own actions, the onus is also on government and industry to minimize the potential harm and create a safe gambling environment. As a result, Australian responsible gambling strategies focus beyond treatment services and prevention programs for individual gamblers. Policies extend to detailed regulation of the gambling environment, including venue design and industry practices.

Accessibility of gambling, particularly electronic gaming machines (EGMs), is now recognized in Australia as directly related to the prevalence of problem gambling (Productivity Commission 1999; Marshall, McMillen, et al. 2004). Evidence from Australia suggests that the principle of 'regulation by scarcity' has been relatively effective in minimiz-

Figure 5.2: Epidemiological framework for problem gambling

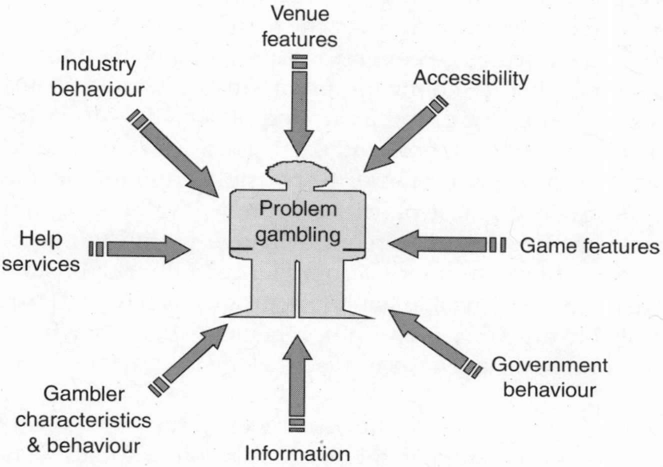

Venue features

Industry behaviour

Accessibility

Problem gambling

Help services

Game features

Government behaviour

Gambler characteristics & behaviour

Information

Source: Productivity Commission 1999, 6.23.

ing the harm of machine gaming. Where this principle has not been rigorously applied (e.g., NSW, Australian Capital Territory), problem gambling and other regulatory risks have been more common than in jurisdictions where a more managed, regulated approach has been adopted (e.g., Queensland, Tasmania, Northern Territory) (Table 5.1). Similarly, where market entry has been denied (e.g., EGMs in Western Australia), problem gambling prevalence and the level of harm are demonstrably lower than where machine gaming is more accessible and competitive.

Over time, gambling can change the nature of cities and have serious social and economic consequences in vulnerable communities. Consequently, regulators in several Australian jurisdictions require industry applicants seeking additional gaming machines or new licences to submit community impact statements on the aggregate potential impact in local communities.[8] If the impact statement process is properly conducted with clear guidelines and informed assessment of applications by authorities, it is a powerful regulatory tool that at the very least encourages industry sensitivity to the potential impacts of their business and community participation in the licensing process (McMillen 2000c). If the process of social impact assessment is mismanaged or deficient, however, it can become merely a token gesture that masks and legitimates decisions contrary to the public interest.

In many respects the implementation and the regulation of Australian responsible gambling strategies go beyond anything in other countries. Internationally, responsible gambling programs in the United States and Canadian provinces include similar strategies such as self-exclusion programs, consumer information, and community awareness campaigns (see chapter 3 for a discussion of responsible gambling in the Canadian context). However, those policies are rarely developed within a regulatory framework designed to require change within the gambling industry and achieve industry's compliance with responsible practices. All Australian responsible gambling programs have a statutory base, and they are arguably more comprehensive than elsewhere. In effect, harm minimization is seen as industry's legislated responsibility.[9]

Typical of federal systems of government, however, the pattern varies from state to state. Responsible gambling regulation in Australia is characterized by a mixture of voluntary self-regulation and government prescription. In some states and territories extensive legislative measures have been introduced, while in others a more self-regulatory approach is being taken. For example, some state authorities have mandated industry codes of practice (South Australia, the Australian Capital Territory, Northern Territory); some have left program development and implementation to key industry providers (NSW, Tasmania); others have been able to achieve considerably more through cooperation and collaboration (Queensland). Programs in some states (e.g., Queensland, Victoria, and South Australia) also are more progressive and coherent than in others. In the case of Queensland, for instance, a comprehensive 'whole of industry' program was achieved by a collaborative partnership between industry, government, and the community.[10]

In all Australian jurisdictions, however, action by governments and/ or the prospect of direct regulatory intervention was required before all industry sectors accepted that changes to past practices were necessary. Some gambling operators have been more willing to embrace the objectives of harm minimization while others have resisted reform. A small number of gambling operators continue to demand scientific evidence to support policy change. But in the main, the Australian industry has embraced the rhetoric of responsible gambling, if not always the practice, while simultaneously seeking to achieve a regulatory environment conducive to profitable markets.

In the context of reform and re-regulation, Australian gambling has become a highly politicized environment. Political lobbying and the influence of industry at the level of grass-roots and elite party politics have undermined regulatory standards established when operators were first licensed. For example, casinos have been able to negotiate considerable tax concessions to allow them to compete; casino table games have been progressively replaced by more profitable EGMs; large venues have increased the number of machines and betting limits; and regulations for money laundering have been loosely applied at times (McMillen and Woolley 2000).

Industry groups have also formed powerful national organizations that actively conduct research and lobby governments (e.g., the Australian Casino Association, Australian Gaming Council). In NSW, an industry alliance (Gaming Industry Operators Group [GIO]) commissioned research specifically to address the regulator's proposed changes to gaming machine features (Blaszcynski, Walker, et al. 2002; Centre for International Economics 2001). Another recent trend has been recruitment of experienced professional counsellors from community agencies to develop responsible gambling programs for commercial gaming providers.

Similarly, community groups that feel excluded from the policy and research process have joined forces to express their social objection to gambling (e.g., the Interchurch Taskforce in Victoria); and anti-gambling critics have convened conferences to promote their cause (Duty of Care Inc. 2005). A small number of associated researchers, mainly from Victoria, have published highly critical perspectives on gambling policy and impacts (e.g., Borrell 2004; Doughney 2002, 2007; Livingstone 2001; Livingstone and Woolley 2007). In many cases, however, it has become increasingly difficult to distinguish between research and advocacy, with both sides of the political debate resorting to ideologically driven claims and counter-claims.

It must also be said that there is little evidence to indicate whether responsible gambling policies have achieved their main objectives (reduction in the level of problem gambling prevalence and community harm), or which harm-minimization strategies are effective in reducing gambling problems and which are not. Independent evaluation of support programs for gamblers has begun in only a small number of jurisdictions (e.g., Queensland, Victoria, South Australia) where it is too soon to reach any firm conclusions. Available information, however, suggests that Australians are not inclined to seek gambling counselling, even when services are readily available. Most people turn to families and friends for help with gambling problems, and self-recovery is common (Jackson 2002; McMillen et al. 2004a).

Where assessment has been undertaken of other harm-minimization strategies (e.g., restrictions on venue opening hours, limits on cash payment of winnings), research has indicated that the measures in place have had little positive effect, often because venues and patrons take advantage of fundamental flaws and deficiencies in policy design (ACNielsen 2005; McMillen and Pitt 2005). Moreover, restrictions and standards are not always enforced (Independent Pricing and Regulatory Tribunal [IPART] 2004).

The likely effect of some harm-minimization policies is more contentious. Emerging evidence indicates that some policies can have unanticipated consequences. For example, the NSW and Queensland governments introduced different 'trading schemes' to encourage venues to transfer licences and reduce the number of EGMs. Reduction in the total number of EGMs in NSW has not reduced spending, however. Under the NSW government's trading scheme, many EGMs have been relocated to hotels in high-expenditure areas where they generate more revenue (e.g., moved from country to city venues).

More targeted efforts to reduce EGM numbers also have had questionable effect. In 2001, the Victorian government introduced limits on the number of EGMs in disadvantaged communities (McMillen and Doran 2006; South Australian Centre for Economic Studies 2005); and more recently South Australia introduced a controversial reduction in the number of EGMs already licensed (Independent Gambling Authority 2004).

The Australian experience suggests that limiting the number of gaming machines (at the level of venues, regions, or statewide) is a weak regulatory strategy to minimize harm. The concept of 'access' is complex, involving much more than simply the number or density of gambling opportunities (McMillen and Doran 2006; Productivity Commission 1999). Rather, features of gaming machines themselves (e.g., line betting configuration, bet sizes, scale of prizes, game speed, note acceptors; see Livingstone and Woolley 2008), the *type* of gaming venues (e.g., venues offering a range of recreational facilities versus venues that rely heavily on gaming), and their *location* (e.g., 'destination' venues away from residential areas versus venues close to areas of community congregation) have become critical considerations by licensing authorities in Queensland and Victoria.

Underlying the lack of policy evaluation is the precarious state of funding for independent gambling research. Corporatization of the Australian university sector in the 1990s and subsequent budget cuts have produced a general crisis of academic resources and research independence. Australian universities do not normally provide funding for gambling research; as a general rule, research centres are self-funded and individual researchers must generate their own research grants. Funding from independent academic sources such as the Australian Research Council is highly competitive and difficult to obtain; and government-funded research is periodic, unpredictable, and narrowly defined to address strategic goals.

The problem is compounded by the practical difficulties facing researchers committed to critical theory and social issues. A good deal is at stake in the professional rivalry that has developed around funding for gambling research. A potential danger for researchers is the emerging imperative to conduct research *for* (rather than with) private industry and government. At worst this could lead to a dollar-driven erosion of academic principles and standards to keep the funding agencies happy. The risks of 'capture' and loss of credibility are acute. The Australian public has expressed very real concerns about the academic independence of gambling research; and some media have promoted the view that research partnerships with government or industry will inevitably corrupt or taint the research.

Current Trends

Uncertainty about the efficacy of harm-minimization measures is no reason for not using the best available information and research to attempt to address the problem in policy and regulation. Since 2000 Australian gambling policy has been characterized by a general, largely unstated policy of containment. Rather than waiting for conclusive evidence, some (but not all) Australian regulatory agencies have begun to apply the 'precautionary principle' to gambling policy. This contrasts with the regulation of gambling in the Canadian context, where, as discussed by Ray MacNeil (chapter 7), the precautionary principle has never been adopted. The principle requires a new way of thinking about gambling policy, involving *anticipation* of possible harm and an integrated approach to harm minimization.

First, the precautionary principle tells us that action should be taken to protect consumers and communities in advance of conclusive evidence that harm will occur – that is, when there is reasonable evidence that damage may occur. Second, using the best available information and consideration of a public interest test, it asks us to weigh up potential benefits from a decision about gambling policy against the potential damage. Third, it requires application of protective measures that can be applied to enable gambling to proceed.

The precautionary principle requires wise deliberation and informed judgment as part of the democratic process. Keeping a watchful eye on gambling impact trends is one general measure for the application of precaution. Informed by such objectives, regulatory commitment to prevention of problem gambling is progressively being introduced in some states/territories. For example, although evidence directly linking the use of automatic teller machines (ATMs) to problem gambling is limited (KPMG 2002; McMillen, Murphy, et al. 2004), restrictions on ATM location and daily withdrawals have been introduced in most states. Similarly, two jurisdictions (Queensland and the ACT) have reduced the denomination of EGM note acceptors from $100 to $20; and the Victorian government will require changes to EGMs permitting gamblers to set personal loss limits from 2010.

More boldly, the Queensland government has amended the object of all gambling legislation to include a statement that gambling, on balance, should be of community benefit. In stark contrast to the hostile relationships that have existed in some jurisdictions (e.g., NSW, Victoria), support for this important 2002 initiative was achieved through a partnership between the state government, all industry sectors, and community groups (Queensland Government Treasury, undated). This signals a new regulatory approach that contrasts with the command and control policies of the past. While the Queensland government is committed to research and program evaluation to monitor the implementation and impacts of this innovative strategy, it remains to be seen if it will achieve its stated objectives of community engagement and democratic outcomes.

Despite barriers to market growth since 1999, Australian gambling expenditure has continued to rise. During 2005–6 Australian gambling losses totalled $17.57 billion or around AUD$1,123 per adult. As in previous years, growth was mainly in the gaming sector, with EGMs accounting for 60 per cent of all gambling activity. Gambling expenditure varies across jurisdictions, however, reflecting the availability and spending of EGMs. Almost half the total spending on EGMs occurred in NSW. Total gambling expenditure also was highest in NSW

(AUD$1,357 per adult – 3.56 per cent of HDI) and lowest in Western Australia (AUD$551 per adult – 1.46 per cent of HDI).[11]

However, the *rate* of industry growth has slowed since 1999. At a national level, real annual expenditure since 1998–9 has grown by AUD$1.36 billion, compared to growth of AUD$7.8 billion in the seven years before 1999. Further, overall per capita spending has flattened; and gambling expenditure as a proportion of household discretionary income has continued to decline from 3.16 per cent in 1999–2000 to 2.93 per cent in 2005–6.

Overall growth in tax revenues also has slowed. Since 1999–2000 real tax revenue from gambling has declined in several jurisdictions. NSW gambling taxes comprise 32 per cent of the national total, primarily because of high EGM expenditure in that state. Two attempts by the NSW government to increase gaming taxes to bring them into line with other states were blocked by strong industry opposition (McMillen and Wright 2008). The Victorian government, in contrast, was willing to sacrifice a temporary decline in revenue to implement its reform program.

Significantly, there is no firm evidence that problem gambling has diminished, contrary to claims by some politicians and industry groups that problem gambling has been reduced since 1999. Although prevalence surveys have been conducted in several Australian states since the national study (Table 5.1), they have used different and inconsistent prevalence measures, making direct comparisons invalid (Banks 2007). Two Queensland surveys, using the same screen and large samples, provide the most reliable indication of trends and suggest any apparent reduction in problem gambling is insignificant (Queensland Government Treasury 2002, 2004).

Periodic reviews by the chair of the Productivity Commission continue to call for more interventionist regulation over industry practices and EGMs (Banks 2002, 2007). There is no evidence to suggest that self-regulation by any operator has achieved the standards now expected by governments and the Australian community; and in all states, the reform process has exposed the tensions and contradictory functions of government in gambling policy. The uncertain effects of post-1999 reforms have prompted renewed debates about how far governments are prepared to steer gambling development to minimize the social harm that can occur.

Australian gambling has experienced many of the regulatory risks that confront Canadian authorities (McMullen and Perrier 2007; International Gambling Studies 2007, 2:233–52). Ad hoc decisions by policy makers, slanted by their mutual objective with industry to maintain or increase revenues, have allowed the market to expand beyond community expectations. While this policy focus has facilitated industry expansion, it has exposed flaws and risks in the regulatory systems (McMillen 2006; Miers 2003, 2004). Regulatory failure is more likely to occur as governments abandon their traditional responsibility to manage and restrict the market.

Perhaps the most important achievement in the process of Australian re-regulation, however, has been steady progress towards a coordinated national approach to research and policy development. Significantly, this has been achieved by increased consultation between the states and territories, rather than with Commonwealth involvement. On the contrary, the Commonwealth's role in gambling regulation continues to be contested, not least by state governments wary of federal intervention.

Following the 1999 national inquiry by the Productivity Commission, a national Ministerial Council was established to bring together all states and territories and the Commonwealth to regularly discuss policy options. That process has been far from smooth. Potential cooperation between the two levels of government suffered a serious setback in 2001 when the Commonwealth legislated unilaterally to restrict development of Internet gambling services licensed by the states (McMillen 2003).[12]

The deep political tensions that inevitably emerged over that issue were exacerbated by persistent Commonwealth attacks on state gambling policies. Efforts to achieve uniform national regulation of ATMs also faltered when the Commonwealth refused to use its powers over financial institutions to assist the states. Conversely, states and territories rejected the Commonwealth's proposal to establish a national gambling research institute jointly funded by industry.

The states and territories, in stark contrast, have begun to cooperate over research and policy as never before. A Regulators' Responsible Gambling Working Party, comprised of representatives from all Australian jurisdictions and New Zealand, meets regularly to discuss issues and strategies for responsible gambling. In 2003 a National Gambling Research Working Party was established, comprised of state and territory governments, which has developed a nationally coordinated research program to identify gambling-related problems in the Australian community and to assess reform options.[13] Although Commonwealth representatives have observer status at these forums, the resulting initiatives remain with states and territories.

Most states and territories also have their own research program directed to particular strategic and policy issues. Queensland, Victoria, and South Australia, in particular, have invested considerable resources in gambling research programs linked to evidence-based policy development. The most important policy impact has been to obtain a better understanding of the prevalence and nature of problem gambling.[14] The Commonwealth, through the Department of Families and Community Services (FaCS), also developed a national gambling research framework, but this has produced little of policy import to date.[15]

Against all the odds, the states and territories have revived the oft-neglected principle of cooperative federalism with promising effect. But it took sustained public protests and Commonwealth intervention, in the form of the Productivity Commission inquiry, to shake regional governments out of their complacency.

Election of an Australian Labor Party national government in November 2007 after eleven years of conservative rule has again placed gambling regulation and policy on the national political agenda. The new prime minister has indicated that a more coordinated, national approach to gambling policy is required. His government has moved quickly to establish mechanisms that open the way for genuine cooperation and negotiation between the Commonwealth and the states. Forthcoming changes to the composition of the Senate in July 2008 will shift the balance of power in the upper house to minority parties and independents advocating gambling reform, further ensuring that the momentum for reform is maintained.

In combination, the current tide of public opinion and the political alignment of Australian state and national governments provide the best opportunity in decades for nationally consistent gambling reform. Undoubtedly, some governments with entrenched structural problems and strong links to industry groups could be more resistant to change than progressive states. As occurred in 1999, however, public scrutiny and debate could drive governments further than they might otherwise be inclined to go.

Yet the current mood for cooperative reform may be short-lived. At the time of writing, traditional disputes between the states and territories have resurfaced over cross-border Internet betting exchanges (McMillen 2003; The Australian 2005; High Court of Australia 2008).

The prospect of a genuinely national and lasting approach to Australian gambling policy will remain out of reach while disparate and hostile state governments compete for political authority over new markets. Attempts to harmonize gambling policies require a greater level of trust and common purpose than has existed to date.

Conclusions

Contemporary gambling in Canada and Australia has been shaped by the interconnected dynamics between society, government, and an increasingly global market. In this general context, the variable nature of federal systems and regional differences continue to shape the character and structure of both Canadian and Australian gambling. Governments in both countries have been confronted with a range of contradictory policy options. This process has been managed in different ways in different places.

In Australia, while casino gambling and gaming machines have become the dominant forms of gambling in each state where they have been introduced, gambling policies and practices still reveal significant state differences. These interstate variations derive mainly from the way each government has responded to local pressures, concerns, and expectations. Key defining influences have been social and cultural values that accept gambling as a legitimate recreational activity; a federal political system in which state governments determine their own gambling policies but at the same time learn from the experience in other states; changing economic conditions and trends, which have facilitated legalization of new gambling products; and the impact of technological innovation.

Since 1999 there has been a pronounced shift towards evidence-based policy development. Governments and industry are being held accountable for decisions about gambling as never before. Yet although recent research has provided spectacular gains in our understanding of gambling impacts and the effects of policies on gambling processes, there is still much that we do not know. We still have only partial knowledge of gambling behaviour and the diverse ways that gambling problems are experienced (Smith et al. 2007). Gambling behaviour and impacts in different social contexts are even more complex and not understood.

Many decision makers would like a quantitative formula for determining the need for regulation in specific situations, and for allocation of resources. But the level of scientific uncertainty about the interaction between gambling and the community is relatively high. No matter how sophisticated the scientific methods or how hard researchers try to anticipate problems, there will always be surprises when least expected.

The terrain of gambling regulation is inherently dynamic, further complicating the task. For example, historical definitions distinguishing gaming and betting have been blurred as gambling providers invest in technology that enables development of interactive games and Internet gambling. These innovations have significantly diminished state governments' control over gambling and challenge the principles of state sovereignty (McMillen 2003). Such changes have required Australian states to rapidly develop a range of pioneering regulations to deal with emerging forms of cross-jurisdictional gambling.

Some analysts, including myself, have long argued for national co-ordination of Australian gambling regulation to remedy inconsistencies and policy failures, and to establish uniform standards of consumer protection for all Australians, regardless of where they live. Traditional localized, site-specific, and diverse gambling regulations are ill equipped to deal with an increasingly national and international industry (McMillen 2000c). Importantly, however, globalized gambling does not mean the end of state autonomy or the inevitability of adopting models from other countries. National institutions continue to provide the necessary conditions for the existence of legalized gambling. Each government has the political-legal capacity to constrain and manage the gambling market, to set distinctive conditions and levels of development, and to establish national limits.

A strong national commitment to long-term monitoring of key parameters also will give early warning of possible damaging change and allow necessary responses. At present, Australia lacks such firm commitment. Research is not institutionalized over the long term and is uncoordinated (McMillen 2005a). In some places resources are wasted through duplication and incremental steps in knowledge. Overall, enormous policy gaps remain before Australia can claim that gambling is being understood, regulated, and managed in the public interest.

While much remains to be done in Australia, however, the achievements of the past few years have been remarkable. After two decades of relatively unconstrained market growth, national and community values are once again central to policy processes seeking to refashion stronger, responsive regulation that meets the expectations of civil society.

NOTES

1 In all states, gambling revenue was used to fund public hospitals, public housing, and major projects (e.g., the Sydney Harbour Bridge, the Sydney Opera House, cultural centres) until the 1970s, when the direct nexus with welfare was progressively dismantled. However, Lotterywest continues to direct the large majority of its revenue to community programs. See <http://www.lotterywest.wa.gov.au>.

2 Over time, constitutional challenges to the High Court have occurred, mainly on the rights of interstate trade under section 92 of the Constitution.

3 The only exception was Tattersalls lottery, owned and operated by the George Adams family trust and based in Victoria. See <http://www.tattersalls.com.au>.

4 Australian clubs are non-profit community organizations with social or sporting functions. In contrast, hotels are privately owned, often by large corporations.

5 In Western Australia EGMs are restricted to Perth's Burswood Resort Casino.

6 Australian Bureau of Statistics 1999. *Gambling Industries*, cat. 8684.0.

7 At the time, the Commonwealth government was formed by a Liberal-National Party coalition, while the Australian Labor Party formed all state and territory governments.

8 See, for example, Guidelines for Community Impact Statements, Queensland Gaming Commission, available at <http://www.qogr.qld.au/commission/qgc.guidelines.shtml>.

9 Major reforms in New Zealand in 2003 also incorporated harm minimization as a central objective of all gambling legislation.

10 See <http://www.responsiblegambling.qld.gov.au>.

11 Northern Territory expenditure figures are relatively high but are inflated by the presence of several Internet gambling providers who accept bets from overseas gamblers.

12 The only previous Commonwealth intervention into gambling regulation occurred in 1903 when the then newly formed national government attempted (unsuccessfully) to stop interstate sale of lottery tickets through the post (McMillen et al. 1999).

13 Available at <http://www.justice.vic.gov.au>.

14 Since 1999 large prevalence studies have been conducted in the ACT (5,479 respondents); Queensland (2001 – 13,000 respondents; 2004 – 30,000 respondents); Victoria (2003 – 8,749 respondents); and South Australia (2005 – 18,000 respondents). Smaller prevalence studies have been conducted in NSW and Tasmania.

15 Available at <http://facs.gov.au>.

PART THREE

Governments and Gambling Policy

6 The Policies of Gambling Legitimation and Expansion in Ontario

THOMAS R. KLASSEN AND JAMES F. COSGRAVE[1]

In the past several decades public policies have legitimized many forms of gambling and made them part of mass culture, albeit under the regulatory umbrella of the state. In this chapter we examine how governments have sought to secure and solidify gambling as a legitimate activity – for both individuals and the state – as well as to set the stage for further expansion. Specifically, we analyse how, in its interest in using gambling as a source of revenue, the state developed a series of policies designed to secure this source of revenue. The fact that provinces have jurisdiction for gambling policy in Canada means that there is variation in the forms of lawful gambling and their regulation (Black 1996; Fortin 1996; see also chapter 4). We use the province of Ontario as our case study, because it is the most populous sub-national jurisdiction in Canada and as such has the most extensive capacity to pursue its gambling-related policies.

In the chapter we demonstrate and explain how the province has (1) eliminated competition from charitable and other groups for gambling venues, (2) co-opted groups in society that resisted and opposed gambling expansion, and (3) developed allies so that the expansion of gambling can proceed. Although our analysis encompasses various types of gambling, the focus is on commercial casinos and slot machines, which emerged in Ontario, and indeed in North America (outside of Las Vegas and Atlantic City), only in the past two decades.

We begin our analysis with a brief outline of the dynamics of gambling expansion in Ontario during the past thirty years, with a particular focus on the dramatic rise of casino gambling in the past decade. The second section of the chapter reviews how decision makers have manoeuvred policy levers to protect this source of revenues from a number of threats. In the third section we examine the implications of the state's role in gambling and conclude with a discussion of its future in Ontario.

History

In the twentieth century, with the exception of betting at racetracks and small wagers at charitable games such as bingo and raffles, gambling in Canada was illegal under the *Criminal Code* until 1969 (Morton 2003). The state actively enforced this prohibition for many forms of gambling, such that in a one-year period the Canadian Post Office intercepted 150,000 pieces of mail of which 55 per cent contained tickets for a lottery in Jamaica (Ontario Attorney General 1961, 115). In 1969, at the urging of the Quebec government, which required funds to pay for the 1967 World's Fair and the 1976 Olympics in Montreal, and also to modernize some of the Victorian moral prohibitions, the *Criminal Code* was amended to allow for state-run lotteries (Campbell 1997). Lotteries were attractive to sub-national jurisdictions because they were low risk, required low investment, and could be implemented quickly (Weinstein and Deitch 1974). Lotteries generate more profits per dollar than other types of gambling, such as casinos, because of low payroll and other costs. Ontario established the Ontario Lottery Corporation in 1975, whose offerings have grown from modest beginnings to a dizzying array including bingo, sports betting, instant, and on-line games. In 2005, lotteries generated $2.4 billion in revenues, of which $1.3 billion was set aside for prizes (Ontario Lottery and Gaming Corporation 2006).

By 1976, all provinces had their own lotteries so that in 1985 the federal government formally transferred jurisdiction for gambling entirely to the provinces, and also removed the prohibition against slot machines and other mechanical gaming devices. This transfer of jurisdiction was an important policy decision, which has contributed to the expansion of state sanctioned and operated gambling (Campbell and Smith 1998; Osborne and Campbell 1988; also chapter 4 of this volume). Provinces, compared to the federal government, have considerably more constrained powers to raise revenues, particularly in their limited access to personal and corporate taxes; as such, non-tax sources of revenues are particularly valued. The beginning of the 1990s saw provincial governments facing a downloading of costs and responsibilities from the federal level, and pressures to reduce tax levels. Additionally,

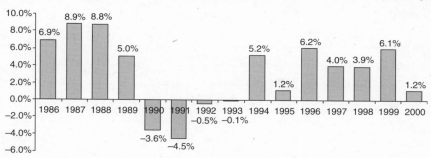

Figure 6.1: Percentage change Ontario annual GDP, 1986–2000 (1992$)

sub-national governments faced high deficits and a deep recession. In their search for revenue, provinces especially sought new forms of non-tax revenues. Most aggressive in this regard was the province of Manitoba, which, under a New Democratic government, approved the first government-run year-round casino in Canada, which opened in Winnipeg in 1989 (Hutchinson 1999; Black 1996).

Ontario was unusually affected by the recession of the early 1990s as its industrial base adjusted to the Canada–United States Free Trade Agreement (1988) and the North American Free Trade Agreement (1993). As shown in Figure 6.1, for four years (1990 to 1993) the economy contracted in real terms, with a resulting increase in unemployment, and a doubling of social assistance cases between 1990 and 1993. At the same time, notwithstanding that demand for government services was high, government revenues were declining, as illustrated in Figure 6.2.

Because of the economic conditions, and its ambitious social policy agenda, the New Democratic government in Ontario, which was elected in 1990, was exceptionally desperate for new sources of income. Ideologically the party was not predisposed to dramatically restrict funding for social programs, which further intensified the quest for new sources of revenues (Fairbrother 2003). In 1991 and 1992, provincial bureaucrats charged with generating more non-tax revenue identified how profitable (for state governments) the casinos in Nevada and Atlantic City were, especially in how their source of revenues came predominantly from tourists arriving from the northeastern states of the United States (Mandal and Doelen 1999, 32–56). The successful and profitable Manitoba extension of casino and video lottery terminals of

Figure 6.2: Ontario provincial revenue, 1986–2000 (billions 1992$)

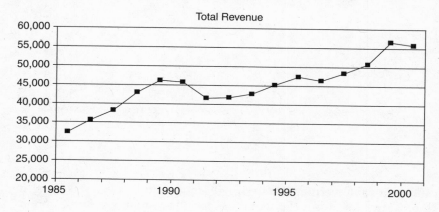

the late 1980s and first years of the 1990s was well known to a cadre of deputy ministers and other senior civil servants in Ontario, who had served with the Manitoba NDP government before being recruited by the Ontario New Democrats in 1990. Reflecting the driving force for allowing casinos in the province – namely, generating revenues – the formal decision was announced in the 1992 provincial budget.

Policy makers at Queen's Park carefully selected the city of Windsor as the site for the first major commercial Las Vegas–style casino, primarily because of its location across the border from the United States. The mainly Francophone Catholic community historically had a high degree of gambling involvement, in comparison with the other mostly Protestant areas of southern Ontario, and the city had acquired the status as the bingo capital of Canada, along with a reputation for illegal 24-hour high-stakes card games. Furthermore, its high unemployment rate in 1992 (officially at 14 per cent, but unofficially at 20 per cent) lowered community opposition to the venture. Nevertheless, there was opposition to the legalization of casinos, to the extent that one NDP member of the Legislature resigned from the caucus in protest (Brady 1993).

Notwithstanding favourable revenue projections from the casino, the policy makers proceeded only with an interim casino, which opened in May 1994. It proved so successful, especially with American tourists, that a second interim facility opened in December 1995. It too proved far more profitable than projected so that a much larger version (100,000 square feet) replaced the interim casinos in July 1998. It included a 398-room four-star hotel and three restaurants, an entertainment lounge, and a sports bar. In mid-2008 the casino was christened Caesars Windsor after a $400 million facelift. The further expansion of casinos in other parts of the province that was to occur is described in the next section.

As Table 6.1 shows, the expansion of gambling has provided a steady and increasing stream of revenues for government coffers. In 1992, the funds amounted to 3.2 per cent of indirect taxes, while a decade later the percentage had more than doubled to slightly more than 7 per cent. By 2002, gaming profits were the fourth largest component of Ontario's revenues from 'production and imports,' exceeded in size only by direct taxes on products (retail and provincial sales tax, and excise taxes), payroll taxes, and the gasoline tax (Statistics Canada, Provincial Economic Accounts 2004, Table 12, p. 188).

State Strategies

To quickly solidify and protect its role in gambling legitimation and expansion, especially with regard to casinos and the slot machines that are the core of such venues, the Ontario government has pursued three strategies. The first was to consolidate its role as a monopolist by eliminating competitors for gambling expenditures by individuals. The second was to co-opt resistance and opposition to state regulated and operated gambling, which, if successfully accomplished, would allow further gambling expansion. The last strategy was to develop allies that support the state in its growing role vis-à-vis gambling.

In ensuring that state-operated gambling became and remained a steady source of revenue, the state has had to curtail competition from other, private, yet legal, forms of gambling. Gambling for charitable purposes – via bingos, raffles, and travelling monte carlo casinos – has a long history in many parts of Ontario, typically in community halls and church basements (Morton 2003). The profits from such gambling flow directly to non-profit groups, rather than the state. Additionally, racetrack betting is a privately operated gambling activity whose profits do not flow to the state. A logical strategy for the state in its own expansion of gambling would be to limit and gradually reduce such competing forms of gambling and thereby minimize the leakage of funds to those games.

The very expansion of state gambling activities has meant greater

Table 6.1
Ontario gaming profits and total indirect taxes, 1992–2002 (billions $)

	1992	1993	1994	1995	1996	1997	1998	1999	2000	2001	2002
Gaming profits	529	581	794	953	914	1,286	1,453	1,580	1,836	1,959	2,017
Total indirect taxes	16,613	17,284	18,523	19,182	19,981	21,831	23,546	25,560	26,989	28,102	28,455

Source: Provincial Economic Accounts, Statistics Canada, various years.

competition for charitable gambling. Community raffles, bingos, and other games cannot match the prizes, marketing, and technological sophistication of casinos and province-wide state lotteries. In Ontario, in 1996 the newly elected Progressive Conservative government concurrently announced new government charitable casinos and the banning of long-standing community roving charity casinos. The government publicized the ban as a means to restrict gaming to those activities under regulatory control, and as a means to generate more funding for charities. The self-serving rationale resulted in the small business people who ran the roving casinos suing the government. Additionally, charitable groups were troubled that they would no longer have access to local sources of revenues.

Racetrack betting, which also has a long tradition in many parts of Ontario, has been in decline for some decades as the province urbanized. However, as with charitable gaming, the increase in state-sponsored gambling has further exacerbated the decline as gamblers no longer need to travel to racetracks at specified times but can gamble, sometimes in simulated horse-race games, in casinos. Not surprisingly, during the 1990s revenue from racetracks plummeted from $536 million in 1989 to only $348 million in 1997 (Marshall 1998). In Ontario, the decline in horse betting provided the state an opportunity to rescue the faltering horse-racing industry by installing slot machines at racetracks, of which a small portion of the profits are allocated to the racing industry (Hutchinson 1999, 154). As a result, most racetracks in Ontario now have slot machines (9,300 in total), with horse racing itself a marginal activity. Many of these racetrack slot facilities are open 24 hours per day for most of the week, effectively transforming them into mini-casinos.

The racinos often are found in municipalities that have explicitly rejected a more traditional casino. For example, Canada's largest racetrack, Woodbine, located in the city of Toronto, has 1,700 slot machines (staffed by 900 workers) ranging from 25 cents to $5, and is open 24 hours a day, 365 days a year. The result is that racetracks, which might have competed to some degree with state-run gambling, are now part of the state gambling system.

Competition to the government's efforts to maximize revenues arises not only from existing legal games, but also from other jurisdictions. It is not surprising that most of Ontario's casinos are located near its border with the United States, with four casinos being literally across a bridge. For the Windsor Casino, 80 per cent of its patrons are Americans; of the two casinos in Niagara Falls, 50 per cent of patrons are from south of the border. In such an environment, however, other jurisdictions will engage in tactics to repatriate their own gambling citizens, and attract those from outside their borders. Casinos have opened in Detroit, across from Windsor, and casinos on Native lands have opened in New York State to compete with Ontario's. The Quebec government strategically built its Casino du Lac-Leamy, with 1,870 slot machines and 64 gaming tables, in Hull, just across the river from Ottawa, with the explicit intent of luring Ontario gamblers (Fortin 1996).

A challenge for the state in expanding gambling opportunities as a source of revenues has been to minimize resistance to its strategy, since resistance not only threatens the revenue stream but also the legitimacy of the state. There are two issues that have the potential to allow coalitions of anti-gambling, and especially anti-casino and anti-electronic gaming machine, groups to coalesce around: problem gambling and the impact of state gambling on charitable groups.

There continues to be considerable anti-gambling sentiment, especially vis-à-vis the expansion of casinos and video lottery terminals. Referenda and plebiscites, sometimes initiated by grass-roots opposition, in numerous Canadian jurisdictions (including Alberta, Prince Edward Island, and Ontario) have often yielded results that oppose gambling expansion, and in some cases have forced governments to remove video lottery terminals and curtail expansion plans (Canada West Foundation 1997). In Nova Scotia, opposition to video lottery terminals, based on the concern that youth were becoming addicted to gambling, resulted in the government removing them from corner stores, and limiting them to age-restricted premises.

Given this sentiment, the Ontario government has had to tread carefully vis-à-vis its expansion of gambling. When the New Democrats were replaced by the Progressive Conservatives in 1995, some expected that gambling expansion would cease or at least slow. After all, the Conservatives were far more anti-government than the NDP and represented rural and traditional small-town Ontario where one would have expected anti-gambling sentiment to be strongest. However, in 1996 the government announced that 44 new casinos were to be built. These would be charity casinos, which differed from the large casinos in Windsor and Niagara Falls only in their smaller scale and lower betting limits. Public outcry forced the government to retreat, so that only five have been built to date. As shown in Figures 6.1 and 6.2, the province's economic and revenue conditions had improved considerably by 1996, which should have made gambling revenues less pressing for the government. However, the Progressive Conservatives were committed to reducing personal and corporate taxes. As such, the higher the gambling revenues, the greater the ability of government to finesse tax cuts, especially for higher-income individuals and corporations, without having to decrease expenditures, or increase other taxes.

Even to establish these five casinos required considerable subtlety on the part of the state to co-opt those who resisted or opposed gambling expansion. In particular, the government has had to demonstrate that the problems associated with the plan are minor, and that the state has adequate policies to address these issues. Because casinos, unlike lotteries, are spatially located in a particular community, they require that such a community bear most of the social and individual costs (Room, Turner, and Ialomiteanu 1999). This characteristic of casinos allows anti-gambling groups greater scope to mobilize in order to oppose state expansion plans. Gambling behaviour in casinos is considerably more concentrated and intensive, given the hours of operation, the variety of games and general nature of the physical environment, and the possibility for addictive behaviour.

In abandoning the ambitious expansion of casinos, however, the government settled for the creation of racinos. The horse breeders and racers and the track owners were co-opted by being allocated 10 per cent each of revenues from slot machines. Municipal governments are given 5 per cent of revenues from the first 450 slot machines and 2 per cent from additional ones. The provincial government has promised to increase the municipal share to 5 per cent of all slot machines, should a charity casino be co-located at a host racetrack municipality. This financial incentive means that some of the current 16 racinos will metamorphose into full-blown casinos over the next decade, with more slots and higher betting limits.

To illustrate that negative aspects of increased gambling opportunities could be managed, the Ontario government began in the early 1990s to provide problem gambling counselling services as part of the state-provided health-care system. By doing so, it gained control over previously independent community-based agencies that sought to help individuals with gambling problems and educate the public on the addictive nature of gambling. The incorporation of problem gambling into the medical establishment has meant that such behaviour has become medicalized and treated as a psychological mental health disorder, rather than as a social phenomenon influenced, and to a degree created, by state decisions to expand gambling and increase accessibility (Castellani 2000). As discussed in the next section, a related strategy was also to incorporate groups previously independent and critical of gambling into allies.

Minimizing resistance to gambling expansion through the availability of treatment is particularly important for frequent players who contribute a much greater share of profits than casual players. For instance, a casual video lottery player in Nova Scotia bets $1.49 per month, while a problem player bets $808.00 per month (a typical player bets about $100 per month).[2] In Ontario, 4.8 per cent of gamblers account for 36 per cent of gambling revenues (Williams and Wood 2007). As such, on the one hand, the state is under pressure to increase revenues by introducing more addictive gambling opportunities, including games with higher betting limits, faster slot machines, technologically more advanced games, and more advertising for casinos and lotteries; yet, on the other hand, such policies will heighten the social problems associated with gambling. These problems, if left unattended, could ultimately endanger gambling revenues by acting as catalysts for calls for less gambling.

A general strategy used by most jurisdictions, including Ontario, is to rebrand gambling as gaming. In other words, the gambling industry and the state have sought to differentiate gambling (which was previously illegal and counter to dominant Protestant beliefs) from the new gaming, which the state is actively promoting. Indeed, the term gambling is now used only when addressing problems associated with gambling, such as problem gambling (Barker and Britz 2000, 10). Even the term problem gambling is being obscured by the emphasis placed by lottery and casino corporations, as well as state-sponsored gambling-related agencies, on 'responsible gambling' or 'responsible gaming,' thus completing, on a symbolic level, the process of sanitizing an activity with previously deviant connotations. While such terms are used by government and industry, they indicate the objective of policy makers and government gaming officials to influence public discourse and shape gambling behaviour. The responsible gambling message is seen more frequently now, in advertisements for gambling activities and practices that also enjoin individuals to 'know your limit.'

Not only has the state had to demonstrate that it assists those who become problem gamblers – primarily through the funding of awareness, prevention, and treatment programs – but also that it is studying problem gambling and its implications. In 2000, the province created the Ontario Problem Gambling Research Centre, which reports to the Ministry of Health, and distributes about $2.5 million per year for research. The research centre not only allows the state to demonstrate its awareness of, and concern with, problem gambling but also provides a state-sanctioned mechanism for researchers to study problem gambling. The research projects that receive funding tend to conceptualize problem gambling as primarily a personal, psychological, and medical condition, rather than a broader social issue, while research projects that might reflect adversely on gambling, such as benefit-cost analyses, are typically not funded.

Finally, the research centre allows the state to exercise a degree of influence over the discourse on problem gambling, which is a component of the gambling legitimation strategy. The relatively recent study of gambling behaviours in Ontario (problem and non-problem behaviours) is to a great extent the study of social behaviours produced by the state-run system of legal gambling and its particular modes of social organization. The knowledge generated by state-funded studies of gambling behaviour contributes to the normalization and risk management of gambling behaviours and markets (see chapter 3).

A second issue around which gambling opponents have coalesced, especially those who wish to stop the expansion of casinos, is the decrease in funds available to charitable and religious groups as community bingos, small raffles, and local lotteries faced mounting competition from casinos. These community fund-raising efforts are unable to compete with the appeal of large-scale casinos and lotteries. The solution in Ontario was to establish the Trillium Foundation, which in 1999 began to distribute $100 million annually of government funding. According to government rhetoric, this funding comes directly from gambling profits. However, since all gambling revenues are deposited in the government's general revenues, there is no direct linkage between the Trillium Foundation expenditures and gambling revenues. The $100 million amount remained unchanged until 2007, at which time, due to inflation, it was worth the equivalent of $85 million, notwithstanding that during the same time period profits from gambling increased by more than 20 per cent. The increase in 2007 of the Trillium funds to $105 million did little to stem the gradual erosion of funding for charities. The role of the Trillium Foundation ostensibly is to replace the funds that organizations previously raised with their own charitable gambling efforts. However, not only has this strategy made community and charitable groups reliant on the state for funding, but it also allows the state to direct funds to some groups, and not others, based on political considerations. A final outcome is that the granting agency provides the state with a venue to announce how gambling profits spawn benefits for communities, and allows state-sponsored gambling to be viewed as a socially positive activity.

In the spread of gambling, the state has employed policies that ensure it has allies who will aid it in further gambling expansion. Three groups have been nurtured by the state for this purpose: gambling operators and retailers, municipalities, and Native groups. In addition, groups that promote 'responsible' gambling have been fostered by the state to support gambling expansion, and finally the general public is a potential ally of the state.

With respect to lottery games in Ontario, individual retailers have become extraordinarily dependent on this source of revenues. Corner convenience (mom and pop) stores in the city of Toronto derive between one-fifth and nearly one-half of their profits from commissions earned from sales of Ontario Lottery and Gaming Commission products. The smaller the store, the more of its profits were generated from gaming commissions.[3] In 2005, there were 10,800 retail sites across the province that sold lottery products (Ontario Lottery and Gaming Corporation 2006).

Casino operators, whether private sector multinational corporations that manage the commercial casinos – such as Harrah's Entertainment, which, with other private sector partners, operates Casino Windsor, and Penn National, which operates Casino Rama, just north of Toronto – or the Ontario Lottery and Casino Corporation, which manages the charity casinos, become powerful allies for the state once lotteries, casinos, and other games are operating (see also chapter 4). The Ontario Lottery and Gaming Corporation employs 8,500 staff, while the contract management companies that operate the major casinos hire an additional 11,500 workers. As such, it and its counterparts in other provinces have become forceful advocates, within the state, for additional gambling. For instance, it was the Crown corporations that advocated for changes to the *Criminal Code* in 1999 to legalize gambling on cruise ships and previously banned dice games, such as craps (Ontario Casino Corporation 1999; Hutchinson 1999). These changes to legislation were made solely to allow Canadian casinos and tourism operators to compete better with American jurisdictions in attracting gamblers. The monopoly of state interests is 'circumscribed only by the *Criminal Code* and the social conscience of legislators' (Campbell and Smith 1998, 34).

The global nature of the gambling operating industry, especially for casino operations, has created a group of large and powerful companies that operate the majority of casinos (McMillen 1996; Schwartz 2003). These corporations, with annual revenues in the billions of dollars, hold considerable influence regarding the operational policies of casinos, as well as the economic power to play one jurisdiction off another. The overall result is that substantial power flows to state and private interests in policy making since the gambling public has no institutionalized voice in setting gambling policy (Walker 1998, 28–9).

The decentralization of state decision making has been to the advantage of groups favouring additional gambling. At the same time, it works to the detriment of those (usually opponents of gambling) who argue for a holistic perspective on gambling policy. For instance, the diffusion of responsibility is apparent in that between 2002 and 2005 the Ontario Lottery and Gaming Corporation reported to four different ministries. In 2002, it was under the jurisdiction of the Ministry of Tourism, Culture, and Recreation; and then moved in 2003 to the Ministry of the Attorney General and Ministry Responsible for Native Affairs. In 2004, responsibility for the Crown corporation was shifted to the Ministry of Economic Development and Trade, and most recently to the Ministry of Public Infrastructure Renewal.

That ministerial responsibility for the Crown corporation is unstable suggests that there is no agreement on how closely lottery and gaming activities should be overseen by politicians, and the extent to which political direction is given. The lack of a stable reporting relationship means that within government there is little opportunity for policy expertise to be developed about the impacts of the activities of the Crown corporation. Finally, critics and stakeholders have less opportunity to influence strategic government gambling policy when each year a different minister and bureaucratic office holds the formal reins. The result is that over the past several years the Ontario Lottery and Gaming Corporation has acquired more autonomy from its supposed political masters than would be the case had it had a constant reporting relationship.

The regulation of gambling is the responsibility of the Alcohol and Gaming Commission and the Ontario Racing Commission, which report to the Ministry of Consumer and Business Services, and the Ontario Illegal Gaming Enforcement Unit, reporting to the Ministry of Community Safety and Correctional Services. Treatment programs are with the Ministry of Health. Lastly the distribution of a small portion of the gambling profits is undertaken by the Ontario Trillium Foundation, which is an agency of the Ministry of Culture, although it previously reported to the Ministry of Tourism.

One outcome of such a disjointed policy framework is that casinos increasingly use 'comps,' that is, complimentary gifts to casino gamblers including tropical cruises, free hotel accommodation, expensive watches based on their level of spending – the more spending the more lavish the gifts. In total, between $200 and $300 million per year is provided to frequent gamblers in this manner (Chung 2005b). However, there is no oversight by the provincial government of these promotional allowances, or accountability by casino operators or the Ontario Lottery and Gaming Corporation to provincial policy makers.

The lax oversight allowed the Ontario Lottery and Gaming Corporation to effectively place the interests of its retailers ahead of gamblers. As a result, in early 2007, the government had to take the unprecedented step of appointing the associate secretary of the provincial Cabinet as the interim CEO of the corporation to restore public trust. This followed evidence that the corporation allowed lottery retailers and other insiders to collect at least $100 in fraudulent prizes. The 69-page ombudsman report on the matter found 'incontrovertible' evidence that over several years the lottery corporation 'was shirking its responsibility in protecting against fraudulent insider wins' (Marin 2007, 3). The scandal shook confidence in the lotteries, caused the resignation of senior officials at the corporation, and led to calls for a special inquiry (Ferguson 2007). However, the government was able to ultimately refute demands by opposition politicians for independent supervision and regulation of the lottery and gaming corporation.

As noted in the previous section, a second group that has been nurtured as an ally by the provincial governments are municipalities, especially with respect to slot machines and casinos. Municipalities, after all, must approve the zoning and construction of a casino, while having considerable ability to mobilize citizens for, or against, a new casino (Klassen and Cosgrave 2002). Municipalities are offered a 5 per cent cut of revenues from the first 450 slot machines to ensure their silence, if not support. Casinos in a particular community will also contribute funds to various local charitable causes as goodwill gestures to demonstrate that they are good citizens and garner community backing.

The state has managed to craft an alliance with Native groups in intensifying casino gambling, especially in regions where local governments and grass-roots groups have opposed gambling expansion. Some

Native bands, with autonomy over land use on their reserves and less bound by legislation, have been eager to utilize casinos as a means to create employment and bring visitors to their economically depressed areas that have few if any other avenues of capitalist development. In the bargain, the state gains considerable revenues, extends its control over Natives by setting the rules of the gambling operation, and ensures that gambling expansion proceeds even in regions where there is opposition by community groups. In Ontario, the large commercial Casino Rama and the smaller charity Blue Heron, both near Toronto, are on Native lands. However, in practice both are indistinguishable in their focus on profit maximization, games offered, and other features from casinos on non-Native lands. Indeed, in early 2008 the province's Aboriginal communities signed a deal with the government that guarantees them 1.7 per cent of gaming revenues annually for the next twenty-five years. In return, Aboriginal communities gave up their rights to revenues from Casino Rama (Puxley 2008). The arrangement further solidified the role of the state in gambling policy and continued its strategy of offering a slice of gambling revenues to groups whose support is imperative.

In Ontario, the previously grass-roots Canadian Foundation on Compulsive Gambling became, in 2001, the Responsible Gambling Council, now entirely funded by the government through the Ministry of Health. Along with the name change, the objective of the organization also shifted, from one focused on assisting individuals who had become compulsive gamblers, to one that primarily promotes responsible gambling by teaching individuals how to be self-regulating bettors (Responsible Gambling Council of Ontario 2002). The organization that was previously highly critical of government's role in gambling has been transformed into 'one that takes no position on controversial gambling practices, does not publicly criticize government, and no longer advocates for problem gamblers' (Chung 2005a, A16). Forty per cent of the members of the board of directors are from the gaming industry. The effect is that a group that was formerly a counterweight to government gambling policies now is charged with teaching citizens, including high school students, how to gamble responsibly.

A final group that must be made an ally of gambling are citizens, or some portion thereof. In this regard, the very nature of gambling ensures that those who wish or need a windfall are supportive of games of chance. Nevertheless, the state can aid this process. For instance, winning limits were increased in the newly opened Niagara Falls mega-casino, such that shortly after its opening the largest slot-machine jack-pot in Canadian history, $5.8 million, was paid at the casino. Intensive media advertising by the Ontario Lottery and Gaming Corporation further fuels demand for gambling. In this regard, it is interesting to note that lawmakers have essentially prevented the private sector from advertising tobacco and alcohol, but allow the state to undertake such advertising for gambling.

Conclusions

Gambling represents a unique activity in that the state is the regulator, supplier, and promoter and also receives the revenues. This chapter has illustrated, using Ontario as the case study, that the recent expansion of gambling, especially casinos, was driven primarily by the desire of the state to acquire non-tax revenue. As such, the state has constituted gambling 'as a mass leisure activity' and brought 'gambling into the fold of "legitimate" business enterprise' (Reith 1999, 90). In orchestrating the expansion and institutionalization, Ontario, governed since 1990 in turn by the New Democrats, Progressive Conservatives, and Liberals, has utilized a series of policy decisions that significantly enlarged the role of the state in cultural activities that were previously not directly under the regulatory domain of the state, except by prohibition.

The legalization of gambling in Ontario has been a selective legalization, as the structure of legal gambling, including the types of games allowed and the ability of these games to generate revenues, benefits and serves the needs of the state (Abt 1996). This suggests that the expansion and legitimation of gambling is not a process that has occurred naturally as an expression of civil society, of consumer demand, or even as an explicit demand of capital, but rather has been initiated and supported by state policies for its own purposes.

The events that we have reviewed raise four key considerations, not only for future developments in Ontario, but also for a more in-depth understanding of gambling in Canadian society. First, technology now makes lotteries and other forms of gambling a more immediate and, at the same time, widespread phenomenon. On-line games now account for 65 per cent of lottery sales in Ontario (Ontario Lottery and Gaming Corporation 2006, 17). Internet technology now makes it possible for lottery tickets to be sold on-line rather than via the traditional retailers, and for draws to be held almost continuously. Telecommunications and related technology are increasingly freeing gambling activities and behaviour from some of their spatial and temporal constraints. The reaction of the state to this is yet unclear, although, as our analysis demonstrates, the protection of its market and its monopolistic position is a key consideration for decision makers.

Second, lotteries and other forms of gambling are no longer used to support specific and identifiable public projects. In the past, citizens could choose to purchase tickets for one lottery, rather than another, in order to support the charitable cause of their choice. Today, lottery funds join all other funds raised by government to be allocated depending on political priorities. Indeed, revenues from gambling allow the government to reduce revenues from other more traditional sources, such as progressive income tax and corporate taxes. The operation of the Trillium Foundation means that there is no longer a spatial or other connection between a gambler's wager and any return to his or her community. If opposition to gambling were to increase (for whatever reasons), or indeed if the state was to seek to expand gambling, it may well seek to more closely link the revenues from gambling to specific expenditures.

Third, gambling in Ontario is increasingly dominated by the existence of large-scale casinos. The dramatic rise of casinos in the 1990s carried substantially more risks for the state, demanding more extensive policies (Thompson 1997). Casinos require considerable state investment – financial, political, and policy – to establish, without a guarantee that costs will exceed benefits (Henrikson 1996). The new Fallsview Niagara Falls casino completed in 2004 was one of the largest privately funded commercial development projects in Canada at a cost of nearly $1 billion. Its 150 gaming tables, 3,000 slot machines, and 368-room hotel – operated by a consortium of the Hyatt Group, Highland Gaming Inc., Shiplake Gaming Corporation, Olympic V Inc., and 3048505 Nova Scotia Company – represent a commitment by the provincial government to ensure that casinos remain an important component of its revenue stream. Not surprisingly, shortly after the casino's opening, the Liberal premier stated, 'There is no doubt about it, we have come to rely on gambling revenues. Perhaps in a better world we wouldn't, but the fact of the matter [is] it's here, it's here to stay' (Brennan 2004).

Fourth, the manner in which governments have pursued gambling expansion helps to illuminate a major debate in public policy: whether, and to what degree, nation states are now less able to make policy. Observers such as Ohmae (1991), Strange (1996), Teeple (1995), and others propose that due to globalization and related developments, nation states have steadily lost power to make both economic and social policy. However, the extent of this loss, especially with regard to social policy, is subject to debate, and the matter is far from settled (Fairbrother 2003; Mishra 1999). Our analysis of gambling policy in Ontario demonstrates that governments, in particular provinces, retain considerable social policy levers, which have been used to react to the loss of some economic policy power.

This chapter highlights that within a neo-liberal political climate, the 'liberalization of gaming [has] presupposed a stronger state, not a weaker one' (Kingma 1996, 218). However, the pursuit of a regressive source of income such as gambling suggests that the state is adopting policies of governing that require individual self-regulation. The social problems that arise as a result of such policies are viewed not so much as social costs, but rather as economic risks to be managed.

The successful expansion and promotion of gambling in Ontario demonstrates that the state continues to have the necessary machinery to shape public opinion, manage dissent, and create new institutions, namely those required to regulate, manage, and promote gambling. However, that the state has had to rely on such a regressive source of income raises questions about the objectives of both social and economic policy. In other words, expanding and utilizing gambling as a source of state moneys has meant preying on the most vulnerable citizens – those least able to afford additional expenditures.

In successfully culling gambling as a source of revenues, the state has demonstrated that it retains considerable power. It is not unreasonable to suggest that under conditions similar to those that existed in the early 1990s (high deficits, limited room to raise tax revenues, and pressures for greater public expenditures, possibly from an aging population) state officials might again find ways to increase gambling revenues or turn to other vices in their search for revenues. One option with respect to gambling would be to entirely decriminalize the activity and simply allow it to be regulated by provincial governments (Patrick 2001). This would provide provinces with increased scope to introduce new types of gambling, such as Internet gaming.

Alternatively, governments might seek new sources of non-tax revenues from currently prohibited behaviours. State-operated recreational drug clinics and brothels exist in European nations, and may be viewed as a model. In Canada, there have been proposals in the past for the state to apply a pornography tax. Thus, it is not impossible that pornography, prostitution, and marijuana use could be selected in a similar manner to gambling as means to generate revenues. If this is the case, the experience with gambling suggests that the state will seek to eliminate competition, co-opt resistance, and develop allies to support its revenue generation strategy.

NOTES

1 We extend thanks to the eight government officials, representatives of health agencies and gambling corporations in Ontario, as well as four officials in Nova Scotia, and two in British Columbia, who were interviewed in person during 2002 and 2003. This research was funded by research grants from York University and Trent University. The research assistance of Anna Kim is gratefully acknowledged.
2 Data obtained from interviews with government officials in Nova Scotia, August 2002.
3 The figures are from the authors' own calculations using a sample of 10 convenience stores in the city of Toronto for the 2003 calendar year. The annual net profit (including gaming) for these stores ranged from $24,000 to $61,000.

7 Government as Gambling Regulator and Operator: The Case of Electronic Gaming Machines

RAY MACNEIL

It is impossible to analyse the recent history of gambling proliferation in Canada without concurrently discussing, in some detail, the role of the state. The complexities of governmental structures and functions, and their operation, are interrelated with the rise of the modern gambling infrastructure. As a long-time government employee and bureaucrat, it is my hope that this chapter will provide useful insights that are not always brought forth in more academic treatments of this issue. In particular, the chapter analyses critical aspects of gambling oversight, regulation, and promotion in Canada.

To understand current developments, it is useful to recall two facts. First, the era since about 1990 is dramatically different from the pre-gambling expansion era. By any account, the post-1990 period shares few qualities with any other period in the history of gambling. The timing of this expansion is partly related to the rise of microcomputer and other technology that permitted the invention of a specific type of gambling product, namely electronic gaming machines in the form of slot machines or video lottery terminals (VLTs). The machines represent the most problematic and controversial form of gambling in Canada. In 2005, there were 88,615 legal electronic gaming machines in Canada, with British Columbia having the fewest per capita (221.1/100,000 people +18) and Manitoba having more than four times that number (Canadian Partnership for Responsible Gambling 2007, table 4).

Second, and perhaps more importantly, not all gambling is created equal. Reporters, politicians, bureaucrats, the general public, and even researchers often make the same mistake of treating all gambling products or 'opportunities' as equal in terms of their impact. I will argue that this error reduces the quality and sensitivity of the debate surrounding vital policy issues, especially with respect to electronic gaming machines.

Gambling Expansion Era

The gambling industry in Canada, and worldwide for that matter, prior to 1990 was a markedly different one from that which arose in the early 1990s and with which we interact today. These two periods in history bear little resemblance to each other, and – while Atlantic City and Las Vegas still exist – the proliferation of casinos, slot machines, video lottery terminals, and other forms of gambling in the intervening years has generated remarkable social change. The impact of this change is still for the most part uncertain because some of its harmful effects, for example, on crime (see chapter 8) or youth (see chapter 9), may not be evident for decades. While some citizens have already drawn their own conclusions, how Canadians will remember their governments' role in this expansionist period is yet to be determined.

As an example, consider the gaming industry in Nova Scotia prior to 1990, which did not include a single electronic gaming machine or casino. Local charity bingos were a predominant form of gambling as were lotteries and scratch tickets, which were introduced in Nova Scotia in the early 1980s. Contrast this with the post-1990 era where electronic gaming machines, in the form of VLTs, now represent 70 per cent of the total gaming revenue in Nova Scotia, with 2,361 VLTs in 456 bars and lounges in addition to over 1,000 slot machines in casinos (CPRG 2007). Nova Scotians will soon likely see increasing levels of regulated on-line or machine-based gambling, such as the PlaySphere on-line gambling product and mega-bingos. The expansion of these forms of gambling is taking place when research suggests that, when compared to other forms of gambling, a larger than usual proportion of on-line gamblers are problem gamblers (Ladd and Petry 2002).

While it may sound simplistic that not all gambling opportunities are created equal, it is absolutely fundamental to bear in mind that the characteristics of each gambling product or game are unique and present specific challenges to public policy and the management of problem gambling prevalence. The precise characteristics of a particular game or machine will make it more or less addictive. Unfortunately, the properties that make games addictive can be the very same properties that make them exciting to play (Dickerson 2003). This fact alone results in a contradiction for operators that wish to make their machines less addictive while maintaining their appeal to gamblers. In other words, there is evidence that some products cannot be made less problematic without also reducing their general appeal and excitement for a broad range of gamblers (Dickerson 2003).

The term gambling (or gaming) can be misleading in that it encompasses a range of products and devices so broad as to have little in common. Semantically speaking, from the perspective of problem gambling, it is a poor taxonomic descriptor. Individual games bring with them their own unique qualities, each potentially contributing, to a greater or lesser degree, to problem gambling. According to the latest prevalence estimates, in Nova Scotia it is reported that almost 90 per cent of adults (approximately 576,000) participated in the past year in some form of gambling (Schellinck and Schrans 2003). At the same time, based on the Canadian Problem Gambling Index, 6.9 per cent of all adults are reported to be either at risk (4.8 per cent) or problem (2.1 per cent) gamblers (Schellinck and Schrans 2003).

From a policy perspective it might be argued that a rate of 2.1 per cent of either moderate or severe problem gamblers is quite reasonable, when weighed against the entertainment/leisure and economic benefits of gambling at the community level. Unfortunately, this rate masks the more specific and important underlying issues associated with the prevalence of problem gambling. According to research completed by the Nova Scotia Department of Health in 2003, VLTs are associated with over half of all past and current self-reported gambling problems despite the fact that only about 5 per cent of adults are regularly involved in the activity each month (Schellinck and Schrans 2003). A large percentage of problem gambling in Nova Scotia and Canada today is associated with electronic gaming machines (EGMs) and specifically VLTs. This finding is partly due to their accessibility, with over 456 VLT locations in Nova Scotia, for example, and more than 7,200 across Canada (CPRG 2007), and the machine's distinctive and inherent illusion-creating properties.

Serge Chevalier et al. (2004) have discussed the 'gambling offer' as a way to address the measurement of dangerous gambling products. Their work attempts to quantify the extent of gambling opportunities in a jurisdiction based on specific qualities of games that may predict problematic gambling (for example, accessibility, speed of betting, rate of money loss, etc). While this work is in its early stages, it represents an important concept that may in the future allow governments to measure the extent of current and (perhaps more importantly) future gambling opportunities in a jurisdiction. Compared to today's standards, the work of Chevalier et al. represents an important initial attempt to design a more systematic and accurate method of quantifying the expansion of gambling products. It is also an opportunity to improve our ability to forecast the potential contribution each new gambling opportunity presents to problem gambling.

Public sentiment can be unkind to problem gamblers, particularly electronic machine gamblers. It is often a simplistic approach that drives this condemnation, such as 'these people should know better.' Particularly where VLTs are concerned, though, it must be remembered that these machines are in many provinces highly accessible (in terms of dispersion, number of machines, hours that the machines are available, short and low learning curve), with well-developed features of illusion (high speed of play, near misses, etc.), and the potential to extract considerable money from a gambler quickly (with a new bet every seven seconds). As a result of the various features, the gambler is led to believe that a large win is imminent, thereby encouraging the chasing of loses, one of the primary behaviours that scientists associate with problem gambling.

Gambling expansion in Canada has presented significant social policy challenges for governments. In Nova Scotia, the public has, from time to time, enunciated overwhelming support for increased controls on VLT accessibility. At the same time, public support plummets for such controls if they are associated with an increase in personal taxes or a decrease in public services. This reflects a historical dichotomy of the public interest in gambling issues. Generally, political parties across Canada have accepted the notion that gambling is here to stay, and for the most part, that notion goes unchallenged. While there are outcries around seminal events, the public seems prepared to support the notion that gambling is a necessary evil.

The remainder of this chapter will focus on the implications of machine gambling. As advances in technology allow the industry to experiment with more convenient and accessible ways for citizens to gamble there will no doubt be other products that will contribute to the prevalence of problem gambling. Today, however, and for the foreseeable future, a major cause of problem gambling is machine gambling (see also chapter 9).

The Precautionary Principle

In modern times the state is required to address many complex social and economic issues. Conflicts often arise between social and economic objectives, such as between expansionist economic development agendas and ecological or environmental protection agendas.

There are few people in my experience, gambling opponents or otherwise, that fault the original decision to engage in machine gambling in Canada. While it is possible that there were some in the industry who may have had knowledge of their addictive potential, few would suggest that government leaders had any sense of the issues that would be facing us today as a result of decisions to engage in machine gambling. That being said, even with the aid of two decades of research, debate, and experience, a new approach is required, one that is based on a precautionary principle.

Although there is no consensus definition as to what is termed the precautionary principle, one oft-mentioned statement, from the 1998 Wingspread Conference in Racine, Wisconsin, aptly sums it up:

> When an activity raises threats of harm to human health or the environment, precautionary measures should be taken even if some cause and effect relationships are not fully established scientifically. In this context the proponent of an activity, rather than the public, bears the burden of proof. (Raffensperger et al. 1998, n.p.)

The important relationship here is that between (1) the uncertainty of a cause and effect relationship between a product or activity and human health and (2) the precautionary reaction to that uncertainty. This approach has been used extensively in the literature on environmental risk where the advocates of the precautionary principle argue that existing risk assessments of industrial chemicals err in that they ignore the longitudinal and interactive properties. In other words, the harmful effects may not be known for decades or may be evident only in combination, making existing forms of risk evaluation static and faulty. The same might also apply to electronic gambling machines and other types of gambling, such as electronic bingo or Internet gaming.

Canadian governments have never chosen a precautionary approach to the expansion of gambling. This contrasts with Australia where, as discussed by Jan McMillen in chapter 5, this approach has been adopted by some regulators. In fact, during the 1980s and 1990s, government officials in Canada knew very little about electronic gambling machines, yet seemed eager to participate in experimentation (see also chapters 4 and 6). In part this had to do with the prevailing values among officials and industry leaders at the time, which continue to exist to a degree to this day. When all jurisdictions are expanding gambling, not to do so is to be out of step with modern practice. In many jurisdictions there was a further perception that not getting into the gambling business at a level equal to your neighbour actually meant that there would be a negative economic impact. This is because those dollars that would have otherwise been spent on a gambling industry within a jurisdiction would leave to gambling-friendly neighbours. As a consequence, not only was there no strong argument to prevent expansion, but there is actually an enticing rationale to continue it.

A precautionary approach is a necessary strategy if the goal is to generate the social and economic balance that is sought by many stakeholders in this industry. Utilizing a precautionary principle is important to gambling policy first and foremost because government's ultimate objective must be to safeguard and enhance the health and welfare of its citizens. Governments undertake this commitment using a variety of means and through the provision of a complex array of services. These services, of course, require financing. Government officials often see gambling revenues, in the absence of gambling's social costs, as providing much-needed financing to their provinces that may be hard pressed without it. However, the financing of government services in and of itself cannot and should not supersede the primary edict of protecting the health and welfare of citizens from dangerous activities, including gambling and particularly electronic machines. Recently, the Nova Scotia government developed a policy paper that described a framework for future development of a sustainable gaming industry. In their response to this strategy, the directors of addictions programs and services in the province provided the following feedback expressing their concern about the absence of a precautionary approach: '[The policy paper] appears predicated on the fallacious thinking that public health and social policy objectives are to be construed as taking their place within a larger, somehow more compelling, "gaming sector" vision and policy framework' (Devine et al. 2004).

This concern is part of a broader debate recognizing the need for an approach predicated on consumer protection principles, particularly with respect to electronic gambling. Recently two important organizations have joined the debate concerning the structure of the gaming industry in Canada: the Canada Safety Council (2004) and the Law Commission of Canada (2005). Both organizations expressed serious reservations concerning how gaming is currently operated in Canada. The importance of the Canada Safety Council's voice is in its public identity as a consumer protection leader in Canada. The reframing of gaming issues in terms of consumer protection requires the active engagement of such organizations.

The implication of a consumer protection approach is that if a product, by its very nature, is dangerous to the public's health, then providing (downstream) treatment services and (upstream) prevention services is insufficient. Dickerson (2004) has pointed out that impaired control is common among electronic machine gamblers, such as the inability of a gambler to either agree to or enforce time and/or money limits on play. In fact, he argues further that impaired control is not a symptom of pathology, but instead is a natural response to sophisticated gaming machines. If Dickerson is correct, then this is a strong argument supporting a change of tack where EGMs are concerned, supporting the adoption of a strategy based on consumer protection principles, and recognizing that the machines are inherently problematic in their current configuration. Governments must also recognize that public expectations of 'duty of care' are higher for government-run enterprises than they would be for a privately run gambling enterprise.

Government Structure and Function

Government policy development is typically a difficult, sometimes even disorganized, endeavour characterized by weak processes, poor information, and, if not outright political influence, then certainly significant competing interests. Without strong and coherent processes, those who seek to influence the policy are at an advantage, and undue influence can go unchecked. These issues are exacerbated when in the complex of the gaming regulation/operation portfolio. That government decision-making processes are not always optimal should not be a surprise and is not necessarily a criticism. Unfortunately, though, the consequences in the gambling milieu can be significant.

Over the past two decades, there have been a variety of both planned and serendipitous policy shifts that provide at least partial explanation as to why government gaming operations are currently structured as they are. Some of these changes have resulted in structural impediments that restrict the development of socially and economically balanced gaming policy. As well, these impediments must often be managed by government organizations whose mandates reflect competing goals: particularly those of continued revenue growth versus harm reduction.

The regulatory environment in which this industry operates is the result of a patchwork of changes to the *Criminal Code* occurring over more than half a century. This has caused what the Law Commission of Canada has referred to as a balkanization of the *Criminal Code*, with each lottery and gaming corporation developing its unique interpretation of the legislation (Campbell et al. 2005). The result is a hodgepodge of structures and gaming products across Canada, such as outlined in previous chapters. In Prince Edward Island alone, a province of just 138,000 people, there are four organizations that have some responsibility for gaming regulation.

Questions have been raised recently as to whether all provinces are even working within the boundaries of the *Criminal Code* (Campbell et al. 2005). If there is too great a divergence from the *Criminal Code*, federal law reform may be essential as a way to establish a more uniform national policy framework for gaming activities. Of course, federalism and the jurisdiction that provinces hold with regard to gambling will make this difficult to attain unless there is considerable public pressure.

As described earlier, the lack of well-defined and robust policy development processes is another structural impediment to gambling reform. While it is not unusual to the gambling portfolio, it nonetheless impedes the percolation of the public interest into state decision making. This concern is exacerbated in gaming policy by the complexity of departments, agencies, and officials that are typically involved in gaming policy development. These departments and agencies are asked to share responsibility for policy development and to coordinate their activities when their mandates have them working at cross-purposes. While the public perceives government as a monolithic structure, in reality it is an agglomeration of smaller organizational units, with diverse and at times opposing mandates. Clearly the level to which objectives are shared among state bodies in regard to gambling is limited because of the incompatibility of continued annual revenue growth and the minimization of gambling harm.

A third important structural influence is the natural location of power within the state apparatus. The Department of Finance wields significant authority and influence within government. In most Canadian provinces, decisions taken relative to gaming revenue generation are the purview of this ministry, while prevention and treatment services and regulatory responsibilities are divested to other departments. Typically, prevention and treatment are the responsibility of Ministry of Health or addictions treatment organizations, while regulatory authority is the responsibility of a range of other organizations depending on the province.

The natural result of this structure is a greater emphasis on revenue generation and, relatively speaking, a decreased emphasis on health protection. Revenue generation currently takes place in the absence of any measure of social cost. By design, increasing revenue generation naturally supplants other activities, particularly in an ideological and economic environment where revenue from non-tax sources is a major policy concern. The minister of finance is often in the position of being challenged by his or her colleagues to make more money available for programs and services, whereas colleagues are pressured by their constituents to make more money available for programs and services.

Many organizations, including the Canada Safety Council and the Law Commission of Canada, have recognized the inherent conflict of interest that provincial governments are faced with when concurrently acting as gambling operator and regulator. The rebuttal from government so far has been to reiterate that the internal separation of responsibilities ensures that the task of operator does not override the regulatory objectives.

Opponents of the gaming industry contend that increased separation of the regulation and operation functions is necessary for a balance of the economic and social objectives to be attained. This could occur, it is argued, through further privatization of operations while enhancing and strengthening the regulatory role of the government. However, the solution is likely not to be so straightforward. In Nova Scotia, for example, net gaming revenues were approximately $185 million in 2004–5. Changes in structure must take into account the influence that revenues of this magnitude have on the governance system. Adams (2004) suggests that there is a 'natural decay' in democratic systems when the influence of these amounts of money is involved. This is in reference not to illegal activities, but to more subtle distortions resulting from systemic pressures that are a function of the magnitude of profits involved. Thus, changes in the level of privatization, in and of themselves, are unlikely to affect the overall balance of social and economic interests.

To follow with Adams's argument, balance can best be brought to the system when there is a commitment to a significant reduction in revenues. In this case, reduction refers to reductions in total revenues (all profits including gross government profits *and* operator profits). A simple redistribution of existing profits such that the state's share is smaller, as is argued by some industry opponents, would be insufficient to shift government priorities in this policy domain. A commitment to significant total revenue reductions will result in decreased distortions, a lessening in the bias towards increased revenue generation. As a result, I would argue that significant reductions in total revenue should be the focus of any realignment of government gaming organizations and/or functions completed in the interests of social responsibility.

There is recognition of this principle by some governments. In Queensland, Australia, for example, the regulator plays a significant role in determining what features and structures will be present on licensed electronic gaming machines in that jurisdiction. The decisions to license a particular machine for use are based, in part, on a machine's potential contribution to problem gambling levels. The regulator has the authority to prevent certification of a particular machine for use in that jurisdiction, based purely on its potential vis-à-vis problem gambling. Some of the most problematic and controversial features of EGMs, common in many jurisdictions, are illegal in Queensland. This strategy reflects the beginnings of a precautionary approach. While many regulators are responsible for ensuring EGMs function within certain operational boundaries, the example described above is one in which current research and practice has been utilized to make problem gambling considerations an inherent part of the regulatory process.

A topic that is discussed with alarming infrequency is the issue of performance measurement and evaluation, as it relates to efforts to curb problem gambling. The notion that the industry should actually evaluate its measures of social responsibility against some clear, unambiguous, agreed-upon, and publicly stated targets is still a new concept. For example, what is a reasonable level of problem gambling? If over 50 per cent of all the revenue of a particular product is being collected from problem gamblers, as is the case with VLTs in Canada, and if this is unacceptable public policy, then what targets should our governments set for the reduction of that financial contribution by problem gamblers? In other words, what level of profit should be derived from problem gamblers? There are measures that can be applied to these questions. By enunciating targets and goals, greater accountability and an increased likelihood of meeting those targets will result. Performance measurement, evaluation, and accountability as it relates to measuring, monitoring, and addressing the industry response to problem gambling must take a higher priority.

The Social Policy Challenge

Governments are faced with the dilemma in gambling policy of recon-
ciling social responsibility (regulation) and gambling revenue generation (operation). The Canada Safety Council has referred to the dual
role of operator/regulator in gaming as a glaring conflict of interest
(Canada Safety Council 2004). In response to reports that gambling-
related suicides could be as high as 360 per year, Emile Therien, president of the Canada Safety Council, stated, 'If you have an average of
one person a day killing themselves because of an addiction, it's
become a public health and safety issue' (Canadian Broadcasting Corporation 2004). The state, with less than two decades of experience relative to its role in balancing these forces of social responsibility and
revenue generation, continues to experiment in how to achieve the
appropriate balance.

There is a view among some political leaders that gambling, in its
current form, is inevitable (see the previous chapters). Contrasting this
position with that of the Canada Safety Council and other groups
reveals significant divergence in how the direction of gambling policy
should proceed. The Canadian gambling regulatory framework, most
of which was instituted in the early 1990s, was created without the
knowledge, research, and evidence currently available concerning
problem gambling. Jurisdictions are now able to reassess their gambling offerings, and make adjustments to product offerings that are
defensible and in the best interests of gambling consumers and their citizens generally. In short, there are no obvious edicts or criteria that support the need to maintain the industry in its current form.

The political intransigence that some jurisdictions witness has
unlikely brethren. In a parliamentary democracy, it is said that the responsibility of the opposition parties is to oppose. Unfortunately this
responsibility, originating from our adversarial system of government,
results in a ritual of sorts. In this ritual, the opposition parties support
the position that gambling is an evil and should be abolished, or accessibility significantly reduced. The party in power, on the other hand,
supports either the status quo or, worse, gambling expansion. The ritual
plays itself out, regardless of which party is in power. This posturing is
at least partly at fault for the general public's ambivalence towards gambling as a social issue. A layperson would be excused for believing that
this polarization is sometimes even encouraged by opposition politicians, eager to leverage gambling as a political fulcrum to aid in their

election. To say the least, these actions do not contribute to the development of a long-term sustainable industry and are perceived by the public as hypocritical.

Provincial governments are, nonetheless, expected to provide a regulatory framework for gaming that is progressive with respect to product integrity, consumer security, and consumer protection. Sadly, the current approach contributes to an environment where provincial governments are not only the operator and regulator of gambling, but are also the largest promoters of gambling. The marketing and promotion of gambling by the state should be of great concern; unfortunately few, if any, statistics are available from the industry concerning marketing costs versus treatment and prevention expenditures.

Of the many issues that could be discussed under the heading of gambling social policy, there is one further to raise. That is the role that sound research plays in the development of sound social policy. Briefly I will elaborate on two key issues: the Reno Model, and gambling prevalence studies.

An analysis of gambling policy in twenty-first century Canada would be incomplete without at least a cursory discussion of the Reno Model (Blaszczynski, Ladouceur, and Shaffer 2004). Developed by a team of scholars from Canada, the United States, and Australia, it is the first attempt at a comprehensive framework that would lay out, in a formal sense, the groundwork for developing reasoned, balanced social policy in the gambling industry.

The model is an attempt to outline 'a strategic framework, or blueprint for action, to advance and coordinate efforts to limit gambling-related problems' (Blaszczynski, Ladouceur, and Shaffer 2004, 302). The principles of the model are to guide gambling operators, health service and other welfare providers, community groups, consumers, and government agencies in matters related to responsible gambling initiatives. The primary goals of the Reno Model are: (1) design responsible gambling initiatives, and (2) ensure a dialogue about responsible gambling among stakeholders. The authors point out the inherent conflicts that exist for an industry that, while driven by revenue like a private industry, is expected to exclude its most lucrative customers: the problem gamblers.

The authors, however, also make a critical error, one that was referred to earlier in this chapter, when they suggest that the 'majority of the adult population gambles responsibly' so that only a small minority of the population develops gambling-related harm (Blaszczynski, Ladouceur, and Shaffer 2004, 309). This notion is a misinterpretation of the relationship between the revenue contributions of problem gamblers and specific products within the gambling industry, particularly electronic machines. This has the unfortunate effect of trivializing it. Using Nova Scotia as an example, the majority of adults are not problem gamblers because they either (1) are not gamblers or (2) do not participate in EGM gambling. Only 23 per cent of adults gambled on VLTs in 2000, and only 5.7 per cent of all adults played them regularly (i.e., once a month). Of this 5.7 per cent, 16 per cent of them (0.9 per cent of all adults) are problem gamblers (Schellinck and Schrans 2000). Clearly this is, as the authors have pointed out, a small minority of adults. However, over 95 per cent of all calls to the Nova Scotia Problem Gambling Helpline concern VLT use. This 0.9 per cent of adults is also responsible for over 50 per cent of total VLT revenue in Nova Scotia and approximately 25 per cent of total gambling revenue (from all products). If you are a regular (at least once a month) VLT gambler in Nova Scotia, there is a one in six chance that you are a problem gambler.

The findings that electronic machine revenues reflect a significant contribution to total gambling revenues and that a small minority of these gamblers contribute significantly to total electronic machine revenue are both stable measures across most jurisdictions in Canada. The conclusion to draw from this is that the reason why only a small number of adults become problem gamblers is because a minority of adults gamble with electronic machines. This percentage (0.9 per cent of all adults are problem gamblers in Nova Scotia) might be acceptable on some scale of harm relative to other public health issues, if it were not for the fact that the major share of machine revenues (over 50 per cent in Nova Scotia) comes from this small minority.

The Reno Model is nonetheless an important milestone in the development of a theoretical basis for both gambling treatment and prevention, and the research that must inform it. It makes a strong connection between scientific method and prevention and treatment efforts. In addition, it encourages all interested parties to ensure that there is a scientific basis for those efforts. The model also commits all parties to document priorities, thereby making them both public and accountable, along with measuring and evaluating those priorities. The authors (2004) provide a set of basic assumptions that underlie the Reno Model and its approach to responsible gambling. These assumptions include: (1) safe levels of gambling are possible; (2) gambling provides benefits to individuals and to the community; (3) some gamblers suffer significant harm; (4) total social benefits must exceed the total social costs; (5) abstinence is not a necessary goal for problem gamblers; and (6) some problem gamblers can return to safe levels of play (Blaszczynski, Ladouceur, and Shaffer 2004, 309).

Schellinck and Schrans (2004) have offered five additional assumptions for consideration in a framework for responsible gambling: (1) gambling product design does impact on product safety; (2) marketing and venue design may also impact on the incidence of problem gambling; (3) there is a basic conflict between marketing practices of the gambling provider and responsible gambling that needs to be resolved; (4) there are gambling products and services where no amount of information will be sufficient to allow the gambler to make an informed choice; and (5) consumers of gambling products and services should expect them to be safe by a clearly defined standard.

These additional assumptions, encapsulated in a framework that Schellinck and Schrans (2004) refer to as the 'Halifax Model,' impress upon the model several important additions: it is possible to develop an inherently dangerous gambling product that will in its natural course put all regular users at risk, and a consumer protection approach that includes the concepts of the precautionary principle can be adopted.

It is important to understand what level of effort, time, and resources may be required for science to fulfil the vision of the Reno Model. The field of alcohol addiction, for example, has seen some forty years of alcohol treatment and prevention research funding. In spite of this investment, the transfer of treatment research findings into practical use has been limited (Miller 1995). This same result is likely in problem gambling treatment, at least in part since the same systems and organizations that provide alcohol addiction treatment and treatment services in Canada provide the same services for problem gamblers.

Lastly, a debate has been heard in Canada recently concerning gambling prevalence research. Prevalence studies are typically sample-based surveys, often conducted using traditional market research technologies, frequently phone-based. Their prime objective is to measure, in the general population, the existence of problem gamblers and gamblers 'at risk' of becoming one. At first glance it may not be obvious why the measurement of gambling prevalence would be a controversial topic. Measuring the incidence and prevalence of public health issues is a matter of course in the health-care system, and the information gleaned from this activity is a necessary and fundamental input for decision making. Why then would the measurement of problem gambling prevalence be controversial?

Problem gambling prevalence rates are typically reported as general population measures. That is to say, the prevalence of problem gambling is reported as a percentage of the total adult population of that jurisdiction using a single aggregate measure for all products. Critics argue that reporting prevalence in this manner 'plays into the hands' of industry expansionists by minimizing the problem gambling rate and subsequent negative effects of specific, dangerous products. In the first instance, it is argued that the *total* adult population should not be the denominator for such measures because only a small percentage of the population ever gambles at a rate that would put them at risk of suffering significant harm and subsequently scoring high enough, on any standard scale, to be classified as an at-risk or problem gambler. However, from a public health perspective, this method is accepted practice and in fact allows for the comparability, within a jurisdiction, of the prevalence rates of various indices of public health. While these general population measures are criticized, it is actually not the presence of these measures that should be of concern, but the absence of other more detailed measures related to specific products.

The second argument concerning prevalence measurement is that the prevalence of problem gambling should not be reported as a single measure for all products due to the unique characteristics of each product that make them more or less risky to use. James Cosgrave, in chapter 3 of this volume, describes this diversity using the dichotomy of 'risky consumption' versus 'consumption of risk.' Using Cosgrave's analogy, purchasing a Lotto 6/49 ticket in Canada would constitute 'consumption of risk' while playing VLTs would be considered 'risky consumption.' These are very different products and reflect not only different levels of risk, but very different types of risk as well. This is reflected in the different rates of problem gambling that are derived for these products via prevalence studies, and supports the notion that rates of prevalence should be reported for individual products in conjunction with the more 'general' rates of prevalence. This is in fact the reporting method that progressive jurisdictions currently employ.

A further criticism of prevalence studies is that problem gambling prevalence rates are extremely stable and consistent across similar jurisdictions. When rates of prevalence and incidence are stable (low variance over subsequent measures) and consistent (similar across similar jurisdictions) concerns are expressed about the expense of doing such research and whether this funding (typically $150,000 or more per study) could be put to better use. This is a reasonable criticism, but difficult to respond to because gambling prevalence studies are varied in their approach and intent. To suggest that governments should not be measuring the prevalence of problem gambling would be irresponsible. There are best practices that allow prevalence research to have maximum impact on the prevention and treatment efforts that it is intended to support. By measuring the rates of problem gambling for specific products and demographic segments (women, the elderly, for example), prevalence studies can be an important tool to inform current prevention and treatment work and future product safety strategies.

The role of prevalence studies as communications tools is also often underestimated. During the release of prevalence study results, the problem gambling debate almost always percolates to the top of the public agenda. As a result, public leaders, in some cases industry leaders, community health advocates, and gambling opponents all are asked to critique the findings of such research. These responses often require leaders to take public positions on important matters related to problem gambling. In this sense, it is one of the few seminal moments in the debate where, in a public forum, citizens are able to reassess and inform their views on problem gambling. This in and of itself is an important role for this research and is often a hidden benefit.

Conclusions

The forces of globalization and technology are interrelated in such a way that, at any one time, each plays the role of protagonist. While it may be more obvious that technology supports increased globalization, the reverse is also true. Globalization and its economic imperative also create a demand for technology. The gambling industry is not only increasingly reliant on technology as measured, for example, by the increasing proportion of revenues derived from electronic gambling machines, but it is at the same time an increasingly global industry. There are already many examples of this worldwide convergence. Free trade agreements as tools of globalization have already had an impact on the gambling industry. The most prominent example is the recent World Trade Organization (WTO) case brought forward by Antigua, the home of many of the world's suppliers of Internet gambling, which filed a formal complaint against the United States for prohibition of Internet gambling.

The effect of these forces is complex, but there is concern that they may result in a reduction in local jurisdictional autonomy over gambling regulatory issues. As gambling becomes increasingly technology-based and increasingly global, traditional sovereign control over gambling infrastructure may transfer to international, non-elected administrative bodies over which nation states have minimal authority. This is especially true in Canada where gambling is a provincial responsibility. Provincial governments have a small role in, and effect on, issues related to international trade, and as such an increase in globalization in this industry could reduce the capacity of governments to effect regulatory change.

We may be entering a period of litigation with regard to problem gambling as the number of lawsuits brought against gaming operators in Canada appears to be on the rise. These legal challenges are being brought forth on primarily two fronts: duty of care and fraud. The duty of care suits are based on the notion that gambling providers have been negligent in how they have operated gambling venues – for example, the manner in which odds (of a particular product) are disclosed. The fraud argument highlights the manner in which oversight is provided for some products, and questions whether some products are open to systematic, fraudulent manipulation.

If the gambling industry is found to be negligent or even fraudulent in a manner reminiscent of the tobacco industry's tribulations, governments will be inextricably tied to the industry's defence. At the same time governments may find themselves in the unusual position of wanting or needing to support the cause of citizens' groups taking legal action against the industry. Colin Campbell, in chapter 4, has sufficiently described the murky road in which the industry currently travels concerning the *Criminal Code*. As proposed, the precautionary principle offers the best policy solution, especially coupled with increased scientific knowledge of gambling and its implications. A first step would be the recognition that not all gambling is created equal and that responsible gambling or problem gambling should be further analysed and policies applied to specific types of gambling, rather than in a general manner. This is because the rates of problem gambling prevalence vary markedly from product to product. In fact, most products present very low risk to the gambler. However, there are products, such as electronic gaming, that present a specific and serious danger to users in their current configuration. Applying the precautionary principle to public policy related to machine gambling – by no means a simple undertaking as debates in environmental protection demonstrate – nevertheless will ensure a better balance between social responsibility and revenue generation.

PART FOUR

Gambling and Social Issues

8 Gambling-Related Crime in a Major Canadian City

GARRY J. SMITH, TIMOTHY F. HARTNAGEL,
AND HAROLD WYNNE

Studies from various regions worldwide suggest an association between criminal activity and easily accessible gambling. Yet, despite spectacular growth in the Canadian commercial gambling industry as discussed in previous chapters, surprisingly little is known about the nature, extent, or impact of gambling-related crime in Canada. The present study provides a general overview of the topic and investigates the relationship between crime and gambling in a major Canadian metropolitan area, the city of Edmonton, Alberta.

Legal gambling offerings in Canada were sparse until several decades ago when the *Criminal Code* amendments in 1969 and 1985 changed the situation dramatically. These amendments led to a profusion of new games and gambling outlets, as well as relaxed regulations that permit gambling venues extended hours of operation, higher betting limits, on-site automated teller machines, gambling floor liquor consumption, and concessions to First Nations groups (Campbell and Smith 2003). The burgeoning of the Canadian gambling industry was prompted by recognition of the revenue opportunities for provincial governments and indicative of a more permissive attitude towards a previously frowned upon social vice. A presumed cost of widespread gambling is higher crime rates. Lynch (2002) noted several inherent features of legalized gambling that opportunistic criminals can exploit, namely, many cash transactions; the wide potential for dishonesty in gambling transactions and the cash handling process; the operator's information advantage; and the gambler's reliance on the operator's honesty.

Law enforcement officials concur that gambling expansion inevitably leads to 'an increase in enterprise crime and money laundering activity particularly relating to casinos ... and an increase in illegal activities such as loan sharking, extortion and frauds' (Proke 1994). Public opinion polls reflect the perception that an association exists between widely available gambling and crime (Azmier 2000). However, empirical research has not confirmed this speculated link between crime and gambling. Indeed, gambling proponents argue that 'because gambling leads to job growth in gambling communities, crime may actually go down' (Gazel, Rickman, and Thompson 2001). The lack of substantial evidence for a gambling and crime connection is a result of police files seldom identifying gambling as a factor in the commission of a crime (Crofts 2002) and because some gambling-related criminal offences are not urgent matters for Canadian law enforcement agencies (Smith and Wynne 1999).

Anecdotal data from Canadian municipal police and the Royal Canadian Mounted Police (RCMP) authorities suggest there is ongoing gambling-related crime activity, but due to shifting priorities and dwindling resources, the issue does not get their full attention. In general, western Canadian police officials concurred that some forms of illegal gambling thrive because of the activity's diminishing social stigma and because police agencies and the judicial system overlook it (ibid.). Moreover, they maintain that economic crimes (e.g., fraud, embezzlement, forgery, and counterfeiting) committed by 'disordered' gamblers to support their habits are increasing (ibid.).

The present study begins to address these issues by documenting and analysing linkages between gambling and criminal activity in the city of Edmonton, Alberta. Our aim was to determine the nature and scope of gambling-related crime, how such crime was monitored and enforced, its fiscal and human resource costs, and the policy implications of these findings.

Edmonton is replete with legal gambling opportunities; when this research was conducted there were four casinos (not counting one on the city's northern outskirts, a temporary licensed casino during the annual summer fair, and an under-construction First Nations casino adjacent to the city's western boundary); 17 bingo halls; a major racetrack; 1,181 VLTs in 243 locations; 2,352 slot machines in five locations; 492 lottery ticket terminals; not to mention assorted raffles, sports pools, and pull ticket outlets (Alberta Gaming and Liquor Commission 2002).

Previous Research

One of the difficulties in pursuing gambling-related crime research is that there is no accepted definition of gambling-related crime, nor is there a recognized classification system for the different offences. Obviously, there is direct and indirect gambling-related criminal activity; for example, an instance where out-of-control gambling makes a person desperate enough to commit a financial crime to stay in action (direct), versus a crime occurring in a gambling venue that may just as easily have been perpetrated in another location and is only peripherally related to the gambling activity (indirect). However, even this distinction can be imprecise; for example, a losing slot machine player expresses his discontent by vandalizing the casino washroom: Is this a direct or indirect gambling-related crime? On the one hand, it could be argued that the gambling losses produced pent-up frustration that led to the destruction of casino property; had the person not gambled, the vandalism may not have occurred. Conversely, gambling losses may have been only one of several factors causing the player's frustration (e.g., a bad day at work, relationship difficulties, poor coping skills, etc.), which suggests the crime cannot be attributed to gambling losses alone. Also, the fact that the crime took place in a casino could be incidental; the anger might just as easily have been displaced in another fashion, at a different place or time.

Recognizing the limitations of assigning criminogenic characteristics to individual gambling behaviour or particular gambling scenes, we provide the following categories to differentiate among gambling-related crimes.

1 Illegal gambling refers to gambling activity that is counter to the *Criminal Code* (CC) statutes, such as bookmaking, keeping a common gaming house, and providing unauthorized electronic gambling machines.
2 Crimes committed in order to finance gambling activities (e.g., forgery, embezzlement, fraud, and other forms of property crime).
3 Crimes associated with widespread legal gambling (e.g., street crime such as larceny theft and property crime such as burglary and break and enter).
4 Crimes that are spatially or situationally co-incidental or co-symptomatic with gambling expansion or particular gambling venues (e.g., loan sharking, money laundering, profit skimming, passing counterfeit currency, prostitution, drug trafficking, and theft).
5 Crimes that occur in the course of otherwise legal gambling operations (e.g., cheating at play, employee theft, and intentional player overpayment).
6 Crimes that are behaviourally co-incidental or co-symptomatic with

an individual's gambling involvement (e.g., domestic violence, child neglect, suicide).
7 Graft and corruption designed to expedite permits and licences, relax the enforcement of gaming laws/regulations, use gaming funds inappropriately, or win lucrative contracts (e.g., kickbacks, bribes, influence peddling, and extortion).

Although an extensive gambling-related crime literature has been produced by American, Australian, and German authors in particular, space limitations require that we restrict our discussion to Canada (Smith, Wynne, and Hartnagel 2003). In the following section, Canadian-based gambling-related crime research is reviewed under the previously discussed categories. The CC of Canada explicitly forbids certain gambling formats or operations such as three-card monte and keeping a common gaming house; in addition, any gambling format not covered by CC provisions is deemed illegal. Morton (2003) noted how illegal gambling flourished in Canada's largest cities prior to, during, and after the Second World War, with horse-race bookmaking and unauthorized casinos being the most popular forms. Public concerns about illegal gambling at the time were reflected in (1) an Ontario police agency establishing a permanent anti-gambling squad; (2) judicial inquiries establishing links between illegal gambling operations and organized crime; (3) collusion between criminals, police, and politicians; and (4) a lack of police, judicial, and political will to enforce illegal gambling laws, particularly in Vancouver and Montreal. In Morton's view, the public objection to illegal gambling was not so much the moral consequences of engaging in the activity, but 'the way it could contaminate the police force and municipal government and support organized crime' (Morton 2003, 165).

A pioneering investigation of illegal gambling in a lower-class Toronto neighbourhood revealed that illegal gambling clubs had been operating openly without conviction (Garry and Sangster 1968). It was disclosed that the inability of Toronto law enforcers to deter illegal gambling resulted in the gamblers and the police acting under conditions of silence to reduce any conflicts between them. The authors concluded that the extensive illegal gambling in Toronto's tenderloin district had both functional and dysfunctional impacts on the community. On the one hand, gambling was a form of recreation and a distraction from the hardships faced by the underclass. Conversely, uncontrolled gambling took a toll on the mental and physical health of the degenerate gamblers and those close to them. The authors reckoned that when neighbourhood gamblers neglected their social, job, and family obligations the social cohesion of the community was jeopardized.

Recently the Criminal Intelligence Service Canada (1999 and 2000) identified the following trends concerning illegal gambling in Canada: tremendous profits for organized crime groups with few significant deterrents; rapid growth in on-line gambling; and significant profits produced from illegal gambling machines, with this undeclared income used by criminals to support drug trafficking, money laundering, and enterprise crime operations.

A study of gambling and crime in western Canada concluded that illegal gambling was extensive in the four largest cities – Vancouver, Calgary, Edmonton, and Winnipeg – but less so in medium-sized cities, and a minor concern in rural areas (Smith and Wynne 1999). This study also identified sports betting with a bookmaker, unauthorized card clubs, unlicensed VLTs, and offshore lottery sales as the most prominent western Canadian illegal gambling formats. Ironically, these are versions of legal gambling offerings that compete well with their legal counterparts because they provide more attractive wagering propositions and customer services such as credit, better odds, higher-stakes action, and telephone betting. Since credit is often available to illegal gambling patrons, there is an increased likelihood of gamblers getting in over their heads and becoming vulnerable to loan sharks, blackmailers, extortionists, and so forth.

The most detailed measure of illegal gambling in a Canadian region comes from Ontario's Illegal Gaming Enforcement Unit. From its inception in 1997 up until 2001, the unit recorded 1,370 occurrences, 2,069 persons charged, 3,517 charges laid, and 2,034 machines seized at a value of $6,016,505. In addition, cash worth $1,233,763 was seized and $2,839,533 worth of fines and forfeitures were imposed (Moodie 2002).

Problem gambling refers to gambling behaviour that creates negative consequences for the gambler, and others in the gambler's social network or community (Ferris, Wynne, and Single 1999). Readily accessible legal gambling (especially continuous gambling formats) is associated with increased numbers of problem gamblers (Walker 1997). A major social and economic impact of problem gambling is illegal acts committed to obtain money to gamble or pay gambling-related debts (Volberg 2001). Since electronic gambling machines have been shown to be the most addictive gambling format (Breen and Zimmerman 2002; Dickerson 2003; Smith and Wynne 2004), logic suggests that the presence of electronic machine gambling in a jurisdiction will add to the crime rate.

Anecdotal evidence from clinical, welfare, and judicial sources links problem gambling to criminal behaviour, whereas data from general population surveys show only a modest association between problem gambling severity and the commission of criminal acts. Data from Gamblers Anonymous (GA) members, problem gamblers in treatment, and incarcerated populations indicate a much closer correspondence between the two behaviours. For example, in two general population surveys, respondents were asked if they ever had trouble with the law because of their gambling activities. Only 2 per cent (Wynne Resources 1998) and 4.3 per cent (Smith and Wynne 2002) of the problem gamblers admitted to having committed illegal acts to support their gambling participation. On the contrary, 68 per cent of a GA sample reported committing illegal acts to finance their gambling (Ladouceur et al. 1994). The incidence and extent of gambling-related criminal activity may be more acute than general population survey estimates suggest because gambling is seldom identified in official records as underlying the offence. Not all gambling-related offences are detected or offenders apprehended, and some victims, especially family members, friends, and employers, are often reluctant to press charges.

The following casino impact studies have been conducted in Canada. In a one-year review of Casino Windsor prepared by KPMG Management Consulting (1995) for the Ontario Casino Corporation, Casino Windsor's impact on crime in the local community was considered minimal. Two factors helping to explain this finding were Casino Windsor's pre-emptive funding of twenty-five new full-time Windsor Police Department positions to work within a five-block radius of the casino and the fact that most (approximately 80 per cent) of the casino patrons came from across the Canada–U.S. border, which is only two miles away.

Room, Turner, and Ialomiteanu (1999) surveyed adults in Niagara Falls, Canada, before the destination casino opened in 1995 and a year following its first year of operation. Prior to the casino opening, 77 per cent of respondents predicted an increase in the number of serious crimes; a year after the casino opening, only 44 per cent of the sample believed that this expected crime wave had actually happened. As with the other two Ontario mega-casinos (Windsor and Rama), the Ontario Casino Corporation paid for twenty-five new police officers to patrol the casino area.

Piscitelli and Albanese (2000) examined trends in the number of criminally inadmissible persons seeking entry to Canada via western New York State border crossings in connection with the opening of Casino Niagara. Their findings showed that total crossings of the four bridges connecting Canada to western New York State increased by 10 per cent the year after the casino opening; the number of criminals denied entry to Canada by Canada Customs officials increased initially by 100 per cent and by 300 per cent one year after the casino opened; and the proportion of criminals seeking entry to Canada that had convictions related to organized crime dropped from 80 per cent prior to the casino opening to 60 per cent after. In effect, more criminals sought entry into Canada from western New York State after Casino Niagara opened, but a smaller percentage of these criminals had committed offences related to organized crime.

Morton (2003) used 'space' as a construct to compare and contrast historical gambling patterns in major Canadian cities according to gender, age, ethnicity, and social class; for example, illegal gambling, long an integral part of traditional male culture, was conducted in demarcated male spaces (pool rooms, barber shops, bars, and tobacco stands). Besides catering to gamblers, these male preserves attracted hoodlums and were associated with violence, commercial sex, and drinking. Bingo, on the other hand, was patronized mainly by middle-aged, working-class women and rarely linked with other vices or criminal activity. Indeed, criticism of the bingo milieu centred on bingo players as neglectful mothers. With the advent of legal gambling and changing views on gender roles, gambling became less spatially defined by gender; nevertheless, gambling formats and ambiences still attract different participants and hangers-on, thus rendering some gambling venues more susceptible to criminal activity than others.

Some gambling venue criminal activity is tangential to the gambling action per se and more a result of opportunistic criminal types attracted by the free-flowing cash, throngs of customers, and relative ease with which the proceeds of crime can be legitimated (Smith and Wynne 1999). Racetracks and casinos have been cited as popular locations for money-laundering schemes (Beare and Schneider 1990). Despite a law requiring an official report for cash transactions over $10,000, casino money launderers avoid detection by making several smaller cash exchanges so as not to arouse suspicion (Smith and Wynne 1999). Casinos are also focal points for crimes such as robbery, passing counterfeit currency, prostitution, pandering, and drug trafficking (Calgary Police

Service 1996) along with VLT gambling, which has been associated with an increase in criminal activity (McDonald 1998). Employee theft is common in gambling venues and attributed to the volatile combination of low-paid workers exposed to the temptation of large amounts of rapidly circulating legal tender.

Some criminal behaviour in gambling venues is a by-product of the games themselves; for example, cheating at play generally occurs in the following ways: tampering with the instruments of gambling (e.g., marking cards, using loaded dice, recalibrating gaming machines, unbalancing roulette wheels, drugging horses, etc.); player-employee collusion (e.g., signalling the dealer's hole card in blackjack, introducing an unshuffled deck, race fixing involving jockey-trainer conspiracies, etc.); and miscellaneous scams such as altering bets after the outcome is known, using a computer or mechanical device to keep track of cards played, and overpaying winners, again, a prearranged gambit between player and dealer.

Pathological gambling is often coincidental with other disorders such as depression, bipolar personality, panic and anxiety, and anti-social conduct and is associated with substance abuse and chemical dependency (Volberg 2001). Complications arising from a gambling addiction include financial distress (staggering debt, loss of savings, and bankruptcy); marital and familial problems (lack of trust, poor problem-solving and communication skills, child neglect/abuse, spousal abuse, and divorce); and health concerns such as insomnia, intestinal disorders, high blood pressure, cardiac problems, and suicide rates three times higher than the general population (Smith and Wynne 2002). Taken together, these stressors can combine to affect the gambler's judgment and self-control and result in criminal behaviour.

While seldom the subject of academic investigation, Canada has seen a number of gambling-related political scandals in the past decade. In what has been called a 'recipe for disaster,' Hutchinson (1999) contended that an explosive cocktail is created when ultra-competitive gambling promoters aggressively lobby cash-strapped, morally challenged provincial governments. For example, a former British Columbia finance minister was convicted for fraudulently channelling gambling proceeds into party coffers, and a sitting British Columbia premier resigned under allegations of influence peddling and accepting bribes to help a friend secure a casino licence. The ex-premier was exonerated of the criminal charges, while the friend was found guilty on six counts, including attempt to influence a public official. Conspicuously absent in the court ruling was how it was that a substandard casino licence application, which was initially rejected, later received approval. Political indiscretions such as patronage, conflict of interest, undue influence, misappropriation of funds, and questionable business practices have been central to gambling-related controversies in Nova Scotia (ibid.), Saskatchewan (Saskatchewan Provincial Auditor 2001), and Alberta (Kent 2000).

Gambling-Related Criminological Theory

Much of the gambling-related crime research we reviewed lacked an explicit theoretical underpinning. Given the exploratory nature of this study, specific criminology theories were not tested. However, to emphasize the need for future theory-based research on the topic, we briefly review criminology theory for the purpose of identifying the most plausible interpretations of gambling-related crime. Based on our findings, in the final section of the paper we speculate on theoretical approaches worth pursuing in future studies.

What does criminology tell us about the nature of the crime and gambling nexus? Does gambling cause crime, contribute to crime, or is it inconsequential to crime? To what extent does criminological theory improve our power to predict gambling-related crime? Numerous attempts to systematically study the causes and correlates of crime have shown that no single theory accounts for all criminality. Also noteworthy is that criminological theoretical approaches are not necessarily distinct; some, in fact, are complementary and amenable to integration.

Criminology typically distinguishes different levels of explanation with respect to any criminal behaviour. These levels include the individual, interactional, and social structural. The individual level of explanation focuses on characteristics of persons that contribute to their behaviour, including criminal behaviour. Examples include genetically inherited predispositions, intelligence level, and personality defects. The interactional level examines personal social relationships, particularly those significant to the individual; classic examples include peer and family relationships. The social structural level is concerned with the impact of societal forces that can affect the amount and distribution of crime in a society. For example, unemployment rates or the degree of income inequality in a society may contribute to the overall crime rate and its concentration within certain segments such as inner-city poverty-stricken neighbourhoods.

These levels of explanation are as pertinent to gambling-related crime as to other forms of criminal behaviour. At the individual level, the focus is on the person who engages in gambling-related crime, seeking, for example, to explain why certain individuals engage in illegal gambling or why others commit crimes to support a gambling addiction. It may be that certain individuals have inherited and/or developed psychophysiological characteristics that cause them to seek excitement and engage in high-risk behaviours. Others may be relatively immune from learning from the consequences of their behaviours. At the interactional level, some persons fail to acquire social bonds to conventional society that might constrain their behaviour, thus freeing them to participate in illegal gambling or commit crimes to support a gambling habit. Others develop social relationships that revolve around illicit activity, which may include illegal gambling or crimes associated with legal gambling venues, such as money laundering or drug sales. Finally, at the structural level, key variables might be the over-representation of certain segments of society in illegal gambling activity or the distribution of certain crimes in areas where legal gambling venues are concentrated. The issues here pertain to the cultural values and/or social supports of certain groups that encourage and facilitate illegal gambling; the demographic and social characteristics related to higher rates of gambling-related crime; and the distinguishing features of city areas that may facilitate and/or attract such gambling-related crimes.

Before reviewing several criminology perspectives that help explain illegal gambling and gambling-related crime, it is useful to differentiate key categories of gambling crime offences and offenders since it is likely that specific explanations are more applicable to some kinds of crimes and criminals than to others. We first distinguish among illegal gambling (gaming and betting offences); 'ordinary crimes' related to gambling activity (e.g., fraud, embezzlement, family violence); and 'ordinary crimes' related to gambling venues (e.g., drug deals, money laundering, loan sharking). With respect to offenders, the following categories are likely to involve somewhat different explanations: 'problem' or 'addicted' gamblers; 'career' and 'petty' criminals; those involved in 'organized' crime; and conventional, law-abiding individuals who gamble illegally. Obviously, these distinctions are not mutually exclusive since a given offender could belong to more than one such category and a given 'type' of offender could commit more than one of these gambling-related crimes. Table 8.1 depicts crime categories and likely types of offenders and is used as an organizing tool for applying the various criminological theoretical perspectives.

Conventional, generally law-abiding individuals who engage in illegal gambling and betting offences (e.g., sports betting, card games, etc.) are likely following a rational choice model of behaviour. This perspective holds that individuals make rational choices with an expectation of maximizing their profits or benefits and minimizing costs or losses. These benefits may be social or psychic as well as economic. Decisions are based upon the individual's expected effort and reward compared with the likelihood and severity of punishment and other costs of the criminal behaviour (Cornish and Clarke 1986). Individuals engaging in such activities as illegal sports betting or card games, according to this perspective, have rationally concluded that the benefits or rewards anticipated from these activities sufficiently exceed the risk of legal and informal punishment and other costs to justify pursuing these behaviours.

Social learning theory is also useful in explaining the illegal gambling and betting activity of conventional, generally law-abiding individuals. Social learning theory avers that criminal behaviour is instilled according to the same general principles of learning that apply to all behaviours; only the content of the learning is different. Criminal behaviour is acquired, repeated, and changed by the same process as conforming behaviour (Akers 1997). Thus, criminal acts are learned both through direct experience of their consequences (positive and negative reinforcement), as well as through imitating others.

Applying these assumptions to illegal gambling and betting, it is likely that individuals engaging in these behaviours have initially been exposed to them through the conduct of parents and/or peers. By observing their gambling activity and the psychic, social, and material rewards they obtain, individuals acquire positive dispositions towards these illegal activities. If they find themselves in situations conducive to engaging in these activities, they are then likely to do so. The consequences they experience resulting from their illegal gambling influence the likelihood of their continued involvement in these behaviours.

The rational choice model is also germane to the operators of illegal gambling and betting establishments. These individuals are best seen as entrepreneurs providing a desired, but illegal, service. The operators seemingly have made a business decision that the profits to be attained from these crimes are sufficient enough to assume the risk involved in providing the illegal service. A similar rationale applies to so-called

Table 8.1
Gambling-related crime

	Types of Offenders			
	Problem	Career/petty	Organized	Conventional
Illegal gambling	May or may not partake in depending on accessibility and format (e.g., Internet gambling is likely to exacerbate problem gambling).	Frequenting illegal card clubs, pool halls, etc. (part of deviant lifestyle).	Ownership, control, or partners in illegal gambling operations.	Betting with bookmaker, playing at an illegal card club.
Gambling-related ordinary crime	Fraud, forgery, embezzlement, theft, domestic violence, and suicide.	Drug dealing, fencing stolen goods, cheating at play, theft, money laundering, and fraud.	Money laundering, drug dealing, loan sharking, extortion, assault, and homicide.	Unlikely to be involved.

'organized crime' involvement in these activities. Deterrence theory posits that increasing the costs of deviant conduct, particularly through enhanced certainty and severity of legal punishment, should inhibit 'rational actors' from continuing to supply these services or for 'conventional' individuals to partake in them (Zimring and Hawkins 1973). However, the penalties must be perceived to be sufficiently certain (most important) and severe to offset the rewards anticipated from these illegal behaviours. Such 'tipping points' are likely much higher for the operators and organized criminals than for the more 'conventional' participants in these types of illegal acts, but informal sanctions (e.g., social disapproval from significant others) are more effective for the latter.

While the rational choice perspective may also help explain the involvement of so-called career and petty criminals in illegal gambling and betting offences, aspects of social learning theory are also cogent. These individuals are likely to be associated with a deviant peer group that encourages and compensates their participation in these as well as other types of illegal acts as part of a particular lifestyle. Such behaviour may even help define membership in these deviant peer groups, and the positive reinforcement received from other members perpetuates such activity.

Social learning theory also applies to the habitual or addictive illegal gambling of problem gamblers; that is, their repetitive participation in illegal gambling and betting activity may result from the same processes of acquisition, performance, and repetition of behaviour described earlier for conventional gamblers. What distinguishes so-called problem gamblers, then, is the frequency or extent of their involvement in illegal gambling and their lack of control, rather than the processes or mechanisms by which they became involved. There may be a fine line distinguishing the illegal gambling/betting of problem gamblers and at least some conventional gamblers.

Some argue that both the illegal gambling and gambling-related crimes (e.g., fraud, theft, etc.) by so-called problem or addicted gamblers are the product of personality problems or character defects of one kind or another. These have been attributed to abnormal emotional adjustments resulting primarily from negative early childhood experiences such as neglect or abuse. However, these personality defects may also involve psychophysiological abnormalities with their source in some combination of genetic and environmental factors. One version of this explanation of criminal behaviour regards it as the expression of such traits as impulsiveness, aggressiveness, sensation seeking, rebel-liousness, hostility, and so on (Akers 1997). These traits, in turn, would be manifest in the illegal gambling and gambling-related crime of 'problem' gamblers.

In contrast to personality trait explanations, Gottfredson and Hirschi (1990) developed an interactional theory of crime based upon the con-cept of self-control. Their contention is that individuals have a differen-tial tendency to avoid criminal acts whatever circumstances they find themselves in. Individuals with high self-control are much less likely to ever engage in crimes, while those with low self-control are more likely to commit crimes. However, Gottfredson and Hirschi recognize that circumstances or opportunities affect the likelihood that low self-con-trol will result in criminal acts, although they did not specify the precise nature of these circumstances. These authors locate the source of low self-control in ineffective or incomplete socialization, especially ineffec-tive child rearing, and claim that the degree of self-control acquired in childhood remains relatively stable throughout a person's life (Akers 1997). Furthermore, Gottfredson and Hirschi maintain that low self-control explains not only crime but also such analogous behaviour as smoking, drinking, drug use, illicit sex, and being accident prone. From this perspective, then, both problem gambling and gambling-related crime/illegal gambling result from low self-control ostensibly stem-ming from poor early socialization.

Self-control is related to the more general concept of social control. A number of control theories of crime (Reiss 1951; Nye 1958; Hirschi 1969) share the general assumption that individuals conform to the rules of society because various controls prevent them from violating these rules. Hirschi's (1969) social bonds theory is the most prominent of these, professing that crime results when an individual's bond to society is weak or broken. There are four components of this bond: attachment, commitment, involvement, and beliefs. Attachment relates to close ties to significant others whose opinions and expectations are valued; com-mitment refers to an individual's investment in conventional behaviour or 'stake in conformity' (Toby 1957), which is jeopardized by commit-ting a crime; involvement pertains to participation in conventional activities that consume an individual's time; and belief is defined as the endorsement of conventional values and norms, especially the convic-tion that laws and society's rules in general are morally correct and should be obeyed (Akers 1997). These four components are interlaced such that the collapse of one puts strain on the others. The weaker these bonds or ties to others and to society's institutions, the more likely it is that the individual will engage in lawbreaking behaviour. Thus, gambling-related crimes committed by problem gamblers would result from a weakening of one or more of these social bonds. For example, a problem gambler who has not established close, affective ties with significant others such as a spouse, employer, or fellow employees, has few leisure pursuits other than gambling, and/or who is under/unemployed or has low occupational aspirations is at greater risk of turning to criminal behaviour as a way of coping with financial or interpersonal problems resulting from excessive gambling. Control theories, then, emphasize the breakdown of social restraints rather than the strength of the motivations to explain the occurrence of criminal acts.

Discussion so far has focused on individual and interactional levels of analysis, indicating how particular criminological theories interpret involvement in illegal gambling and betting by several categories of gamblers as well as the gambling-related crimes of problem gamblers. Another issue concerns the geographic distribution within city areas of illegal gambling activity and other criminal behaviour that may be related to the characteristics of locations, particularly the presence of legal gambling venues. For example, thefts from motor vehicles may be related to the location of large legal gambling venues such as race-tracks, bingo halls, or casinos, at least in part because of their poorly supervised parking lots with large numbers of cars. Also, illicit drug sales and money laundering may cluster in and around these same gambling venues. Illegal gambling activities are related to certain demographic and/or social characteristics of city areas and are often located in areas with high concentrations of particular ethnic groups (Morton 2003).

Criminological theories, particularly those that focus on the individual or interactional level of analysis, emphasize criminal motivations: those individual characteristics or social factors that induce people to commit criminal acts. However, these motivations may not, in and of themselves, explain the occurrence of crimes; potential offenders must also encounter opportunities that allow these criminal inclinations to be expressed in overt acts (Sacco and Kennedy 1994); for example, one of Albanese's (2000) criminal opportunity types seems particularly suited to explaining certain gambling venue crimes: those providing opportunity to access illicit funds without incurring high risk.

Several opportunity-based theories have arisen to explain how variations in the levels of crime from place to place or over time are related to variations in opportunities to commit crime. Routine activities theory (Cohen and Felson 1979) is well suited to explain the physical location of these crimes. The gist of this theory is that the likelihood of a crime occurring increases when there is a convergence in space and time of a motivated offender, a suitable target, and the absence of formal or informal guardians to deter the potential offender. This coming together is related to the normal, legal, routine activities of individuals; and the spatial and temporal structures of these routine activities play an important role in determining the location, type, and quantity of illegal acts (ibid.).

While originally formulated to explain predatory offences such as robbery, personal theft, and assaults (Felson 1994), the theory was extended to cover such offences as illegal consumption of alcohol and drug sales. Hence, the theory is likely also applicable to illegal gambling and other gambling-related crimes. As evidenced by the times and places at which crimes occur, leisure pursuits, in particular, provide opportunities for criminal events of various types (Sacco and Kennedy 1994). In general, leisure behaviour can be part of a risky lifestyle that has dangerous consequences (Kennedy and Forde 1990). Much personal victimization occurs during evenings and weekends, and disproportionately in leisure settings such as taverns and the city blocks where they are located (Luckinbill 1977; Roncek and Maier 1991). Gambling venues such as casinos and taverns/restaurants with VLTs and their immediate environs are leisure locations that may attract a higher proportion of the criminally motivated, while also being informal settings where the usual social controls are less operative. These settings also present suitable targets in the form of potential victims of crimes such as theft or violence, as well as the venues themselves being advantageous sites for drug dealing, money laundering, loan sharking, frauds, and so forth.

Another theoretical model with utility for explicating gambling-related crime integrates three key elements: opportunity factors, criminal environment, and skills or access required to conduct the criminal activity (Albanese 2000). For example, a typical cheating at play scenario in a casino may involve free-flowing cash and lax enforcement (opportunity factors), combined with an aspiring cheater and an unscrupulous dealer (criminal environment), who have the requisite dexterity (special skills) to make the scam work. Similarly, a problem-gambling accountant who embezzles from his employer has the opportunity (access to the books, signing authority, and employer trust), the criminal intent (e.g., the need for money to pay gambling debts), and the skills (bookkeeping acumen) to cover up the crime.

The Edmonton Gambling-Related Crime Project

What follows is an attempt to empirically assess the nature and scope of gambling-related crime in the city of Edmonton, Alberta. At the time of the study, the population of the city was 666,000, making it the fifth-largest municipality in Canada.

The following research questions guided this study.

1 What is the magnitude of gambling-related crime in Edmonton?
2 Which legal gambling formats are most associated with criminal activity in Edmonton?
3 Which criminal activities are typically associated with gambling in Edmonton?
4 What types of crimes are committed in and around Edmonton's major gambling venues?
5 How, and to what extent, is gambling-related crime monitored and enforced in Edmonton?

Research Methodology

This was a preliminary, descriptive study of the nature and extent of gambling-related crime in the city of Edmonton during the period January 2001 to 31 August 2002, and an investigation of law enforcement policy pertaining to gambling and crime. Several types of data were utilized to address the five research questions. These include Edmonton Police Service (EPS) crime occurrence files, a summary of the Alberta Gaming and Liquor Commission (AGLC) investigations files, a gambling occurrence report form used by the EPS, relevant EPS documents, and interviews with EPS and RCMP officers and supervisors and gambling venue security personnel.

All of the content in EPS crime occurrence files selected from the 'violation/incident type code' categories deemed most likely to contain gambling-related crime occurrences was read. In some crime categories 100 per cent of the files for the 2001 calendar year were reviewed; in others a 20 per cent random selection was inspected because either the total number of files was too large for a 100 per cent review or the category was considered less likely to render gambling-related occurrences.

Table 8.2
EPS *Criminal Code* categories searched

100% sample

Code	Violation/incident type	Total files available	Total files reviewed
10101	1st Degree Murder	3	3
10102	2nd Degree Murder	15	15
10103	Attempted Murder	3	3
10105	Manslaughter	2	2
10201	Extortion	31	28
20220	Counterfeiting	487	482
20225	Fraud – Cheque	730	677
20230	Fraud – Credit Card	1246	1210
20235	Fraud – Other	1338	1210
20423	Betting House	0	0
20430	Gaming House	0	0
20441	Other Gaming & Betting	2	2
20851–20855	Organized Crime Types	0	0
40110	Suicides	95	95
40115	Attempted Suicides	45	45
	Total	3997	3772

20% sample

Code	Violation/incident type	Total files available	Total files reviewed
10205	Robbery – Firearm	153	35
10206	Robbery – Offensive Weapon	476	84
10210	Robbery	714	140
21151	Cocaine Trafficking	312	71
50115	Family Disputes	5546	1094
	Total	7201	1424

Table 8.2 shows the EPS violation/incident CC categories searched and the numbers of files in each that were analysed. For 2001, a total of 11,198 possible gambling-related crime files were available for review, and of these 5,196 were examined. Details of each gambling-related occurrence were entered into a computer database for subsequent content analysis.

We attempted to collect prospective data on gambling-related crime by developing a gambling-related occurrence report (GOR) form for use by EPS investigating officers during the seven-month period 1 February 2002 through 31 August 2002. The GOR was developed in consultation with EPS supervisors and based on a similar EPS domestic violence report form. Officers investigating any complaint during these seven months were asked to determine whether gambling was in any way a factor in the occurrence. If so, they were to complete the GOR as part of their normal investigation and reporting routines. When the relevant occurrence report subsequently reached EPS Central Records for coding, the GOR was flagged as a file wherein gambling was related to the alleged crime. These files were then content analysed in the same manner as the 2001 files.

The AGLC Investigations Branch also conducts investigations into suspected *Criminal Code* gambling offences and, where applicable, makes arrests. To obtain a broader scope of gambling-related crime for this study it was necessary to access AGLC 2001–2 criminal investigation files of incidents that took place in Edmonton. An AGLC summary printout of investigations from 1 January 2001 to 31 August 2002 was analysed using the same procedures as described above for EPS files.

Interviews with key informants were conducted to determine how gambling-related crime was being monitored, enforced, and tracked and how the various law enforcement agencies deployed their resources in carrying out these functions. Also explored were the points of interaction between these agencies and their interrelationships with provincial gambling regulators. Ten key informant interviews were conducted (six with law enforcement agency representatives and four with gambling venue security managers). Law enforcement respondents were chosen based on their background in gambling investigations and knowledge of agency policy and represented nearly the total population of relevant Edmonton-based police potential interviewees.

Findings

Traditionally, enforcing the CC statutes pertaining to illegal gambling has been the responsibility of the EPS Vice unit. Table 8.3 provides data on the number of illegal gambling and betting offences recorded in the Edmonton metropolitan area over the past decade.

Obviously, the number of recorded illegal gambling and betting offences varies widely from year to year, ranging from 2 in 1996 to 42 in 2000. It is important to note that offences in this category depend on police activity to be discovered; there are seldom victims in the usual sense who file complaints with the police. Consequently, the fluctua-

Table 8.3
Edmonton metro area gaming and betting
offences (1991–2000)

Year	Offences
2000	42
1999	5
1998	6
1997	16
1996	2
1995	7
1994	5
1993	7
1992	37
1991	5

Source: Statistics Canada, Canadian
Centre for Justice Statistics, Data Libera-
tion Initiative n.d., Common Offences,
Census Metropolitan Areas, 1991–2000.

tion from year to year in the number of offences known to the police is
largely a function of police efforts to root out such offences. For example, the 42 offences in 2000 all stemmed from a single joint forces raid
on illegal card clubs. Had the raids not been conducted, zero gambling
and betting offences would have been recorded that year.

When this research was conducted the EPS Vice unit was ostensibly
still responsible for monitoring illegal gambling; however, in the previous year and a half, the EPS had dealt with only one illegal gambling
case, the joint forces effort noted above. Illegal gambling investigations
had become a low EPS priority, accounting for an estimated 1 per cent
of the vice unit's time. To compensate for this priority shift, Alberta
Gaming pays a seconded EPS Vice unit member to serve on one of its
gaming investigation teams (GITs). The EPS benefits from this arrangement in that a member is working on illegal gambling investigations,
but not at EPS expense.

Gaming investigation teams now handle illegal gambling surveillance in Edmonton. The Edmonton area team is comprised of two
Alberta Gaming investigators, a seconded EPS Vice unit member, and a
seconded RCMP officer. Illegal gambling complaints received by EPS
are turned over to GITs; EPS will assist if required. One EPS respondent
acknowledged the existence of bookmakers and illegal card rooms

associated with various ethnic communities and pointed out that these operations are concealed and hard to infiltrate, but most importantly, there are few complaints about them. Illegal gambling operations were monitored by the EPS Vice unit up until a decade ago, but dropped in priority because illegal gambling investigations are labour intensive, often involving stakeouts and wiretaps that use up police resources. Moreover, other vices have since gained prominence; for example, child pornography was a lesser concern before the Internet but now occupies one-third of the vice unit's resources. Also, when legal gambling expanded in the early 1990s, the activity lost much of its social stigma. Under the prevailing legal and political climate, the vice unit's time and efforts are perceived to be better spent elsewhere.

In reviewing EPS 2001 files for instances of gambling-related crime, we were struck by the dearth of information on unlawful gambling activities such as bookmaking, illegal gambling houses, and illegal gambling machines, since an earlier study (Smith and Wynne 1999) suggested that these activities were widely practised in western Canada's major urban centres; yet EPS recorded no arrests for these activities in 2001–2. However, as our EPS Vice unit respondent made clear, Alberta Gaming is now policing illegal gambling. One informant commented that the 'policing of illegal gambling is falling through the cracks. I thought AGLC's involvement would solve this problem, but so far it doesn't appear to be so.' He went on to report that the extent of illegal gambling is 'huge, especially among certain ethnic communities.' From his perspective, AGLC investigators do a good job of eliminating illegal gambling machines since these and card rooms have an impact on government gambling profits. Yet, bookmaking operations flourish because no one is monitoring them, which, in his view, is a mistake, because of the potential ties to organized crime.

Depicted in Table 8.4 are the crime categories investigated in the EPS files, the total number of files for each category, number of files searched, and number of gambling-related occurrences identified. On the surface, it appears that with only 208 gambling-related occurrences out of 5,196 files reviewed (4 per cent), gambling played a minor role in Edmonton's overall criminal activity in 2001. This low frequency of gambling-related crime is likely an underestimation, since the majority of crimes known to the police are unresolved. The year 2001 clearance rates (the percentage of all offences known to the police cleared either through laying charges or some other means) according to EPS records were as follows: all CC offences (35 per cent), all property crimes (21

Table 8.4
EPS gambling-related occurrences (2001)

Code	Occurrence type	Total files	Files viewed	Gambling-related occurrences
10101	1st Degree Murder	3	3*	0
10102	2nd Degree Murder	15	15*	0
10103	Attempted Murder	3	3*	0
10105	Manslaughter	2	2*	0
10201	Extortion	31	28***	0
10205	Robbery – Firearm	153	35**	4
10206	Robbery – Offensive Weapon	476	84**	0
10210	Robbery	714	140**	5
20220	Counterfeiting	487	482***	130
20225	Fraud – Cheque	730	677***	9
20230	Fraud – Credit Card	1246	1210***	17
20235	Fraud – Other	1338	1210***	20
20423	Betting House	0	0	0
20430	Gaming House	0	0	0
20441	Other Gaming & Betting	2	2	2
20851–20855	Organized Crime Occurrence Types	0	0	0
21151	Cocaine Trafficking	312	71**	1
40110	Suicides	95	95	3
40115	Attempted Suicides	45	45	1
50115	Family Disputes	5546	1094**	16
	Total	11,198	5,196	208

* These files were classified and were reviewed by homicide personnel.
** Sample = 20 per cent of total files available.
*** Total of files available to view from sample, as some files were not available during investigation (i.e., due to ongoing investigations, warrants, etc.).

per cent), all fraud crimes (51 per cent), and all gaming and betting crimes (63 per cent).

It is important to recognize that clearance rates are affected by how police learn about offences; to wit, most property crimes are reported by the victim well after the occurrence, thus making it difficult for the police to apprehend offenders. Most gaming and betting offences are encountered directly by the police, as opposed to 'victim' reporting, making it easier to clear the case because the offender is often known.

Upon reviewing the economic crime files we noted numerous credit card offences involving theft and unauthorized use. Why the credit card was stolen and how it was used was seldom mentioned, even when an arrest was made. Gambling may have factored into some of these incidents, but to what extent is unknown. Existing files are usually not descriptive enough to determine whether gambling was involved, and, of course, many offences are unreported and therefore unknown to the police. Undoubtedly, then, 4 per cent represents a conservative approximation of the extent of gambling-related crime in comparison to the total volume of crime in Edmonton.

From the data displayed in Table 8.4, the crime most frequently connected to gambling was passing counterfeit currency, which accounted for 130 of the 208 (63 per cent) gambling-related occurrences. Presumably, criminals see gambling venues as prime locations to make counterfeit transactions because of the likelihood of bogus bills going unnoticed amid the high volume of circulating cash. Twenty-seven per cent of all EPS counterfeiting files in 2001 were gambling-related, with $20 bills the most common denomination and relatively small amounts of money involved.

Of the 3,097 files reviewed in several fraud categories, 46 (1.5 per cent) were gambling-related. Six of the nine fraud cheque occurrences involved attempts to cash stolen cheques; other incidents were for cheque forgery, altering a certified cheque, and writing cheques on a closed account. The perpetrators in six of the nine incidents admitted to having a gambling problem. Substantial amounts of money were involved: up to $20,000 in stolen cheques; and in the case of the altered certified cheque, a new truck was bought with a $52,240 cheque originally issued in the amount of $240.

Gambling-related credit card frauds involved stolen credit or bank cards (9), unauthorized credit or bank card use (6), and fake credit cards (1). In six of the credit card fraud cases the suspect admitted having a gambling problem. The amount of money involved in these frauds ranged from a low of $100 to over $20,000, with the majority of cases in the thousands of dollars. Examples of larger frauds involved individuals attempting to support a gambling addiction and included making false application for six credit cards and using the cards to obtain $21,000; a boyfriend receiving unauthorized cash advances of $15,000 to $20,000 on his girlfriend's credit and bank cards; and an extended home care employee using a resident's bank card to siphon $13,000 from the account.

The dollar amounts involved in some of the 'fraud-other' category offences were also substantial. For example, an insurance representative defrauded 34 elderly clients of $166,000; two bingo-playing acquaintances were taken for $127,000 by a third party; an Alberta woman contributed $60,000 to an illegal lottery in Quebec; a hotel employee stole $31,500 from the business; and two alleged Quebec organized crime associates used fake credit cards to make 'cash calls' for $22,500 at Edmonton casinos. In eight of the cases the accused admitted to having a gambling problem while the other incidents either took place in or were associated with a gambling venue.

A 20 per cent sampling of the family dispute files revealed sixteen gambling-related incidents, approximately 1.5 per cent of the 1,094 files reviewed. One or both party's gambling addiction was the basis for twelve of the incidents; two were attributed to who should control gambling winnings; and two were precipitated by spouses leaving their companions at bingo halls, thus forcing them to walk home.

In addition to analysing EPS 2001 crime files, we attempted to collect 2002 data using the GOR form. In spite of our efforts to have police officers comply with this new protocol, the overall results were less than expected as only twenty-six gambling-related incidents were uncovered using this reporting format. In retrospect, the lack of compliance is understandable; EPS file clerks told us that when a similar domestic violence reporting form was introduced, it took four years to get full participation and consistency.

To augment data-gathering efforts for the seven-month period in 2002, EPS file clerks were asked to identify any gambling-related crime files they came across since, as part of their duties, they comprehensively read all new files for the purpose of assigning code numbers and appropriate cataloguing. With the file clerks' assistance, an additional ninety-three gambling-related crime occurrences were confirmed. While we cannot guarantee that all gambling-related crimes were identified, the clerks did examine every file in all crime categories, not just those most likely to have a gambling connection, as was the case with our 2001 file search. Since there was no record of the total files viewed in each crime category, the percentage of occurrences that were gambling-related could not be calculated.

For the period January through August 2002 a total of 119 gambling-related crime occurrences were identified, 26 through the GOR forms completed by investigating officers and 93 flagged by EPS central records file clerks. As with the 2001 data, the most frequently noted gambling-related crime was passing counterfeit currency, 72 of the 119 incidents (61 per cent), followed by 10 thefts (8 per cent), 8 frauds (7 per cent), 5 family disputes (4 per cent) and a few incidents in other crime categories.

The AGLC Investigations Branch created 182 gambling-related criminal investigation files that encompassed 230 incidents occurring in the city of Edmonton between 1 January 2001 and 31 August 2002. The most common incidents investigated by the AGLC included cheating at play (33), over/underpayment of winnings (33), thefts (33), and illegal gaming (9). Charges were laid in 53 (23 per cent) of the incidents, usually in connection with serious crimes such as fraud, theft, assault, obstructing a police officer, and forgery.

To obtain an industry viewpoint on gambling-related crime, in-depth interviews were conducted with security managers of the city's five largest gambling venues (four casinos and the racetrack). Security-related incidents are duly recorded and categorized in these locations; by way of illustration, for the first six months of 2002 at one of Edmonton's major legal gambling venues, 38 crimes against persons and 60 crimes against property were recorded. Among the crimes against persons, 12 disturbances involving alcohol and 12 other disturbances (including 3 drug-related) were recorded; passing counterfeit currency (37 incidents) was the most frequent property crime.

The resolution of these on-site incidents depended on the perceived severity of the offence. The majority of incidents were dealt with internally; that is, through a warning, removal from the premises, and/or suspension of privileges. Security personnel are empowered to make house arrests, which includes detaining a suspect until the police arrive. A general rule used by gambling venue security managers in handling incidents is the less fuss and publicity the better. While gambling venue interests may be better served by handling criminal activities internally, this approach contributes to an under-reporting of gambling-related crimes, as many on-site occurrences never make it into police files.

Gambling venue security managers candidly discussed the criminal types that frequented their premises; the general view was that 'known criminals are okay as long as they behave themselves.' As one respondent stated, 'They may be gambling with the proceeds of crime but they are spending money not laundering it.' Based upon EPS intelligence, one respondent estimated that 15 per cent to 20 per cent of his casino's high-roller patrons were drug dealers. Generally speaking, downtown venues attract a rougher clientele than do venues in outlying districts. This observation was borne out by the numbers on each venue's banned list. All of the major gambling venues excluded troublesome patrons; depending on the gravity of the misbehaviour, players may be banned for a day, a week, three months, or life. Banned lists in Edmonton's major gambling establishments ranged from 75 to 700 patrons; making the list can result from a single serious incident but is usually due to serial misconduct. One security manager noted that revenue considerations can determine whether or not players make the banned list; for example, improper behaviour by high rollers is tolerated more so than it is from ordinary players.

In regard to money laundering in Edmonton's major gambling venues, the consensus among security managers was that it happens but is seldom done blatantly. One respondent noted that transactions exceeding the $10,000 limit requiring official recording are fairly common. 'We do the paper work and file the reports but nothing really happens with them. I suppose they're on hand for inspection in case an audit trail is required.'

Gambling venue security managers claimed to have good working relationships with the EPS, RCMP, and AGLC investigators. Gambling venue staff report suspicious activity to the police and cooperate with law enforcement officers in mutually beneficial ways. An external law enforcement agency is called in on approximately 10 per cent of the gambling venue incidents: that is, the EPS if an arrest is needed or the AGLC in cases of cheating at play or internal theft.

Conclusions and Implications

The number of crimes directly linked to gambling in the EPS and AGLC files is relatively small; however, as this study has demonstrated, gambling-related crime data are scanty, imprecise, and fragmented. Gambling-related crimes are not identified as such by the police and investigating officers, since they seldom ask about criminal motive or inquire into the underlying causes of a criminal act. Whether or not a crime is gambling-related is often irrelevant to the investigating officer. Furthermore, in a significant number of EPS files no suspect is identified, so unless the crime took place in a gambling venue, there is no way to know if it was gambling-related.

Each law enforcement group responsible for monitoring gambling offences has its own agenda and keeps separate records. Many gambling-related crimes are handled internally by venue security staff and not reported, and, of course, many offences go undetected. The research on problem gamblers in treatment and Gamblers Anonymous members indicates that over 50 per cent of respondents admitted to having engaged in criminal behaviour to support their gambling addictions; however, only 20 per cent report having been convicted for a gambling-related crime. For these reasons we believe our research only scratches the surface of gambling-related crime.

Using the gambling-related crime categories described earlier in the study, we make the following observations based on our findings. The widespread legalization of gambling in Alberta has reduced the stigma of participating in the activity (including illegal formats). That, and the perception of light penalties meted out in court, has resulted in illegal gambling enforcement becoming a low priority for law enforcement agencies. This lack of police oversight prompted the AGLC to expand its investigatory powers to include illegal as well as legal gambling. The upshot of this role transference has resulted in an agency (AGLC) with more manpower (but not necessarily trained in gambling investigations) that selectively enforces illegal gambling statutes. The most common and popular illegal gambling activity, bookmaking, flourishes in this environment.

When government regulators assume the job of investigating illegal gambling operations, there is a potential for conflict of interest because the government agency that sanctions and markets gambling is not only the major recipient of gambling proceeds but is also policing the activity. The possibility exists that gambling-related crimes may be downplayed or covered up to avoid publicity.

In this chapter, the terms 'gambling problem' or 'problem gambler' pertain to the description of a suspect by a police officer, government investigator, witness, or family member. This label may or may not equate to a clinical diagnosis of problem gambling. The majority of crimes committed by problem gamblers were non-violent (the exceptions being a few armed robberies and several domestic disputes). Problem gamblers tend to be law-abiding citizens who, after reaching a crisis state, become so desperate for money to pay gambling debts or recoup gambling losses that they cross the line into criminal behaviour. Seldom physically aggressive or threatening to others, problem gamblers typically acquire money through lying, conning, manipulation, and stealth (McGurrin 1991). These factors are now considered by the courts and reflected in sentences requiring restitution and community service.

Various gambling formats attract different types and degrees of criminal behaviour. For example, few crimes were associated with non-continuous gambling formats such as raffles, lotteries, or sports pool betting. Fast-paced, continuous gambling formats such as VLTs and slot machines are closely associated with problem gambling due to the rapidity of play and the engrossing properties of the machines. (Smith and Wynne 2002); consequently, by extension, crimes associated with problem gambling (fraud, theft, and domestic violence) are closely linked to the gambling formats with the highest addictive potency.

In recognition of this familiar chain of events (electronic machine gambling leads to problem gambling, subsequently causing criminal behaviour), some jurisdictions take precautionary measures with their EGMs such as restricting their location and daily operating hours, banning machines with note acceptors, eliminating on-site ATMs, reducing the maximum wager, calibrating machines for a slower rate of play, automatically stopping EGMs for ten minutes at certain intervals, and limiting player losses to $50 per hour (Hayward and Kliger 2002). These measures are aimed at moderating problem gambling prevalence rates and, in turn, reducing the frequency and severity of crimes committed by problem gamblers.

It was beyond the scope of this study to determine whether or not crime rates increased as a result of gambling expansion. As noted earlier, the city of Edmonton was already replete with gambling opportunities when this study commenced. Consequently, there was no opportunity for pre- and post-gambling expansion comparisons.

Major gambling venues (that is, casinos and racetracks) that attract sizeable crowds and large sums of money are susceptible to crime occurrences such as passing counterfeit currency, credit card fraud, money laundering, loan sharking, assaults, and disruptive behaviour. Criminal events occur in specific locations and are influenced by participants' perceptions of the gambling venue's physical and social milieu. In other words, particular locations and/or ambiences increase or lessen the likelihood of crimes occurring. Moreover, because of the patterns of activity and types of persons attracted to the setting, certain crimes are linked with particular gambling formats. For example, in this study police files cited counterfeiting as the most common crime in gambling venues; gambling venue security officials specified assaults, disruptive behaviour, vandalism, and loan sharking as the main problems they dealt with; and AGLC files noted cheating at play, frauds, and thefts as their primary gambling venue crime concerns. In this regard, gambling venues are somewhat similar to other commercial settings (e.g., shopping malls, night clubs, and sporting events) where people congregate. In each case there is a convergence in space and time of motivated offenders, suitable targets, and minimal perceived deterrents.

One problem with monitoring gambling venue crime in Canada is that there are separate enforcement groups, each with different agendas and modes of operation. For example, gambling venue security officials focus on protecting their business assets, patron and staff safety, and the smooth operation of the games. Consequently, behaviour that interferes with any of the above is dealt with expediently. Municipal police fulfil their mandated peacekeeping role by responding to a gambling venue's call for help; in this regard, a gambling venue is treated the same as a call from any other source. Government regulators are concerned with ensuring the games are honestly and fairly run and that sponsoring charities and gambling providers adhere to the terms and conditions of their licences.

The fact that each enforcement agency performs different roles is reflected in how gambling venue criminal behaviour is handled; for example, crimes such as assault, loan sharking, and vandalism are typically dealt with internally by staff security officers. Unless the offence is considered serious, charges are seldom pressed; perpetrators may be warned, ushered off the premises, possibly suspended or banned. City police investigate gambling-related crimes such as counterfeiting, fraud, and robbery and lay charges if there is supporting evidence (rarely for counterfeiting, more likely for fraud and robbery). Typical offences dealt with by government investigators are cheating at play and employee theft and fraud. Convictions for these crimes often result in job dismissal and fines; usually not a jail sentence unless a substantial dollar amount is involved. In the case of money laundering, other than gambling venue staff filing the requisite forms for transactions over $10,000, little scrutiny is provided by law enforcement agencies or security staff. Many offences dealt with by government investigators in this study featured large dollar amounts (theft and fraud) and were potentially damaging to the integrity of the gambling industry (cheating at play, gambling venue workers engaged in criminal acts, and player overpayments). Gambling venue cheating scams involved casino table game irregularities, tampering with electronic gaming machines, conspiracies between venue staff and players, and employee theft. These crimes were usually detected by 'eye in the sky' surveillance cameras and are a major reason why some jurisdictions (e.g., Ontario and British

Columbia) require an ongoing law enforcement presence at major gambling venues.

Gambling may be just one of several precipitating factors in a domestic violence occurrence; by way of example, an incident may appear to have been triggered by a spouse's intemperate gambling, but the problem gambling may be related to a depressive state brought on by the partner's substance abuse problems. In this instance, emotional disorders entangled with unhealthy behaviours and poor coping skills create a ripple effect resulting in a dysfunctional relationship that ultimately leads to abusive acts and law enforcement intervention. One party's excessive gambling may be part of the volatile mix, but cannot always be singled out as the single causal factor in an incident. No formal charges were laid in any of the gambling-related domestic violence occurrences investigated by EPS. None of the gambling-related crimes uncovered in the time period studied fit into the graft and corruption category.

Our data are not definitive enough to infer that widespread gambling causes crime. We do, however, underscore the point that gambling and crime are associated in three ways. First, problem gamblers commit crimes – many of the gambling-related family disputes and suicides and more than one-half the frauds where charges were laid were associated with one person's problem gambling behaviour. Second, major gambling venues attract opportunistic criminals looking to exploit the scene through activities such as cheating at play, theft, and counterfeiting. Third, popular illegal gambling formats (e.g., bookmaking, card rooms) are flourishing as there are few, if any, strong deterrents.

Gambling-related crime is a concern in Edmonton given the depth and breadth of gambling opportunities (legal and illegal) but could be better contained if police resources were augmented to give more attention to illegal gambling; if gambling-related crime was carefully documented and aggregated by all enforcement agencies; and if tighter restrictions were put on electronic gaming machines (the gambling formats with the highest addictive potency). Furthermore, to enhance the integrity of the gambling industry, the AGLC Investigations Branch should be nonpartisan and autonomous, much like other government watchdog agencies such as the provincial auditor, ombudsman, and ethics commissioner. The current contradictory roles of government gambling profiteer and regulator raise questions of bias, transparency, and accountability and run counter to the public interest (Goodman 1995; Castellani 2000).

Policing gambling-related crime in an optimal fashion in Edmonton would require the EPS to provide additional resources; conceivably, two officers on illegal gambling detail and ten to twelve officers to cover the major gambling venues. By comparison, police services in the area of Ontario's major casinos (Windsor, Rama, and Niagara Falls) each added twenty-five officers when these facilities opened in their communities. Edmonton police officials argued that since gambling-related crime is exacerbated by expanded licensed gambling, additional resources should come from the provincial government. Alternatively, an amendment to the *Criminal Code* removing laws against bookmaking and other illegal gambling offences might be a solution.

Future research on gambling-related crime needs to test the explanatory and predictive power of criminological theories. While hypotheses were not employed in this study, our findings suggest that criminological theories such as 'rational choice' and 'deterrence' are useful in clarifying the motivations of illegal gambling participants, and 'self-control' theory helps to explicate why problem gamblers adhere to self-defeating playing strategies and why excessive losses, coupled with poor coping skills, leads some problem gamblers to commit crimes.

Opportunity-based theories shed light on the criminal activity that occurs in and around major gambling venues; for example, 'routine activities' and 'criminal opportunity' models emphasize the likelihood of a crime occurring when there is a convergence in time and space of a motivated potential offender with the requisite skill set, a suitable target, and an absence of formal or informal guardians to deter the offender. Opportunity theories also help interpret commonplace crimes such as counterfeiting, credit card fraud, money laundering, and loan sharking at major gambling venues, as well as thefts from winning players at VLT establishments.

9 Youth Gambling: A Canadian Perspective

JEFFREY L. DEREVENSKY

As described in earlier chapters in this book, the landscape of gambling within Canada has radically changed since the early 1990s. In spite of the widespread media coverage highlighting problems associated with gambling, most Canadians perceive gambling as a legitimate form of entertainment and appear ambivalent concerning its expansion. The prevailing attitudes of legislators (that gambling is an excellent source of government revenues) and the public at large suggest that new gaming venues (for example, an increased number of provincial casinos/racinos[1] in jurisdictions currently without such forms of gambling) and new technologies in the form of interactive lotteries and Internet gambling will continue to expand rapidly.

Concomitant with provincially regulated and sponsored gambling has come a commitment for renewed research in understanding the impact of gambling expansion, the identification of the risk and protective factors associated with disordered gambling, the development and evaluation of best practices for the treatment and prevention of excessive gambling, and funding for services dedicated to individuals with gambling problems. This commitment, along with the significant increase in funding, has been influential in providing support for researchers, increased availability for treatment of those with problems, the provision of call-in centres for problem gamblers, and the development of several research centres in Canada. Researchers across Canada, largely as a result of substantial funding, remain at the forefront of the field and have been instrumental in advancing our knowledge about problem gambling, shaping research agendas, and promoting responsible social policies throughout the world.

Adolescent Gambling Behaviour

Once viewed as an activity primarily relegated to adults, gambling has become a popular form of recreation for adolescents. While in most cases explicit legislative statutes prohibit children and adolescents from provincially sponsored gambling, their resourcefulness enables many youth to engage in both regulated and non-regulated (e.g., card games, peer sports wagering, etc.) forms of gambling. Gambling behaviour for adolescents, similar to adults, can be best viewed along a continuum ranging from non-gambling to social/occasional/recreational gambling to at-risk gambling to problem/pathological gambling.

Ten studies completed in Canada between 1988 and 2001 revealed prevalence rates for juvenile gambling ranged from 60 to 91 per cent, with a median participation level of 67 per cent, which is comparable to U.S. findings for the same period (Jacobs 2004). More recent studies have generally found similar rates of gambling among adolescents (Derevensky and Gupta 2004). Survey findings and reviews of prevalence studies examining youth gambling behaviour have consistently revealed that adolescents (12–17 years of age) have managed to participate, to some degree, in practically all forms of social, government-sanctioned, and non-regulated gambling available in their homes and communities. Such games include cards, dice, and board games with family and friends; betting with peers on games of personal skill (e.g., pool, bowling, other sports); arcade or video games for money; purchasing lottery tickets; sports betting with friends or through the lottery (e.g., Sports Select, Pro-Line, Mise-O-Jeu); wagering at horse tracks; gambling in bingo halls and card rooms; playing slot machines and table games in casinos; gambling on video lottery terminals (VLTs); wagering on the Internet; and placing bets with a bookmaker.

Wagering behaviours of adolescents are often dependent upon the local availability of games, the geographical proximity of gaming locations, the child's gender and type of game (gambling is more popular among males than females; males prefer sports wagering whereas girls report engaging in bingo more often), age (older adolescents are more likely to engage in VLT and casino playing as it remains easier to access these venues), and cultural/ethnic background.[2]

Notwithstanding the availability of gambling opportunities, the most popular games that emerge repeatedly among youth include cards, dice and board games with family and friends, games of personal skill with

peers, sports betting (primarily with peers but also through lottery outlets and/or with a bookmaker), bingo, and lottery purchases, primarily
scratch cards (Jacobs 2004), with new research suggesting Internet
wagering is becoming a popular activity (Derevensky and Gupta 2007).

Adolescent Problem Gambling

Although there is a lack of consensus as to the actual prevalence rate of
severe gambling[3] involvement by adolescents, a number of large-scale
meta-analyses and reviews have concluded that adolescents as a group
constitute a high-risk population for gambling problems (National
Research Council 1999). Recent research in Canada found that between
70 per cent and 80 per cent of adolescents report having engaged in
some form of gambling during the past year,[4] with most best described
as social, recreational, and occasional gamblers. Nevertheless, there
remains ample evidence that 3 per cent to 8 per cent of adolescents have
a very serious gambling problem, with another 10 per cent to 15 per
cent at risk for the development of a gambling problem. Acknowledg-
ing difficulties in comparisons of the data sets, the National Research
Council report concluded 'the proportion of pathological gamblers
among adolescents in the United States could be more than three times
that of adults (5.0% versus 1.5%)' (National Research Council 1999, 89),
with comparable findings being applied in Canada.

More recently, while there have been a multitude of reviews examining the prevalence rates of serious gambling problems among adolescents, the validity of these data has been questioned (Ladouceur,
Bouchard, et al. 2000). Ladouceur and his colleagues have argued that
the current reported rates of serious gambling problems among adolescents may be overestimated. In a detailed analysis, Derevensky, Gupta,
and Winters (2003) concluded that given the current definitions of
youth gambling problems, prevalence rates are likely not over-inflated
and that a small but appreciable and identifiable number of adolescents
are experiencing significant gambling-related problems.

Derevensky et al. (2003) acknowledge that the wide variability of
reported prevalence rates of youth problem gambling remains troubling from a scientific standpoint, given the reported variability among
prevalence studies of adolescents is generally considerably higher compared to the variability reported for adult rates of problem gambling.
They suggest that whereas one might expect age, gender, and regional differences reflecting variability in youth problem gambling, the

reported variability among prevalence studies cannot be explained merely on the basis of these differences. The sources of such variability may be compounding the confusion as to the accuracy of the prevalence rates. They conclude that differences in prevalence rates may be affected by a number of situational and measurement variables including varying sampling procedures (e.g., telephone surveys vs. school-based screens, community vs. convenience samples), use of different instruments and measures, varying cut-point scores associated with instruments, the use of modified instruments, the lack of consistency in terms of availability and accessibility of gambling venues, gender distributions, the age of the target population, cultural differences, as well as the possibility that adolescent reports are simply more variable than their adult counterparts. Nevertheless, while nomenclature, instrumentation, and methodological issues exist and need to be addressed, there remains considerable consensus that gambling and wagering among youth is a relatively common and popular activity and that a small, identifiable population experiences serious gambling-related problems.

Derevensky and Gupta (2000)[5] found that 91 per cent of adolescent and young adult pathological gamblers reported a preoccupation with gambling; 85 per cent indicated chasing their losses; 70 per cent lied to family members, peers, and friends about their gambling behaviour; 61 per cent used their lunch money and/or allowance for gambling; 61 per cent became tense and restless when trying to reduce their gambling; 57 per cent reported spending increasing amounts of money gambling; 52 per cent indicated gambling as a way of escaping problems; 27 per cent reported missing school (more than five times) to gamble in the past year; 24 per cent stole money from a family member to gamble without their knowledge; 24 per cent sought help for serious financial concerns resulting from their gambling; 21 per cent developed familial problems resulting from their gambling behaviour; and 12 per cent reported having stolen money from outside the family to gamble.

Many of the prevalence studies have identified either at-risk (those individuals exhibiting a number of gambling-related problems but not meeting the minimum scoring criteria for pathological gambler) or pathological gamblers (sometimes referred to as probable pathological gamblers during adolescence) with the inherent general assumption that they are homogeneous groups. Two distinct but complementary classifications have been made. One distinction emphasizes that certain gambling activities and types of games (e.g., casino games, VLTs) attract individuals with a specific profile. As such, diversity of activities with distinct characteristics would likely appeal to different types of individuals who engage in them in disparate ways (Abbott, Volberg, Bellringer, and Reith 2004). It has been suggested that some forms of gambling have a stronger association with problem gambling. For example, Abbott, Volberg, et al. (2004) suggest that activities that are continuous in nature and involve elements of either skill or perceived skill have been more closely associated with problematic gambling. While players prone to engaging in a number of different activities have received considerable investigation in the past (e.g., horse racing, VLTs/EGMs, slot machines, casino gambling), it should be noted that some forms of gambling have had relatively little research to identify their potentially addictive nature (e.g., scratch cards, bingo, and Internet gambling). There is evidence, for adults, that individuals with a preference for and frequent participation in certain forms of gambling (e.g., slots, VLTs or electronic gambling machines, casino card games) may have a higher probability of being a problem gambler (Abbott, Volberg, et al. 2004; Schrans, Schellinck, and Walsh 2000). However, little is currently known about adolescent pathological gamblers with respect to the impact of the attributes of specific games since it has been generally assumed that their playing behaviour is much less stable, transitory, and often more dependent upon their age and the availability of the game.

The second distinction comes from the work of Nower and Blaszczynski (2004), who suggest a pathways model for identifying problem gamblers. This pathways model presupposes that there are three (or more) different subtypes of pathological gamblers, with each subtype having a different etiology and different accompanying pathologies. Behaviourally conditioned problem gamblers, those individuals in pathway 1, are explained as lacking psychiatric pathology but are more likely to succumb to games and activities incorporating a highly addictive schedule of behavioural reinforcement. Emotionally vulnerable problem gamblers, pathway 2, manifest both a biological and psychological vulnerability to pathology, and are characterized by high levels of depression and/or anxiety, a history of poor social support, low self-esteem, and emotional neglect by caregivers. In contrast, individuals in pathway 3, antisocial impulsivist problem gamblers, are more likely to possess vulnerabilities similar to those in pathway 2, but they are more identifiably impulsive, have antisocial behavioural traits, and often exhibit multiple addictions. There is recent data suggesting that early indicators of gambling problems include indices of anxiety and impulsivity (Derevensky, Pratt, et al. 2005; Ste-Marie, Gupta, and Derevensky 2006; Vitaro, Wanner, et al. 2004). Given our current knowledge concerning the constellation of correlates and risk factors associated with adolescent problem gambling, and given some recent analyses concerning gender differences with respect to adolescent pathological gambling, it is likely that different profiles of young problem gamblers exist.

Correlates and Risk Factors Associated with Problem Gambling

Canadian researchers have actively contributed to the growing body of research designed to help identify the risk and protective factors associated with adolescents experiencing gambling problems and to examine the antecedents and consequences associated with problem gambling. Considerable research efforts have focused upon basic issues of assessment of gambling severity; the identification of physiological, psychological, and socio-emotional mechanisms underlying excessive gambling behaviour among youth; understanding why some individuals continue to gamble in spite of repeated losses; and behavioural correlates associated with problem gambling along with how best to educate, prevent, and provide treatment for individuals with a gambling problem.

While our knowledge concerning the risk factors associated with adolescent problem gambling appears to be growing, we still have yet to acquire sufficient information concerning protective factors (Dickson, Derevensky, and Gupta 2008). It is essential to remember that most mental health disorders and social problems have multiple risk factors. Similar to other mental health disorders, problem gambling also has multiple risk factors, and no single constellation of these risk factors can alone predict with a great deal of certainty that a particular problem will exist.[6] It is equally important to note that some risk factors are common to multiple disorders, including gambling, while others are unique to the specific disorder. Abbott, Volberg, et al. (2004) have aptly noted that it is not merely important to identify the risk factors associated with a disorder, but rather it is necessary to ascertain how powerful their effect is, both in absolute terms and relative to other factors. While this is indeed true, it may well be that there are multiple constellations of risk factors that in conjunction with a lack of specific protective factors place certain individuals at high risk for a specific problem. One further point is necessary before presenting the current state of knowledge concerning adolescent risk factors. An important issue to consider may be the interaction effect of risk factors, protective factors, and availability of specific forms of gambling. For example, should the availability of specific gambling opportunities be limited or non-existent, it is plausible that an individual may seek some alternative addictive behaviour other than gambling as a stress/anxiety reduction outlet.

Among adolescents there appears to be a more rapid progression from social, recreational gambling to more problematic gambling compared to adults (Derevensky and Gupta 2004; Gupta and Derevensky 1998a). As well, adolescent problem gamblers report initiating gambling at an early age (approximately 10 years of age) as compared with peers who report gambling but have few gambling-related problems (Wynne et al. 1996).

Adolescent and young adult problem gamblers report consistently chasing their losses such as returning to win back money lost (Hardoon, Derevensky, and Gupta 2001). They have also been found to exhibit erroneous perceptions when gambling; for example, they feel that they can predict the outcome of the game or they perceive to have exaggerated levels of skill (Derevensky and Gupta 2000). Many youth problem gamblers also report having had very early gambling experiences or an early big win (Griffiths 1995; Gupta and Derevensky 1997; Wynne et al. 1996).

The consequences of adolescent problem and pathological gambling have been well documented. Adolescents with excessive gambling problems have been shown to experience increased delinquent and criminal behaviour, poor academic and work performance, and disrupted familial and peer relationships (Gupta and Derevensky 1998a; Hardoon, Derevensky, and Gupta 2002; Magoon, Gupta, and Derevensky in press). As well, youth pathological gamblers have been reported to have high rates of suicide ideation and suicide attempts (Nower, Gupta, Blaszczynski, and Derevensky 2004) and a wide variety of mental health and behavioural problems (Derevensky and Gupta 2004; Hardoon et al. 2004).

While somewhat dependent upon the availability of gambling activities and geographic distribution, a number of consistent findings have been shown to be associated with gambling problems among adolescents. Prevalence study after study has revealed that more male than female adolescents exhibit pathological gambling behaviours. Pathological gambling among male adolescents has been found to be anywhere from two to four times as prevalent as among females (Derevensky and Gupta 2004; Lesieur et al. 1991; Stinchfield 2000; Stinchfield and Winters 1998). Males have also been found to make higher gross wagers and exhibit greater risk-taking behaviour (Derevensky, Gupta, and Della-Cioppa 1996). As well, males have been found to gamble earlier, gamble on more games, gamble more often, spend more time and money, and experience more gambling-related problems than females (Jacobs 2004). It also appears that parents are more likely to encourage their son's gambling, as more males than females report gambling with their parents (Ladouceur et al. 1994) and that gambling remains a significant part of the male culture (Huxley and Carroll 1992).

While there is a paucity of research examining cultural differences among adolescents, Stinchfield (2000) in a large-scale study of Minnesota adolescents reported that 30 per cent of American Indian adolescents gambled weekly, followed by Mexican-American and African-American youth (22 per cent), compared to 4–5 per cent of Asian and Caucasian youth. Wallisch (1993), in sampling adolescents in Texas, reported that Hispanics gambled more frequently than Caucasians. In a recent province-wide survey of addictive behaviours among secondary school children in Quebec, Chevalier et al. (2003) reported that while Francophone adolescents gamble more than non-Francophone adolescents, they reported few gambling-related problems.

The importance of parents and relatives on children's behaviour cannot be underestimated. Considerable reference has been made to families and their potential role in contributing to the initiation of gambling and the development of problem gambling through increasing an individual's exposure to gambling activities, social learning, and heredity (Abbott, Volberg, et al. 2004). Research has shown that adolescent pathological gamblers' initial gambling experiences took place with family members in their own homes (Gupta and Derevensky 1997), with older siblings being an early influence. As children get older, their patterns of gambling change such that youth gamble less with family members and more with friends. Adolescents with gambling problems in general population surveys are also more likely to report having parents who they perceive gamble excessively, are involved in other addictive behaviours, and/or have been involved in illegal activities (Abbott and Volberg 2000; Gupta and Derevensky 1998a; Hardoon et al. 2004; Raylu and Oei 2002).

Children of problem gamblers exhibit a number of mental health, substance abuse, and psychosomatic problems, and are as well at heightened risk for long-term problems (Jacobs et al. 1989). There is evidence suggesting that adolescent pathological gambling is correlated with parental attitudes towards gambling. Fisher (1999) concluded that having a parent who does not care if his or her child gambles increases the child's probability of experiencing significant gambling problems by 50 per cent. These findings are supported by the work of Gupta and Derevensky (1998a). However, the long-term impact of the family on the development and maintenance of an adolescent's gambling behaviour, including relationships and support, has not been extensively examined.

With respect to peer influences, Griffiths (1990) reported that 44 per cent of adolescents participated in gambling activities because their friends were engaging in similar practices. As children get older the results from several studies in Quebec indicate they tend to gamble more with friends in their homes (Gupta and Derevensky 1997). This trend reinforces the notion that, for many youth, gambling is perceived as a socially accepted and entertaining pastime. Fisher's (1993) research uncovered that adolescents reported that gambling made them feel older and that they enjoyed displaying their skills among their peers. Hardoon and Derevensky (2002) further noted that children in grades 4 and 6 (ages 9 and 11) who played a computer-simulated game of roulette, individually and in groups, demonstrated significant changes in their playing behaviours as a result of peer modelling, suggesting a strong social learning component involved in the acquisition of such behaviours. Clinically, there is evidence that adolescents with gambling problems replace old friends with new 'gambling associates' (Gupta and Derevensky 2000, 2004); however, the impact of peers upon the acquisition and/or maintenance of adolescent gambling behaviour and problem gambling is unclear.

Adolescent pathological gamblers have increased physiological resting states, a greater need for sensation seeking, and are more likely aroused and excited when gambling (Nower, Derevensky, and Gupta 2004). They have also been reported to dissociate more frequently when engaged in a variety of gambling activities (Gupta and Derevensky 1998b; Jacobs, Marston, et al. 1989).

Research findings suggest that adolescent probable pathological gamblers are greater risk-takers (Abbott, Volberg, et al. 2004; Derevensky and Gupta 2004; Nower, Derevensky, and Gupta 2004), score higher on measures of impulsivity (Derevensky et al. 2005; Gupta and Derevensky 1997), excitability, extroversion, and state and trait anxiety (Blaszczynski and McConaghy 1989; Ste-Marie et al. 2006), and score lower on measures of conformity and self-discipline (Gupta and Derevensky 1998a; Vitaro, Ferland, Jacques, and Ladouceur 1998). Problem and pathological gamblers are also more self-blaming, guilt prone, anxious, and less emotionally stable (Gupta and Derevensky 2000). While there is some literature suggesting that obsessive compulsive disorders (e.g., Black, Moyer, and Schlosser 2003) and psychoticism, neuroticism, borderline disorders, and histrionic and narcissistic personality disorders have been found to be elevated among adult pathological gamblers (Blaszczynski and Steel 1988; Raylu and Oei 2002), there is no evidence supporting these findings among adolescent problem gamblers.

In general, problem gamblers report having lower self-esteem, higher rates of depression, and greater suicide ideation and suicide attempts compared with other adolescents (Gupta and Derevensky 1998a; Langhinrichsen-Rohling, Rhode, et al. 2004; Nower, Gupta, Blaszczynski, and Derevensky 2004).

In addition to adolescents with severe gambling problems having a history of delinquency (Ladouceur et al. 1994; Magoon et al. in press; Stinchfield 2000; Winters et al. 1993), they are also more likely to experience a multiplicity of school-related problems, including increased truancy and poor academic performance, to have repeated a grade in school (Fisher 1999; Hardoon et al. 2004), and to report a greater frequency of attention deficit hyperactive disorder and conduct-related problems (Derevensky et al. 2005; Hardoon et al. 2004). There is empirical support that adolescent problem gamblers also experience a number of antisocial problematic behaviours including the development of multiple addictions, in particular alcohol and substance abuse disorders (Hardoon et al. 2004; Winters and Anderson 2000).

There is a substantial body of literature examining differences in cognitive processing between individuals with and without gambling disorders. In a review of the literature, Toneatto (1999) provides a comprehensive compendium of the gambling-related cognitive distortions endorsed by adult pathological gamblers. Such findings relate to the erroneous beliefs, cognitive thinking displaying a lack of utilization of independence of events when making judgments, and exaggeration of perceived skill involved in gambling. Similar distortions have been reported for adolescent problem gamblers as well.[7]

Adolescents with gambling problems, compared to their peers, have poor or maladaptive general coping skills (Gupta, Derevensky, and

Marget 2004; Nower, Derevensky, and Gupta 2004). More specifically, problem and pathological gamblers use more emotion and distraction oriented coping styles than non-gamblers. It has been suggested that maladaptive coping may be a mediating factor for addictive behaviours (Bergevin et al. 2005; Gupta, Derevensky, and Marget 2004). Given that adolescents with gambling problems report more daily hassles and major traumatic life events (Bergevin et al. 2005; Kaufman, Derevensky, and Gupta 2002), their lack of implementation of effective coping and adaptive mechanisms remains of concern.

Similar to adults, adolescents view gambling as an enjoyable form of entertainment. Gambling is generally viewed as a relatively benign activity, significantly less harmful than alcohol, drugs, or cigarettes (Dickson, Derevensky, and Gupta 2002). Gambling activities are viewed as highly acceptable activities, a belief that is reflected in the finding that very few children are afraid of getting caught while gambling, with even fewer being afraid as they get older. Research has also indicated that adolescent attitudes and behaviour predict gambling behaviour in later adulthood (Griffiths and Wood 2000).

Situational/Environmental Risk Factors

In addition to individual risk factors, there are a number of situational and/or environmental factors that strongly interact with individual risk factors to create an increasing probability that an individual may become a problematic gambler.

Fisher (1999) in examining adolescent gambling behaviour reported that the availability and easy accessibility of 'fruit machine' gambling (low-stake slot machines, which are legal for children of all ages) in the United Kingdom was directly related to higher rates of gambling and problem gambling. Similar findings were found with adolescents who engage in scratch lottery playing, sports lottery playing, and VLT playing (Felsher et al. 2003, 2004). Jacobs (2004) concluded after reviewing a large number of prevalence studies that there is a direct link between availability, accessibility, and gambling in general, with gambling problems in particular among youth.

It is likely that the structural characteristics of specific games – in particular, electronic gambling machines, which incorporate rapid play, high event frequencies, and are predicated upon intermittent reinforcement schedules – may be highly addictive. Such machines lend themselves to being played continuously. Their 'short payout intervals' result in immediate and rapid feedback, creating ideal environments for repeated and continuous play while simultaneously minimizing the individual's opportunity to cognitively recognize the losses (Abbott, Volberg, et al. 2004). Such features have been associated with the distinction between hard and soft forms of gambling.[8] In addition to the variable ratio payout schedules of these machines, it has been argued that the 'near miss' provides the player with a form of secondary reinforcement by creating an illusion that the player is not constantly losing but rather is nearly winning (Griffiths 1999). Such types of structures are frequently found in gambling machines and scratch lottery tickets, both of which are particularly attractive to youth (Felsher et al. 2004). As well, Griffiths and Wood (2004) have argued that electronic forms of gambling generally possess other structural characteristics, including vivid colours, sounds, music, and lights, making them highly attractive and creating an aura promoting continued gambling. Other evidence exists that suggests the names of the games are both common and particularly attractive to youth. In a large-scale study of adolescent lottery playing, Felsher et al. (2004) reported youth like scratch tickets incorporating games with which they are familiar (i.e., bingo, monopoly) or those that provide an illusion of enormous payouts (e.g., Cash-for-Life). Derevensky, Gupta, Dickson, and Deguire (2001) urged caution in using popular cartoon characters such as Betty Boop on lottery tickets given their widespread appeal to underage individuals.

Technological advances continue to provide new gambling opportunities in the form of Internet gambling and more technologically advanced slot machines, VLTs, interactive lottery games, interactive television games of chance, and telephone wagering (Griffiths and Wood 2000). It is predicted that active participation in Internet gambling will increase tenfold in coming years as accessibility from one's home is easy, Internet gambling has the potential to offer visually exciting effects similar to video games, slot machines, and VLTs, and the event frequency can be very rapid, particularly if the gambler is subscribed to multiple sites (Griffiths and Wood 2000). Given the increasing popularity, accessibility, and familiarity of the Internet, this represents another venue for potential problems for adolescents. There is recent research suggesting that a large number of underage youth have gambled on the Internet without money (a number of Internet gambling sites offer players the opportunity to engage in identical activities without money with the potential for acquiring points and/or a prize), with a smaller number gambling with money (Byrne, Gupta, and Derevensky 2004; Hardoon, Derevensky, and Gupta 2002). Still further, there is evidence that youth who gamble both with and without money are more likely to exhibit gambling problems. Currently, in order to engage in these activities an individual must have a credit card. While many adolescents do not have easy access to a credit card, there remains a concern that these Internet gambling sites that permit individuals to play free games without money are in fact training a generation of youth to gamble with money once they have acquired their own credit card. Derevensky and Gupta (2004) have also suggested that the probability of winning on the free sites might not be the same as when gambling for real money. As more jurisdictions get involved in Internet gaming, there remains a concern that this will become another way in which adolescents can circumvent age restrictions. Other forms of technological advances, including mobile gambling (through cell phones), are on the horizon and represent cause for concern.

Clearly, there is a wide and disparate range of provincially regulated gambling venues in Canada including horse tracks, local convenience stores that sell lottery tickets, casinos, establishments that have VLTs, racinos, and Internet wagering, among others. These environments, in conjunction with the previously mentioned structural characteristics, encourage individuals to engage in repetitive play and loss of self-control. Although adolescents are legally prohibited from entry into many of these venues, their resourcefulness along with a lack of enforcement enables them to engage in otherwise legally prohibited activities.

There is little doubt that youth are particularly susceptible to advertisements in general and are considered an important target by advertisers. Consequently, the advertising and glamorization of gambling is of great concern. For example, the Virginia lottery has advertising campaigns linked with NASCAR racing (a highly popular sport for adolescent and young adult males). Several states have used the cartoon character Betty Boop with their lottery, with opportunities to win Betty Boop leather jackets, and other promotions include the opportunity to win Harley Davidson motorcycles, World Wrestling Federation products, and the use of popular games including baseball and football lottery scratch tickets. Some entertainment personalities have endorsed Internet gambling sites, including actor James Woods, Pamela Anderson, and Nikki Cox. Recently, 'Celebrity Poker' and the 'World Championship of Poker' have achieved enormous television ratings throughout the world with adolescents and young adults. At the International Centre for Youth Gambling Problems and High-Risk Behaviours at McGill University, one of the clients with a poker problem remarked how he tapes all the poker shows and uses the tapes as his 'educational class.' There are recent data that also suggest youth pay particular attention to lottery advertisements and, like adults, are more prone to purchase scratch tickets when they are placed on checkout counters of local convenience stores. With huge advertising budgets, provincial lottery corporations have been able to target adolescents whether directly or indirectly.

Jessor's (1998) general theory of adolescent risk behaviours conceptualizes the interactive nature of risk and protective factors as a way of predicting the likelihood of an adolescent acquiring or maintaining a particular risky behaviour. Although Jessor (1998) did not articulate youth gambling as a particularly risky behaviour, Dickson and her colleagues (2002) incorporated and expanded his model to include excessive adolescent gambling. While there are certainly some specific, unique risk factors associated with problem gambling, many of the risk factors found in adolescents cut across a number of risky behaviours (e.g., drug and alcohol use and abuse, cigarette smoking, unprotected sex, as well as gambling). In a large-scale study with adolescent problem gamblers, Dickson et al. (2008) attempted to test whether specific protective factors common to other adolescent risky behaviours were applicable to youth with gambling problems. Based upon their review of the literature, a number of variables were thought to serve as protective factors. Using self-report measures, they sought to establish whether family cohesion, mentorship, school connectedness, achievement motivation, involvement in prosocial activities, and coping strategies served to act as protective factors for excessive gambling. Their results suggest that poor family and school connectedness was symptomatic of adolescent problem gambling, with family cohesion playing a significant role as a protective factor.

In another study, Lussier, Derevensky, Gupta, Bergevin, and Ellenbogen (2007) examined resilience in the presence of identified risk factors as a possible protective factor for youth gambling problems. The resiliency literature is predicated upon the assumption that some individuals appear more immune to adversity, deprivation, and stress than others. In testing this theory with adolescents, their results suggest that vulnerable youth, those individuals scoring low on measures of resilience, are more likely to meet diagnostic criteria for problem gambling. Adolescents perceived to be vulnerable (high risk/low protective factors) had a mean gambling severity score nine times larger than the resilient group (high risk/high protective factors), eight times larger than the fortunate group (low risk/low protective factors), and thirteen times larger than the ideal group (low risk/high protective factors). Those youth identified as vulnerable were at greatest risk for experiencing gambling problems. The authors further reported that 100 per cent of the youth classified as probable pathological gamblers and 86.7 per cent classified as at risk for problem gambling were within the vulnerable group. Strikingly, only 4.3 per cent of youth identified as resilient were identified as at-risk gamblers, and none were probable pathological gamblers despite their reporting high levels of risk exposure.

It is important to note that resilience is a dynamic process encompassing positive adaptation within the context of significant adversity. Resilience is not a fixed attribute and varies depending upon situational factors, the individual's age and developmental period, and the general surrounding environment. Those youth who have not developed a gambling problem despite unfavourable circumstances have adapted, at that particular time, to the various stressors (risk factors) they face. Resilient youth seem to be able to more effectively cope with stressful situations and emotional distress in ways that enable them to develop appropriate adaptive behaviours and go on to become competent individuals (Garmezy, Masten, and Tellegren 1984).

Prospective Studies

The scientific community has been generally hampered by the lack of prospective studies examining problem gambling from childhood through adulthood. In a small study, Winters, Stinchfield, and Kim (1995) followed 532 Minnesota adolescents, aged 15 to 18 when initially assessed, over a period of eighteen months. While no overall changes in prevalence of problematic gambling occurred, there were some noticeable differences such as an increased preference for more legal/regulated gambling activities (e.g., lotteries and electronic gaming machines) and a decrease in preference for more informal gambling activities (e.g., cards, personal games of skill). In a further follow-up, Winters, Stinchfield, Botzet, and Anderson (2002) found no appreciable changes in gambling behaviour. They did, however, report that the early onset of gambling, before age 12, was related to a modest association with adult at-risk gambling problems. Winters et al. also reported that prior substance misuse and being male were risk factors for future gambling problems, with similar findings in cross-sectional research being reported by Gupta and Derevensky (1998a).

In a recently published prospective study, Vitaro et al. (2004) followed 903 males from ages 11 to 17. They identified three groups of youth based upon their developmental trajectories of gambling behaviour. Low gamblers (62 per cent) reported minimal gambling, chronic high gamblers (22 per cent) initiated gambling by age 11 and maintained or increased their gambling, and late-onset gamblers (16 per cent) did not begin gambling before age 13 but were similar to the chronic high gamblers in their gambling behaviour. Their results show that gambling problems at age 17 were highest among the chronic high gamblers (20 per cent) followed by the late-onset gamblers (15 per cent), compared with the low gamblers (4 per cent). As well, differences were found between the groups with respect to impulsivity and risk-taking measures. Vitaro and his colleagues propose that differential patterns of gamblers likely exist, and treating all adolescent problem gamblers as a homogeneous group may be inappropriate. Their results support the work of Nower and Blaszczynski (2004) suggesting different types and trajectories of problem gambling, ultimately requiring differential treatment approaches.

While a number of individual, situational, and environmental risk and protective factors have been found to be related to youth problem gambling behaviours, the causal links have not yet emerged. Abbott, Volberg, et al. (2004) correctly state that the availability, accessibility, and structural features of specific games most likely combine with an individual's psychosocial characteristics in various ways to create rather complex patterns of risk. To date, our knowledge still remains limited as to the combinations of risk and protective factors that interact to decrease the likelihood of specific individuals engaging in gambling excessively. Similarly, our understanding of those protective factors that may minimize and reduce the risk of excessive gambling remains limited. While we can continue to examine the commonality of risk and protective factors between gambling and other addictive behaviours, only longitudinal and prospective studies will be able to help resolve this issue. Longitudinal and sector-specific studies can identify and elucidate where the lines of risk and resilience intersect, within individuals and the wider population, and their interactions with different forms of gambling (Abbott et al. 2004).

Given the pervasiveness of the problems associated with youth gambling and the concomitant mental health, social, economic, educational, and legal problems, there is a necessity to clearly identify the risk factors associated with problem gambling. We need a better understanding of the effects of accessibility and availability of gaming venues on future gambling behaviours. Specific research also needs to focus on gambling advertisements and their relationship to the onset and maintenance of adolescent gambling and problem gambling.

Treatment

Beginning in the mid-1990s, Canadian provinces began a concerted effort in funding gambling treatment programs, although most were developed for adult problem gamblers (Azmier 2001). While annual expenditures for treatment vary considerably from province to province, the amounts being allocated are considerably higher than in most other countries.[9] The current treatment paradigms for adolescents and young adults have been based upon a number of theoretical approaches that parallel those used for adults, including psychoanalytic or psychodynamic, behavioural, cognitive and cognitive-behavioural, pharmacological, physiological, biological/genetic, addiction-based models or self-help models.[10]

The resulting treatment paradigms incorporate a rather narrow focus depending upon the therapists' theoretical orientation to the etiology of a gambling problem and their background work in the field of addictions. Abbott, Volberg, et al. (2004), in reviewing the treatment literature, concluded that the ability to design effective treatment programs for problem gamblers has been hampered by a lack of theoretical understanding of the etiology underlying problem gambling. They further argue that while the biomedical model has dominated the treatment community within the United States, the cognitive-behavioural model or social learning theory model has been dominant in other countries. Currently, there is a lack of consensus on what constitutes the best practices or empirically validated treatment approaches for treating both adolescents and adults with gambling problems (Nathan 2001; Toneatto and Ladouceur 2003). Too few treatment centres work with adolescents specifically for gambling problems, few underage problem gamblers actually present themselves for treatment, treatment approaches may vary within a centre, and the number of controlled treatment efficacy studies is extremely limited.

There is considerable empirical evidence that gambling involves a complex and dynamic interaction between ecological, psychophysiological, developmental, cognitive, and behavioural components and that problem gamblers are not a homogeneous group. Given these assumptions, Gupta and Derevensky (2000, 2004, 2008) contend that a dynamic interactive approach needs to take into account the multiplicity of interacting factors into a treatment paradigm for youth experiencing significant gambling problems. Empirical support for Jacobs's general theory of addiction for adolescent problem gamblers (Gupta and Derevensky 1998b) further implies that adolescent problem and pathological gamblers exhibit evidence of abnormal physiological resting states, report significantly greater emotional distress and anxiety, have increased levels of dissociation when gambling, and are more likely to have higher rates of comorbidity with other addictive behaviours. As such, Gupta and Derevensky concluded that treating gambling problems in isolation of other social, physiological, developmental, cognitive, and emotional difficulties consuming the adolescent may lead to short-term success, but at the expense of relapsing.

Current treatment studies have generally been case studies with small sample sizes and have been criticized for not being subjected to rigorous scientific standards. Ladouceur and his colleagues have long argued for a cognitive-behavioural approach to treating both adults and youth with gambling problems (e.g., Ladouceur, Sylvain, et al. 1998; Ladouceur and Walker 1998). Underlying the cognitive-behavioural approach is the assumption that pathological gamblers continue to gamble in spite of repeated losses because they maintain an unrealistic belief that losses will be recovered. This perspective also assumes that it is the individual's erroneous beliefs (i.e., a lack of understanding of the notion of independence of events, erroneous perceptions concerning the level of skill required to be successful in predicting the outcome of chance events, and an illusion of personal control and skill) that ultimately foster persistent gambling behaviour. While the empirical literature examining treatment paradigms for adolescents is scant, Ladouceur et al. (1994), using four adolescent male pathological gamblers, implemented a cognitive-behavioural therapy program and reported clinically significant improvements in the individuals' beliefs about the perception of control when gambling and a significant reduction in the number and severity of gambling problems. Six months after treatment, three of the adolescents were reported to have sustained initial treatment gains and were abstinent. Ladouceur and his colleagues concluded that the cognitive-behavioural approach shows promise as a treatment intervention for adolescents with gambling problems.

Gupta and Derevensky (2000, 2004, 2008) have described a treatment model predicated upon their research and clinical findings that youth problem gamblers generally exhibit depressive symptomatology, somatic disorders, anxiety, attention deficits, academic, personal, and familial problems, high risk taking, and poor coping skills, ultimately using gambling as a form of stress-reduction and a way of escaping daily and long-term problems. Gupta and Derevensky acknowledge that these individuals also experience numerous erroneous cognitive beliefs and distortions. They contend that one must effectively deal with their underlying psychological problems as well as the specific gambling problem.

Of great promise is Nower and Blaszczynski's (2004) pathways approach to treating youth gamblers. They suggest that a multifaceted constellation of risk and protective factors differentially influences adolescents, who otherwise display similar phenomenological features and patterns following alternative and distinct pathways towards a gambling disorder. Originally proposed for adult pathological gamblers, the approach suggests that a similar model is plausible for use when explaining adolescent gambling problems. The model, previously discussed, proposes at least three subgroups of adolescent problem and pathological gamblers with distinct clinical features and etiologies. Nower and Blaszczynski (2004) contend that the pathways model is composed of individuals who share certain similar processes and symptomatic features, yet three major but distinct pathways leading to pathological gambling exist, necessitating different therapeutic approaches.

While all youth pathological gamblers are subject to ecological variables, operant and classical conditioning, and cognitive reasoning distortions, Nower and Blaszczynski contend that differences between subgroups have major implications for both diagnosis and treatment. They suggest that pathway 1 youth gamblers are normal in temperament, but lose control when gambling as a result of the intermittent reinforcement schedules and probabilities of success so common in most forms of gambling. In contrast, pathway 2 gamblers are characterized by having disrupted and/or poor familial and personal histories, affective instability and disorders, and inefficient coping and problem-solving skills. As such, these individuals are more likely to view gambling as a means of emotional escape and mood regulation. Finally, those adolescents in pathway 3 are more likely to exhibit distinct biological vulnerabilities towards impulsivity, have heightened arousal-seeking and sensation-seeking behaviours, are more likely to have had an early onset of gambling, and exhibit significant attention deficits and antisocial traits. While empirical research is needed to determine the relative proportion of youth in each pathway and to validate the proposed model and its implications for treatment, identifying the appropriate pathway for youth gamblers will provide a useful clinical framework that should ultimately provide a differential treatment approach and improve treatment outcomes.

Work by Hodgins and his colleagues (Hodgins and el-Guebaly 2000; Hodgins, Currie, and el-Guebaly 2001) has suggested that Prochaska and DiClemente's stages of change model may be useful in helping to understand treatment and natural recovery of pathological gamblers. DiClemente, Story, and Murray (2000) and DiClemente, Delahanty, and Schlundt (2004) have also suggested that a stage theory model[11] represents a viable conceptual framework for explaining a treatment paradigm for adolescent pathological gamblers. While this may have important implications for youth problem gamblers, little empirical support currently exists confirming its utility.

Hodgins and his colleagues have also empirically evaluated short-term brief motivational enhancement therapy and telephone counselling with and without manuals developed for adult pathological gamblers. Their results imply that brief telephone counselling and the use of a home-based manual may be effective, especially for those with less severe gambling problems (Hodgins and el-Guebaly 2000; Hodgins, Currie, and el-Guebaly 2001). Given that many adolescents fail to seek treatment in traditional therapeutic settings, the use of telephone counselling and manuals, which can be mailed to an individual's home, may be an important innovative and promising approach to helping adolescents with gambling problems.[12]

Clearly, the research on the effective treatment of adolescent pathological gamblers is limited and in its early stages. Further research into the efficacy of alternative treatment models for youth problem gamblers is necessary before recommendations for best practices can be reliably established. It may well be that some of the previously established treatment models for other mental health disorders and addictive behaviours can be applied to youth with gambling problems given the significant overlap in risk factors. As with treatment models for other mental health problems, such approaches may require further refinement.

In light of the research on adult problem gambler subtypes, it remains important to determine the efficacy of different interventions and therapeutic approaches for subgroups with differing and diverse needs. Abbott, Volberg, et al. (2004) suggest that given the diverse needs of subtypes of individuals with gambling problems (although they refer to adults, a similar argument can be made for adolescents), it is most unlikely that any one treatment strategy can be maximally beneficial to all. It is highly plausible that some treatment models may be more effective with certain subgroups or subtypes of pathological gamblers. Abbott, Volberg, et al. caution clinical researchers against placing heterogeneous groups together and failing to account for their diversity when analysing outcome measures, as it may well inflate the variance and obscure the potential positive effects of treatment. As well, they recommend substantially increased research on understanding differential treatment effects towards reduced, controlled gambling compared to abstinence.

The issue of natural recovery is increasingly imperative. If the current adolescent rates maintain themselves over time, the percentage of adults with gambling problems may in fact increase. Although this has not yet been the case, there is also some speculation that natural recovery may be the primary reason. Given adult lifetime prevalence rates are always higher than past-year problem gambling rates, and that adolescent prevalence rates are higher than adult rates, many individuals with gambling problems must be stopping on their own. Studies have not yet examined the path that natural recovery takes among adolescents and adults experiencing significant gambling and gambling-related problems and its potential impact for treatment.

Finally, the field of psychopharmacology may provide a complementary strategy for working with adolescents experiencing significant gambling problems. While the current pharmacological strategies for treating pathological gambling in adults suggest the use of mood stabilizers, and naltrexone for adults, little is known about their success with adolescents. Grant, Chambers, and Potenza (2004) contend that while the data point to potentially promising pharmacological treatments for adolescent pathological gambling, recommendations must await completion of controlled treatment studies with adolescents.

As a combination of both behavioural and drug therapies has been demonstrated in other addictive disorders to be superior to either treatment alone (Carroll 1997), and as further research and refinement in matching treatment strategies with gambler typologies is undertaken, it is likely that best practices for treating adolescents with gambling problems will eventually be realized. Nevertheless, Abbott, Volberg, et al. (2004) in their review of treatment outcome studies concluded that it appears that individuals who have received treatment for a myriad of mental health problems and addictions generally do better than controls who did not receive any formal treatment. From the available literature they went on to conclude that, irrespective of the particular type of therapy, most clients who show initial improvement maintain it, albeit that probability of relapse increases with time (Abbott, Volberg, et al. 2004). Further research in understanding the barriers to treatment and treatment efficacy for youth will aid treatment approaches.

Prevention Models

Limited progress has been made in understanding the treatment of problem adolescent gambling and the characteristics of those seeking help, and empirical knowledge concerning prevention of gambling problems and its translation into science-based prevention initiatives is similarly scarce (Derevensky, Gupta, Dickson, and Deguire 2001). Fortunately, prevention specialists in the gambling field have drawn heavily upon the substantial research on prevention of adolescent alcohol and substance abuse and have adapted these programs for adolescents.

Current prevention efforts in the fields of alcohol and drug abuse focus upon the risk and protective factors and their interaction (Dickson et al. 2000). These efforts seek to prevent or limit the effects of risk factors while enhancing resilience through protective factors. Although few scientifically validated prevention initiatives currently exist for problem gambling, the increasingly widespread use of a harm-reduction/harm-minimization approach in the field of alcohol and substance abuse may be a useful strategy in preventing gambling problems (Dickson, Derevensky, and Gupta 2004).[13] Based upon current theoretical and empirical evidence of common risk and protective factors across adolescent risky behaviours, it is advocated that prevention initiatives move towards designing prevention strategies that are inclusive and target multiple risk behaviours (Jessor 1998), including problem gambling (Dickson et al. 2004).

As an overarching framework, harm reduction (also referred to as harm minimization) includes strategies, policies, or programs designed to promote responsible gambling and gambling reduction without requiring abstinence. By definition, this framework includes secondary prevention strategies, predicated upon the assumption that it is not feasible and is highly unlikely that one can prevent individuals from participating in particular risky behaviours (Baer, MacLean, and Marlatt 1998); tertiary prevention strategies (DiClemente 1999); as well as a 'health movement' strategy (Denning and Little 2001). It is important to note that a responsible approach incorporating a harm-minimization approach does not in and of itself preclude abstinence, especially for young children.

Accepting harm reduction as a health paradigm in lieu of, or as an interim step towards, an abstinence model, this approach remains value-neutral and supports strategies aimed at reducing harmful negative consequences incurred through involvement in risky behaviours (Dickson et al. 2004; Messerlian, Derevensky, and Gupta 2004). Underage youth are legally prohibited from accessing regulated gambling venues, consistent with an abstinence model. While these age-related statutes vary from province to province and are dependent upon the specific form of gambling (i.e., lottery purchases in general have lower age restrictions than VLT and casino entry in many jurisdictions), they remain necessary and are in need of stricter enforcement and adherence. Early gambling experiences among children and adolescents occur for both non-regulated forms of gambling (e.g., playing cards for money, placing informal bets among peers on sports events, etc.) as well as all forms of legalized and provincially regulated games (e.g., lottery purchases, casino games). As Dickson et al. (2004) noted, this highlights both the paradox and the confusion as to which primary prevention approach to promote – either abstinence or harm reduction. It may not be realistic to expect youth to stop gambling when there is ample research suggesting that upwards of 80 per cent of adolescents report having gambled during the past year (Jacobs 2004; National Research Council 1999), especially with family members (Gupta and Derevensky 1998a). Still further, gambling has become viewed as a respectable and socially acceptable form of entertainment (Azmier 2000), which is offered and promoted by the state. As with adult gambling, it could be argued that it is unrealistic to expect youth to stop gambling entirely, especially since it is exceedingly difficult to regulate and enforce access to all forms of gambling. In any case, the vast majority of youth who gamble do so without developing any significant gambling-related problems.

The application and the mode of prevention approaches have continuously shifted from abstinence to informed use. Beck (1998) has described the cycle of the 'just say no' approach to the 'just say know' approach that has taken place in the drug prevention movement. He contends that the 'just say no' climate resulted from inaccurate information being conveyed to youth in an attempt to intimidate and persuade them to abstain from drug use. According to Beck, this approach fostered widespread distrust and a resultant discounting of all messages independent of their credibility. In contrast to this approach, the 'just say know' movement appears more viable and closely parallels the harm-reduction model where prevention/education strategies focus upon providing cognitive education and fostering decision-making skills, with the ultimate goal of minimizing the negative consequences associated with drug abuse and dependency. Unfortunately, while these early programs often resulted in significant gains in knowledge, they were found to be generally ineffective both in the reduction of the use of illicit drugs as well as in fostering healthier attitudes towards their use (Schaps, DiBartolo, et al. 1981).

Despite the complexities of using a risk-protective factor model, this model can be used as the theoretical basis of harm reduction because of its role in science-based prevention and its empirical validity in adolescent risk behaviour theory. Changes in risk and protective factors have been shown to account for changes in targeted behaviours, attitudes, and so forth. A strength of the risk-protective factor model is that it quantitatively measures changing rates of harmful consequences of risky behaviours. The model thus enables prevention specialists to create, evaluate, and refine harm-reduction prevention programs.

DiClemente's (1999) theory of intentional behavioural change has also been used to understand the initiation of health-related behaviours including gambling, along with the modification of problem behaviours such as excessive alcohol use and problem gambling (DiClemente et al. 2000, 2004).

In light of the need for prevention programs, a number of gambling-specific curricula materials, videos, student-developed screenplays and productions, poster and public service announcement contests, and CD-ROMS have been developed. Such school-based curricula are generally aimed at secondary school children, although the International Centre for Youth Gambling Problems and High-Risk Behaviours at McGill University has extended its curricula material downward into the later elementary school grades based upon evidence that problem gamblers often report gambling by age 9 or 10 (Derevensky and Gupta 1996; Gupta and Derevensky 1998a). The centre's prevention efforts include empirically validated school-based workshops, a paper-pencil curriculum, award-winning interactive CD-ROMs ('The Amazing Chateau' for primary school; 'Hooked City' for secondary school), a DVD docudrama ('Clean Break'), and poster and public service announcement contests. The Responsible Gambling Council of Ontario has had several student-written screenplays produced and performed throughout Ontario, and the Alberta Alcohol and Drug Abuse Commission, among others, has produced a series of videos focused on adolescent problem gambling.

Many early efforts suggest the positive utility of a general mental health prevention program that addresses multiple adolescent risky behaviours (e.g., substance abuse, gambling, risky driving, smoking, truancy, and risky sexual activity) simultaneously. While adolescent risky behaviours share many common risk factors, the activities themselves can differ on several important dimensions.

Whether harm-reduction prevention programs are designed specifically for problem gambling or incorporated into a general mental health curriculum targeting multiple high-risk behaviours, the need for merging an abstinence approach with a harm-reduction prevention model is exemplified by the apparent contradiction that arises when the principles of the harm-reduction paradigm are applied to adolescents. Research highlights that the age of onset of gambling behaviour represents a significant risk factor, with age of initiation being correlated with the development of gambling-related problems. As a result, delaying the age of onset of gambling experiences may be fundamental in a successful prevention paradigm yet is more appropriate to an abstinence model. On the other hand, teaching responsible gambling through enhancement of emotional and cognitive coping skills and by providing cognitive decision-making tools may be appropriate. School-based programs need to target specific information about gambling to various age groups, educating youth about the forms of gambling they will most likely be exposed to at each particular age (e.g., 9-year-olds are likely exposed to scratch tickets and bingo). One of the central goals of science-based prevention is to promote resilience. Thus, we need to ensure that harm-reduction prevention programs include components that enhance salient protective and resource factors specific to the period of adolescent development. Despite the lack of emphasis on promoting resilience in current harm-reduction prevention programs, both resource factors (those operating independent of risk status) and protective factors (those that interact with risk status) contribute to one's resilience and need to be considered in the design of effective youth gambling prevention programs.

To date, the research community has contributed little to an understanding of the role of protective factors in adolescent gambling problems. Nevertheless, there is ample research to suggest that direct and moderator effects of protection can be used to guide the development of prevention and intervention efforts to help minimize adolescent risky behaviours. An adapted version of Jessor's (1998) adolescent risk behaviour model, delineated by Dickson et al. (2002), provides a useful framework from which to begin the much-needed research that can ultimately lead to the development of effective, science-based prevention initiatives for minimizing problem gambling among youth. It is also vital to note that other forms of prevention have been initiated, including self-exclusion bans for those of legal age to gamble in a casino; extensive training of educators, public health workers, and parents; media campaigns designed to raise awareness that adolescent gambling may not be such a benign behaviour; training programs for vendors; and targeted responsible gambling features on electronic gambling machines.

Conclusions

Adolescence is a developmental period marked by significant physiological, cognitive, and emotional changes. It is a time associated with experimentation and an increase in risk-related behaviours, be it alcohol and drug use, cigarette smoking, and/or gambling. There remains little doubt that adolescents constitute a particularly high-risk group for engaging in a wide variety of potentially risky behaviours. Adolescents are also prone to acquiring gambling problems given their high rates of risk taking, their perceived invulnerability, their lack of recognition that gambling can lead to serious problems, the accessibility of gambling venues, its widespread social acceptability and availability, and the glamorization of gambling.

Given that it takes several years to develop a significant gambling problem, the true social impact and long-term consequences upon youth will likely take years to realize. Today's generation of youth will likely spend their entire life in an environment where gambling is prolific, provincially supported and regulated, and viewed as a socially acceptable form of entertainment. Equally important is that under most governmental statutes children and adolescents are prohibited from engaging in legalized/regulated forms of gambling. Yet, there is ample evidence to suggest that most youth have little difficulty accessing most forms of regulated gambling venues (Felsher, Derevensky, and Gupta 2004; Jacobs 2004). A serious effort must be made to ensure that vendors and gaming operators adhere to existing laws and regulations.

The field of youth gambling is relatively new, and as a result there currently are significant gaps in our knowledge. Much of the research to date has focused on prevalence studies. Unfortunately, large-scale longitudinal research conducted following individuals from youth to adulthood is only beginning. There is ample research from the alcohol, drug, and cigarette-smoking literature to suggest that a risk-resiliency model may have significant benefits for our understanding. Why some individuals appear to be at high risk for developing a significant gambling problem requires further research.

Research is essential to identify common and unique risk and protective factors for gambling problems and other addictive behaviours; and longitudinal research to examine the natural history of pathological gambling from childhood to adolescence through later adulthood is required. Molecular, genetic, and neuropsychological research is necessary to help account for changes in gambling progression. Research assessing whether certain gambling activities may become a gateway to subsequent gambling problems is required; and the development and/or refinement of current instruments used to assess adolescent gambling severity is necessary. A robust understanding of the effects of accessibility and availability of gaming venues on future gambling behaviours has yet to be reached. Similarly, there is a need to examine the impact of gambling advertisements and general availability of gambling opportunities, and their relationship to the onset and maintenance of adolescent gambling and problem gambling. There is little doubt that more basic applied and longitudinal research is necessary to investigate psychosocial, biological, and environmental/situational risk factors associated with youth experiencing gambling problems. Lastly, additional research is also needed to examine the changes in prevalence rates, differences among gambling measurement screens, and cultural and ethnic differences.

From a treatment perspective, funding must be available to continue to help those youth currently experiencing severe gambling and gambling-related behaviours and their families. Along with our current treatment initiatives, we must begin a thorough exploration of best practices for working with youth and alternative ways in which they can be encouraged to seek help for gambling problems.

As previously noted, many other more highly visible adolescent mental health problems have prompted social policy interventions (e.g., cigarette smoking, alcohol and substance use and abuse, increased rates of suicide). Only recently have health professionals, educators, and public policy makers acknowledged the need for the prevention of problem gambling. Reviews of the literature examining prevention initiatives have generally concluded that most pathological gambling prevention programs lack a strong theoretical foundation, and have been implemented without being empirically evaluated. This remains a serious concern as such programs may inadvertently be increasing the appeal of gambling and subsequently an increase in gambling behaviour. While most existing prevention programs are school-based and aimed at children and adolescents, this should not be misinterpreted to suggest that only youth remain at risk for the development of a serious pathological gambling problem. Rather, youth, while vulnerable, represent an easy population to reach for receiving prevention programs.

Problematic gambling during adolescence is an important and growing social and public health issue. While the incidence of severe gambling problems among youth remains relatively small, the large number of children and adolescents gambling is of concern. The long-term consequences and impact upon youth with gambling problems, their families, and friends can be significant. The proliferation of gambling venues and the social acceptability of gambling in light of the lack of widespread prevention initiatives represents an enormous social experiment for which we currently do not know the long-term consequences.

NOTES

1 Racinos are typically horse tracks that have added electronic gambling games including slot machines and/or VLTs.

2 For a comprehensive discussion, see Chevalier, Deguire, Gupta, and Derevensky (2003); Gupta and Derevensky (2004); NORC (1999); NRC (1999).

3 Severe gambling problems have often been termed problem, compulsive, probable/pathological, disordered, pathological, or Level III gambling.

4 See the reviews by Derevensky and Gupta (2004); Jacobs (2004); National Research Council (1999); and the meta-analysis by Shaffer and Hall (1996).

5 Derevensky and Gupta (2000) performed an item analysis on the endorsement rates using the DSM-IV-J (Diagnostic and Statistical Manual, Fourth Edition, for Juveniles) gambling screen. A number of adolescent gambling screens for assessing gambling severity exist. The DSM-IV-J was modelled after the DSM for adult pathological gamblers. This screen was modified from the original screen for adults (American Psychiatric Association 1992).

6 See the work of Jessor (1998) for risk factors associated with a number of adolescent risky behaviours, and Dickson, Derevensky, and Gupta (2002) in its application for problem gambling.

7 See Baboushkin, Hardoon, Derevensky, and Gupta (2001) and Felsher, Derevensky, and Gupta (2004) for examples.

8 See Griffiths (1995) and Griffiths and Wood (2004) for a more thorough discussion.

9 Abbott et al. (2004) provide a comprehensive comparison between countries.

10 For a comprehensive overview of these models, the reader is referred to the reviews by Griffiths (1995); Lesieur (1998); Petry (2005); Rugle, Derevensky, Gupta, Winters, and Stinchfield (2001); and Toneatto and Ladouceur (2003).

11 Specifically, the Transtheoretical Model of Intentional Behaviour Change.

12 See Derevensky, Gupta, and Winters (2003) for a discussion as to why adolescents don't seek treatment for gambling problems.

13 See Abbott et al. (2004) and Derevensky, Gupta, Dickson, and Deguire (2001) for a comprehensive review and list of current programs.

Appendix A
Major Canadian Gambling Resources

Alberta Gaming Research Institute
HUB Mall
University of Alberta
8909S – 112 Street
Edmonton, AB T6G 2C5
Tel.: (780) 492-2856
E-mail: abgaming@ualberta.ca
Web: www.abgaminginstitute.ualberta.ca

British Columbia Partnership for Responsible Gambling
Problem Gambling Program
Gaming Policy and Enforcement Branch
PO Box 9311, Stn Prov Govt
Victoria, BC V8W 9N1
Tel.: (250) 387-0757
Fax: (250) 356-1910
E-mail: info@bcresponsiblegambling.ca
Web: www.bcresponsiblegambling.ca

Canada Safety Council
1020 Thomas Spratt Place
Ottawa, ON K1G 5L5
Tel.: (613) 739-1535
Fax: (613) 739-1566
E-mail: canadasafetycouncil@safety-council.org
Web: www.safety-council.org

Canada West Foundation
Suite 900, 1202 Centre Street S
Calgary, AB T2G 5A5
Tel.: (403) 264-9535
Toll Free: 1-888-TALK CWF (825-5293)
Fax: (403) 269-4776
E-mail: cwf@cwf.ca
Web: www.cwf.ca

International Centre for Youth Gambling Problems and High-Risk
    Behaviours
Duggan House, McGill University
3724 McTavish
Montreal, QC H3A 1Y2
Tel.: (514) 398-1391
Fax: (514) 398-3401
E-mail: ygi@youthgambling.com
Web: www.youthgambling.com

Nova Scotia Gaming Foundation
1660 Hollis Street, Suite 305
PO Box 2392, Halifax CRO
Halifax, NS B3J 3E4
Tel.: (902) 424-0963
Toll Free: 1-866-424-0963
Fax: (902) 424-3601
E-mail: info@nsgamingfoundation.org
Web: www.nsgamingfoundation.org

Ontario Problem Gambling Research Centre
150 Research Park Lane, Suite 104
Guelph, ON N1G 4T2
Tel.: (519) 763-8049, ext. 226
Toll Free: 1-877-882-2204
Fax: (519) 763-8521
E-mail: info@gamblingresearch.org
Web: www.gamblingresearch.org

Responsible Gambling Council of Ontario
3080 Yonge Street, Suite 4070, Box 90

Toronto, ON M4N 3N1
Tel.: (416) 499-9800
Toll Free: 1-888-391-1111
Fax: (416) 499-8260

Appendix B
Problem Gambling Helplines

Alberta Problem Gambling Hotline
Confidential and open 24 hrs. a day. 1-866-33AADAC
(1-866-332-2322)

British Columbia Problem Gambling Helpline
Confidential and open 24 hrs. a day. 1-888-795-6111

Manitoba Problem Gambling Helpline
Confidential and open 24 hrs. a day. 1-800-463-1554

New Brunswick Problem Gambling Helpline
Confidential and open 24 hrs. a day. 1-800-461-1234

Newfoundland and Labrador Helpline
Gambling Crisis Helpline. 1-888-899-4357

Nova Scotia Problem Gambling Helpline
Confidential and open 24 hrs. a day. 1-888-347-8888;
1-888-347-3331 (hearing impaired)

Nunavut Kamatsiaqtut Helpline
Anonymous and confidential telephone counselling
7:00 p.m. to midnight, 7 nights a week
979-3333 (Iqaluit)
1-800-265-3333 (Communities)

Ontario Toll Free Problem Gambling Helpline Number

Confidential and open 24 hrs. a day. Available in English & French.
1-888-230-3505

Prince Edward Island Confidential. 1-888-299-8399

Quebec Gambling Help and Referral Line
Confidential and open 24 hrs. a day. 1-800-461-0140 *or* 1-866-SOS-JEUX
(1-866-767-5389)

Saskatchewan Problem Gambling Helpline
Confidential and open 24 hrs. a day. 1-800-306-6789

Yukon
Confidential and open 24 hrs. a day. 1-800-661-0408

Bibliography

Archival Sources

Attorney General of Alberta. 1919. Deputy Attorney General of Alberta, letter to Rev. Dr Shearer, Social Service League, Toronto, 24 June. Provincial Archives of Alberta, Edmonton, Records of the Attorney General of Alberta, 83.192, file 119.
– 1925. Report by Sgt T. Hidson, Alberta Provincial Police, on 'Alleged gambling joint at Stavely,' 23 October. Provincial Archives of Alberta, Edmonton, Records of the Attorney General of Alberta, 83.192, file 94.
– 1927. Form letter, 'To the Mayor, (City of or Town of _____).' Dated 21 June. Edmonton, Alberta; closing salutation, 'Yours Truly, Deputy Attorney General.' Provincial Archives of Alberta, Edmonton, Records of the Attorney General of Alberta, 83.192, file 119.
Board of Home Missions of the Presbyterian Church in Canada. 1919. Minutes of meeting, 19 March. Library and Archives Canada, Ottawa, RG 13, Vol. 233, file 1919–478.
Cameron, J. McKinley. 1936–9. Notes and correspondence relating to cases of Chinese gambling in Calgary. J. McKinley Cameron fonds, Glenbow Institute Archives, Calgary, M6840, file 799.
Hone, A.W. (St Paul's United Church, Tillsonburg, Ontario). 1928. Letter to Minister of Justice, Ottawa, 21 August. Library and Archives Canada, Ottawa, RG 13, Vol. 1994, file 1432/1928.
Linke, Mrs B.E. (Ferintosh, Alberta). 1920. Letter to Attorney General, Ottawa, 10 April. Library and Archives Canada, Ottawa, RG 13, Vol. 248, file 1920/989.
Macartney, John (Presbyterian minister, Utterson, Ontario). 1924. Letter to Prime Minister W.L. Mackenzie King, 4 March. Library and Archives Canada, Ottawa, RG 13, Vol. 286, file 523/1924.

Maddison, C. Wilmott (Lethbridge, Alberta). 1930. Letter to Minister of Justice, Ottawa, 2 August. Library and Archives Canada, Ottawa, RG 13, Vol. 343, file 1930/1933.

UFWO (United Farm Women of Ontario). 1922. UFWO President's Report (Mrs J.S. Amos), 12 December. Minutes of the United Farm Women of Ontario. Leonard Harman/UCO Collection (XA 1 MS A126005). Archival Collections, University of Guelph Library.

Published Sources

Abbott, M.W., and Volberg, R.A. 2000. *Taking the Pulse on Gambling and Problem Gambling in New Zealand: Phase One of the 1999 National Prevalence Study. Report Number Three of the New Zealand Gaming Survey*. Wellington: Department of Internal Affairs.

Abbott, M.W., Volberg, R.A., Bellringer, M., and Reith, G. 2004. *A Review of Research on Aspects of Problem Gambling. Final Report*. Prepared for the Responsibility in Gambling Trust, London.

Abbott, M.W., Volberg, R.A., and Ronnberg, S. 2004. 'Comparing the New Zealand and Swedish National Surveys of Gambling and Problem Gambling.' *Journal of Gambling Studies* 20: 37–258.

Abt, Vicki. 1996. 'The Role of the State in the Expansion and Growth of Commercial Gambling in the United States.' In Jan McMillen, ed., *Gambling Cultures: Studies in History and Interpretation*. London: Routledge. 179–98.

Abt, V., Smith, J.F., and Christiansen, E.M. 1985. *The Business of Risk: Commercial Gambling in Mainstream America*. Lawrence: University Press of Kansas.

ACNielsen. 2005. 'Evaluation of the 3-Hour Shutdown of NSW Clubs.' Sydney: NSW Department of Gaming and Racing. Available: http://www.olgr.nsw. gov.au/gaming_info_research_reports.asp/. Accessed 16 July 2007.

Adams, P. July 2004. 'Minimizing the Impact of Gambling in the Subtle Degradation of Democratic Systems.' *Journal of Gambling Issues* 11, Available: http://www.camh.net/egambling/archive/pdf/JGI-issue11/JGI-issue11-complete.pdf. Accessed 20 December 2004.

Adlaf, E., and Ialomiteanu, A. 2000. 'Prevalence and Problem Gambling in Adolescents: Findings from the 1999 Ontario Student Drug Use Survey.' *Canadian Journal of Psychiatry* 45: 752–5.

Akers, R. 1985. *Deviant Behavior: A Social Learning Approach*. 3rd Ed. Belmont: Wadsworth.

– 1997. *Criminological Theories*. 2nd Ed. Los Angeles: Roxbury Publishing.

Albanese, J. 2000. 'The Causes of Organized Crime.' *Journal of Contemporary Criminal Justice* 16(4): 409–23.

Alberta Gaming and Liquor Commission. 2002. *2001–2002 Annual Report.* St Albert, AB.

Alberta Gaming Research Institute. 2008. 'Canada Casinos.' Available: www.abgaminginstitute.ualberta.ca. Accessed 19 March 2008.

Alexander, Jeffrey C., Giesen, Bernhard, and Mast, Jason L., eds. 2006. *Social Performance: Symbolic Action, Cultural Pragmatics, and Ritual.* Cambridge: Cambridge University Press.

Alexander, Jeffrey C., and Smith, Philip. 2003. 'The Strong Program in Cultural Sociology: Elements of a Structural Hermeneutics.' In Jeffrey Alexander, ed., *The Meanings of Social Life: A Cultural Sociology.* New York: Oxford University Press. 11–26.

Alfieri, D. 1994. 'The Ontario Casino Project: A Case Study.' In Colin Campbell, ed., *Gambling in Canada: The Bottom Line.* Burnaby, BC: Criminology Research Centre, Simon Fraser University. 85–91.

Allcock, C. 2003. 'A Dinosaur Looks Backwards and Forwards.' In G. Coman, ed., *Proceedings of the 13th National Association for Gambling Studies Annual Conference, Canberra, Australia.* Canberra: National Association for Gambling Studies. 4–11.

Allen, R. 1971. *The Social Passion: Religion and Social Reform in Canada, 1914–1918.* Toronto: University of Toronto Press.

– 1976. 'The Social Gospel as the Religion of Agrarian Revolt.' In C. Berger and R. Cook, eds., *The West and the Nation: Essays in Honour of W.L. Morton.* Toronto: McClelland and Stewart.

American Psychiatric Association. 1992. *Diagnostic and Statistical Manual – Fourth Edition* (DSM-IV). Washington, DC: American Psychiatric Association.

Auditor General of British Columbia. July 2005. *Keeping the Decks Clean: Managing Gaming Integrity Risks in Casinos.* Victoria, BC. Available: http://www.bcauditor.com/AuditorGeneral.htm. Accessed 20 July 2005.

Australian Bureau of Statistics. 1999. *Gambling Industries.* Cat. 8684.0. Canberra, Australia.

Australian Gaming Council. 2007. 'A Database on Australia's Gambling Industries.' Available: http://www.austgamingcouncil.org.au.

Austrin, Terry, and West, Jackie. 2004. 'New Deals in Gambling: Global Markets and Local Regimes of Regulation.' *Research in the Sociology of Work: Globalism/Localism at Work* 13: 143–58.

Azmier, Jason. 2000. *Canadian Gambling Behaviour and Attitudes: Summary Report.* Gambling in Canada Research Report No. 8 (February). Calgary: Canada West Foundation. CWF Publication No. 200001.

– 2001. *Gambling in Canada: An Overview.* Gambling in Canada Research Report

No. 13 (August). Calgary: Canada West Foundation. CWF Publication No. 200107.

– 2001b. *Gambling in Canada: Final Report and Recommendations.* Gambling in Canada Research Report No. 16 (November). Calgary: Canada West Foundation.

– 2005. *Gambling in Canada: Statistics and Context.* Calgary: Canada West Foundation.

Azmier, J., Jepson, V., and Pickup, M. 1998. *Rolling the Dice: Alberta's Experience with Direct Democracy and Video Lottery Terminals.* (September). Calgary: Canada West Foundation.

Azmier, J., Kelley, R., and Todosichuk, P. 2001. *Triumph, Tragedy or Trade Off? Considering the Impact of Gambling.* Research Report No. 14 (August). Calgary: Canada West Foundation. CWF Publication No. 200108.

Azmier, J., and Roach, R. 2000. *The Ethics of Charitable Gambling: A Survey.* Gambling in Canada Research Report No. 10 (December). Calgary: Canada West Foundation.

Azmier, J., Smith, G.J., and the Canada West Foundation. 1998. *The State of Gambling in Canada: An Interprovincial Roadmap of Gambling and Its Impact.* Calgary: Canada West Foundation.

Baboushkin, H., Hardoon, K., Derevensky, J., and Gupta, R. 2001. 'Underlying Cognitions in Gambling Behavior amongst University Students.' *Journal of Applied Social Psychology* 31: 1–23.

Badgley, Kerry. 2000. *Ringing in the Common Love of Good: The United Farmers of Ontario, 1914–1926.* Montreal and Kingston: McGill-Queen's University Press.

Baer, J.S., MacLean, M.G., and Marlatt, G.A. 1998. 'Linking Etiology and Treatment for Adolescent Substance Abuse: Toward a Better Match.' In R. Jessor, ed., *New Perspectives on Adolescent Risk Behaviour.* New York: Cambridge University Press.

Banks, G. 2002. 'The Productivity Commission's Gambling Inquiry: Three Years On.' Presentation to the 12th Annual Conference of the National Association for Gambling Studies, Canberra, Australia. Available: http://www.pc.gov.au/speeches/cs20021121/index.html. Accessed 21 December 2006.

– 2007. 'Gambling in Australia: Are We Balancing the Equation?' Presented to Australian Gaming Expo Conference, Sydney, 19 August. Available: http://www.pc.gov.au/speeches/cs20070819/index.html.

Barker, T., and Britz, M. 2000. *Jokers Wild: Legalized Gambling in the Twenty-First Century.* Westport, CT: Praeger Publishers.

Beare, M., and Schneider, S. 1990. *Tracing of Illicit Funds: Money Laundering in Canada.* Working Paper for the Ministry of the Solicitor General of Canada. Ottawa, ON.

Bebbington, D.W. 2005. *The Dominance of Evangelicalism: The Age of Spurgeon and Moody*. In the series *A History of Evangelicalism: People, Movements and Ideas in the English-Speaking World*. Downers Grove: InterVarsity Press.

Beck, J. 1998. '100 Years of "Just Say No" versus "Just Say Know." Reevaluating Drug Education Goals for the Coming Century.' *Evaluation Review* 22: 15–45.

Beck, Ulrich. [German 1986] 1992. *The Risk Society: Towards a New Modernity*. London: Sage.

– 1995. Trans. Mark A. Ritter. *Ecological Enlightenment: Essays on the Politics of the Risk Society*. New Jersey: Humanities Press.

– 2003. 'Risk Society Revisited: Theory, Politics and Research Programmes.' In Barbara Adam, Ulrich Beck, and Joost Van Loon, eds., *The Risk Society and Beyond: Critical Issues for Social Theory*. London: Sage. 211–29.

Beck, Ulrich, Bonss, Wolfgang, and Lau, Christoph. 2003. 'The Theory of Reflexive Modernization: Problematic, Hypotheses and Research Programme.' *Theory, Culture & Society* 20(2): 1–33.

Beck, Ulrich, Giddens, Anthony, and Lash, Scott. 1994. *Reflexive Modernization: Politics, Tradition and Aesthetics in the Modern Social Order*. Cambridge: Polity Press.

Behiels, Michael. 1985. *Prelude to Quebec's Quiet Revolution: Liberalism versus Neo-Nationalism*. Montreal and Kingston: McGill-Queen's University Press.

Belanger, Yale D. 2006. *Gambling with the Future: The Evolution of Aboriginal Gaming in Canada*. Saskatoon: Purich Publishing.

Berdahl, L.Y. 1999. *Summary Report: The Impact of Gaming upon Canadian Non-Profits: A 1999 Survey of Gaming Grant Recipients*. (July). Calgary: Canada West Foundation.

Bergevin, T., Derevensky, J., Gupta, R., and Kaufman, F. 2005. *Adolescent Problem Gambling: Understanding the Role of Stress and Coping*. Unpublished material, McGill University.

Black, D.W., Moyer, T., and Schlosser, S. 2003. 'Quality of Life and Family History in Pathological Gambling.' *Journal of Nervous and Mental Disease* 191: 124–6.

Black, Errol. 1996. 'Gambling Mania: Lessons from the Manitoba Experience.' *Canadian Public Administration* 39(1): 49–61.

Blaszczynski, A. 1985. 'Pathological Gambling: Illness or Myth?' In Jan McMillen, ed., *Gambling in the 80s. Proceedings of the Inaugural Conference of the National Association of Gambling Studies*, Griffith University, Brisbane, Australia.

Blaszczynski, A., Ladouceur, R., and Shaffer, H.J. 2004. 'The Reno Model: A Science-Based Framework for Responsible Gambling.' *Journal of Gambling Studies* 20(3): 301–7.

Blaszczynski, A., and McConaghy, N. 1989. 'The Medical Model of Pathological Gambling: Current Shortcomings.' *Journal of Gambling Behavior* 5: 42–52.

Blaszczynski, A., Sharpe, L., and Walker, M. 2001. *Assessment of the Impact of the Reconfiguration on Electronic Gaming Machines as Harm Minimisation Strategies for Problem Gambling. Report for the Gaming Industry Operators Group.* University of Sydney.

Blaszczynski, A., and Steel, Z. 1998. 'Personality Disorders among Pathological Gamblers.' *Journal of Gambling Studies* 11: 195–220.

Borrell, J. 2004. 'Alcohol Consumption and Problem Gambling as Forms of Resistance.' *International Journal of Mental Health and Addiction* 2(1): 29–34.

– 2005. 'The Implications of Values in Gambling Research.' Presented at the conference *Public Policy Implications of Gambling Research,* University of Alberta (Sponsored by Alberta Gaming Research Institute), 22 March. Available: http://www.abgaminginstitute.ualberta.ca/2005_program.cfm. Accessed 26 March 2005.

Borrell, Jennifer, and Boulet, Jacques. 2007. 'Values, Objectivity, and Bias in Gambling Research.' In Garry Smith, David C. Hodgins, and Robert J. Williams, eds., *Research and Measurement Issues in Gambling Studies.* Burlington, MA: Academic Press. 568–92.

Bourdieu, Pierre. 1991. *Language and Symbolic Power.* Cambridge: Polity Press.

Bourdieu, Pierre, and Passeron, J.C. 1977. *Reproduction in Education, Society and Culture.* London: Sage.

Brady, Diane. 1993. 'Wheels of Fortune: Casino Due to Open in Windsor, Ontario.' *Maclean's* (12 July) 106(28): 64–5.

Branswell, B. 2002. 'Gamblers Try to Collect a Debt to Society.' *The Toronto Star,* 13 July, J4.

Breen, R., and Zimmerman, M. 2002. 'Rapid Onset of Pathological Gambling in Machine Gamblers.' *Journal of Gambling Studies* 18(1): 31–43.

Brennan, Richard. 2004. 'Addicted to Gambling Revenues: McGuinty Admits Ontario Relies on Gaming Profits.' *The Toronto Star,* 3 November, A2.

British Columbia Lottery Corporation. 2002. *2001–2002 Annual Report.* Kamloops, BC.

Brodeur, J., and Ouellet, G. 2004. 'What Is a Crime? A Secular Answer.' In N. DesRosiers and S. Bittle, eds., *What Is a Crime? Defining Criminal Conduct in Contemporary Society.* Vancouver: UBC Press.

Byrne, A., Gupta, R., and Derevensky, J. 2004. 'Internet Gambling in Canadian Youth.' Paper presented at the annual meeting of the National Council on Problem Gambling, Phoenix.

Caillois, R. 2001. *Man, Play and Games.* Urbana and Chicago: University of Illinois Press.

Caldwell, G., Haig, B., Dickerson, M., and Sylvan, L., eds. *Gambling in Australia*. Sydney: Croom Helm.

Calgary Police Service. 1996. *Current Practices and Policing Issues Related to Calgary Casinos.* Report prepared for the Calgary Police Commission, Calgary, AB.

Campbell, Colin. 1991. 'Gambling in Canada.' In M. Jackson and C. Griffiths, eds., *Canadian Criminology: Perspectives on Crime and Criminality.* Toronto: Harcourt, Brace, Jovanovich.

– 1994. *Canadian Gambling Legislation: The Social Origins of Legalization.* Unpublished doctoral dissertation, Simon Fraser University, Burnaby, BC.

– ed. 1994. *Gambling in Canada: The Bottom Line.* Criminology Research Centre, School of Criminology, Simon Fraser University, Burnaby, BC.

– 1997. 'Under the Halo of Good Causes.' In W.R. Eadington and J.A. Cornelius, eds., *Gambling: Public Policies and the Social Sciences.* Reno: Institute for the Study of Gambling and Commercial Gaming. 607–19.

– 2000. *Non-profits and Gambling Expansion: The British Columbia Experience.* (December). Calgary: Canada West Foundation.

– 2003. 'Gambling, Globalization and British Columbia, Canada.' Paper presented at the International Academic Symposium on Community Governance and Citizen Participation, Shanghai Administrative Institute, Shanghai, China, October.

Campbell, Colin S., and Lowman, John, eds. 1988. *Gambling in Canada: Golden Goose or Trojan Horse? Proceedings of the First National Symposium on Lotteries and Gambling.* Burnaby, BC: School of Criminology, Simon Fraser University.

Campbell, C.S., and Ponting, J.R. 1984. 'The Evolution of Casino Gambling in Alberta, Canada.' *Canadian Public Policy* 10(2): 142–55.

Campbell, C.S., and Smith, G.J. 1998. 'Canadian Gambling: Trends and Public Policy Issues.' *Annals of the American Academy of Political and Social Science* 556: 22–35.

– 2003. 'Gambling in Canada – From Vice to Disease to Responsibility: A Negotiated History.' *Canadian Bulletin of Medical History* 20(1): 121–49.

Campbell, C.S., Smith, G., and Hartnagel, T. 2005. *The Legalization of Gambling and Its Consequences: A Cross-National Comparison.* Ottawa: Law Commission of Canada.

Canada. 2004. *Proceedings of the Standing Senate Committee on Legal and Constitutional Affairs.* (1–2 December). Available: http://www.parl.gc.ca/38/1/parlbus/commbus/senate/Com-e/lega-e/03evb-e.htm?Language. Accessed 10 January 2005.

Canada Safety Council. 2004. *Gambling Problems Risk Further Neglect.* Canadian Safety Council Newsletter. 17 December. Available: http://www.safety-

council.org/news/media/releases/2005/june22-gambling.html. Accessed 20 February 2005.
– 2005. 'Canadian Roulette.' Available: http://www.safety-council.org/info/community/gambling.html. Accessed 6 January 2005.
Canada West Foundation. 1997. *Gambling in the Public Interest?* Calgary.
– 2001. *Gambling in Canada 2001: An Overview.* Calgary.
Canadian Broadcasting Corporation. 2004. 'Put Curbs on Casinos, Safety Council Urges.' Available: http://www.cbc.ca/story/canada/national/2004/12/16/safety-gambling041216.html. Accessed 3 January 2005.
– 2008. 'Problem Gamblers Hit Ontario with $3.5 B Lawsuit.' Available: http://www.cbc.ca/consumer/story/2008/06/11/gambling-lawsuit.html. Accessed 28 July 2008.
Canadian Tax Foundation. 2004. *Tax 101: The Facts Behind the Issues.* Available: http://www.ctf.ca/tax101/tax101.asp. Accessed 8 February 2005.
Carroll, K.M. 1997. 'Integrating Psychotherapy and Pharmacotherapy to Improve Drug Abuse Outcomes.' *Addictive Behaviors* 22: 233–45.
Castellani, Brian. 2000. *Pathological Gambling: The Making of a Medical Problem.* Albany: State University of New York Press.
Centre for International Economics. 2001. *Gaming Machine Revenue at Risk: The Impact of Three Proposed Modifications to Gaming Machines in NSW.* Report for the NSW Gaming Industry Operators Group. Centre for International Economics, Canberra and Sydney.
Chevalier, S., Deguire, A.E., Gupta R., and Derevensky, J. 2003. 'Jeux de hasard et d'argent.' In B. Perron and J. Loiselle, eds., *Où en sont les jeunes face au tabac, à l'acool, aux drogues et au jeu? Enquête québécoise sur le tabagisme chez les élèves su secondaire.* Québec: Institut de la statistique du Québec. 175–203.
Chevalier, S., and Papineau, E. 2004. *The Measurement of the Gambling Offer.* Proceedings of Insight Nova Scotia: International Problem Gambling Conference, Halifax, Nova Scotia.
Chung, Andrew. 2005a. 'Gambling Council under Fire.' *The Toronto Star,* 26 March, A16.
– 2005b. 'Casino High Rollers Hit Freebie Jackpot.' *The Toronto Star,* 10 December, A1.
Clotfelter, C.T., and Cook, P.J. 1989. *Selling Hope: State Lotteries in America.* Cambridge, MA: Harvard University Press.
Cohen, L., and Felson, M. 1979. 'Social Change and Crime Rate Trends: A Routine Activities Approach.' *American Sociological Review* 44: 588–608.
Collins, Alan F. 1996. 'The Pathological Gambler and the Government of Gambling.' *History of the Human Sciences* 9(3): 69–100.

Collins, Peter. 2003. *Gambling and the Public Interest*. Westport, CT: Praeger Books.

– 2003b. 'The Moral Case for Legalizing Gambling.' In G. Reith, ed., *Gambling: Who Wins? Who Loses?* Amherst, NY: Prometheus Books. 322–33.

Cook, S.A. 1995. *Through Sunshine and Shadow: The Woman's Christian Temperance Union, Evangelicalism, and Reform in Ontario, 1874–1930*. Montreal and Kingston: McGill-Queen's University Press.

Cornish, D., and Clarke, R., eds. 1986. *The Reasoning Criminal: Rational Choice Perspectives on Offending*. New York: Springer.

Corrigan, Philip, and Sayer, Derek. 1985. *The Great Arch: English State Formation as Cultural Revolution*. Oxford: Blackwell.

Cosgrave, James F., ed. 2006. *The Sociology of Risk and Gambling Reader*. New York: Routledge.

Cosgrave, Jim, and Klassen, Thomas R. 2001. 'Gambling against the State: The State and the Legitimation of Gambling.' *Current Sociology* 49(5): 1–22.

CPRG (Canadian Partnership for Responsible Gambling). 2007. *Canadian Gambling Digest 2005–2006*. Canadian Partnership for Responsible Gambling. Available: http://www.cprg.ca/articles/Canadian_Gambling_Digest_2005_2006.pdf. Accessed 20 March 2008.

Criminal Intelligence Service Canada. 1999 and 2000. *Annual Reports*. Available: http://www.cisc.gc.ca/Annualreport2000/illegalgaming2000.htm.

Crofts, P. 2002. *Gambling and Criminal Behavior: An Analysis of Local and District Court Files*. Report prepared for the Casino Community Benefit Fund, Sydney, Australia.

Dean, Mitchell. 1999. *Governmentality: Power and Rule in Modern Society*. London: Sage.

Della Sala, Vincent. 2004. 'Les Jeux Sont Fait? The State and Legalized Gambling.' Working Paper, Trent University, School of International Studies. February.

Denning, P., and Little, J. 2001. 'Harm Reduction in Mental Health: The Emerging Work of Harm Reduction Psychotherapy.' *Harm Reduction Communication* 11: 7–10.

Derevensky, J.L., and Gupta, R. 1996. 'Risk Taking and Gambling Behavior among Adolescents: An Empirical Examination.' Paper presented at the Tenth National Conference on Gambling Behavior, Chicago, IL, September.

– 2000. 'Prevalence Estimates of Adolescent Gambling: A Comparison of SOGS-RA, DSM-IV-J, and the GA 20 Questions.' *Journal of Gambling Studies* 16: 227–52.

– 2004. 'Adolescents with Gambling Problems: A Synopsis of Our Current Knowledge.' *eGambling: The Electronic Journal of Gambling Issues* 10.

– 2007. 'Internet Gambling amongst Adolescents: A Growing Concern.' *International Journal of Mental Health and Addictions* 5(2): 93–101.

Derevensky, J.L., Gupta, R., and Della-Cioppa, G. 1996. 'A Developmental Perspective of Gambling Behavior in Children and Adolescents.' *Journal of Gambling Studies* 12: 49–66.

Derevensky, J., Gupta, R., Dickson, L., and Deguire, A-E. 2001. *Prevention Efforts toward Minimizing Gambling Problems.* Report prepared for the National Council for Problem Gambling, Center for Mental Health Services (CMHS), and the Substance Abuse and Mental Health Services Administration (SAMHSA), Washington, DC.

Derevensky, J., Gupta, R., Hardoon, K., Dickson, L., and Deguire, A-E. 2003. 'Youth Gambling: Some Social Policy Issues.' In G. Reith, ed., *Gambling: Who Wins? Who Loses?* New York: Prometheus Books. 239–57.

Derevensky, J., Gupta, R., Messerlian, C., and Gillespie, M. 2004. 'Youth Gambling Problems: A Need for Responsible Social Policy.' In J. Derevensky and R. Gupta, eds., *Gambling Problems in Youth: Theoretical and Applied Perspectives.* New York: Kluwer Academic/Plenum Publishers. 231–52.

Derevensky, J.L., Gupta, R., and Winters, K. 2003. 'Prevalence Rates of Youth Gambling Problems: Are the Current Rates Inflated?' *Journal of Gambling Studies* 19: 405–25.

Derevensky, J., Pratt, L., Hardoon, K., and Gupta, R. 2005. *The Relationship between Gambling Problems and Impulsivity among Adolescents: Some Preliminary Data and Thoughts.* Unpublished manuscript, McGill University.

Devereux, Edward. 1949. *Gambling and the Social Structure.* PhD thesis, Harvard University.

Devine, H., Purvis, G., Harris, E., and Payette, T. 2004. Letter re: Invitation to Provide Feedback regarding New Directions for Gaming in Nova Scotia, 17 September (letter provided by the Directors of Addiction Services in Nova Scotia to a request by the Nova Scotia Gaming Corporation to respond to a paper entitled 'New Directions for Gaming in Nova Scotia,' which set out the Corporation's plans for responsible gaming).

Dickerson, M. 2003. *Exploring the Limits of 'Responsible Gambling': Harm Minimization or Consumer Protection?* Proceedings of the 12th Annual Conference of the National Association for Gambling Studies, Melbourne.

– 2004. *Measurement and Modeling of Impaired Control: Implications for Policy.* Proceedings of Insight Nova Scotia: International Problem Gambling Conference, Halifax, Nova Scotia.

Dickson, L.M., Derevensky, J.L., and Gupta, R. 2002. 'The Prevention of Gambling Problems in Youth: A Conceptual Framework.' *Journal of Gambling Studies* 18: 97–159.

- 2004. 'Youth Gambling Problems: A Harm Reduction Prevention Model.' *Addiction Research and Theory* 12(4): 305–16.
- 2008. 'Youth Gambling Problems: An Examination of Risk and Protective Factors.' *International Gambling Studies* 8: 25–47.
DiClemente, C.C. 1999. 'Prevention and Harm Reduction for Chemical Dependency: A Process Perspective.' *Clinical Psychology Review* 19: 173–86.
DiClemente, C.C., Delahanty, J., and Schlundt, D. 2004. 'A Dynamic Process Perspective on Gambling Problems.' In J. Derevensky and R. Gupta, eds., *Gambling Problems in Youth: Theoretical and Applied Perspectives*. New York: Kluwer Academic/Plenum Publishers. 145–64.
DiClemente, C.C., Story, M., and Murray, K. 2000. 'On a Roll: The Process of Initiation and Cessation of Problem Gambling among Adolescents.' *Journal of Gambling Studies* 16: 289–313.
Dixon, D. 1991. *From Prohibition to Regulation: Bookmaking, Anti-Gambling, and the Law*. Oxford: Oxford University Press.
Dombrink, J. 1996. 'Gambling and the Legalisation of Vice: Social Movements, Public Health and Public Policy in the United States.' In Jan McMillen, ed., *Gambling Cultures: Studies in History and Interpretation*. London: Routledge. 43–63.
Donovan, Kevin. 2005. 'Gaming Officials Demand Casino Shape Up: Niagara Isn't Earning Enough.' *The Toronto Star*, 14 March, A1.
Doughney, J. 2002. *The Poker Machine State: Dilemmas in Ethics, Economics and Governance*. Melbourne: Common Ground Publishing.
- 2007. 'Lies, Damned Lies and "Problem Gambling" Prevalence Rates: The Example of Victoria.' *Journal of Business Systems, Governance and Ethics* 2(1): 41–54.
Douglas, Mary. 1966. *Purity and Danger: An Analysis of Concepts of Pollution and Taboo*. London: Routledge and Kegan Paul.
- 1992. *Risk and Blame: Essays in Cultural Theory*. London: Routledge.
Douglas, Mary, and Wildavsky, Aaron. 1982. *Risk and Culture: An Essay on the Selection of Technological and Environmental Dangers*. Berkeley, CA: University of California Press.
Downes, David, Davies, B.P., David, M.E., and Stone, P. 1976. *Gambling, Work and Leisure: A Study across Three Areas*. London: Routledge and Kegan Paul.
Drury, E.C. 1966. *Farmer Premier: Memoirs of the Honourable E.C. Drury*. Toronto: McClelland and Stewart.
Durkheim, Emile. 1992. *Professional Ethics and Civic Morals*. Trans. Cornelia Brookfield. London: Routledge.
Duty of Care Inc. 2005. *International Pokies Impact Conference*. Adelaide, Novem-

ber. Available: http://www.dutyofcare.org.au/ipic/main.html. Accessed 16 November 2005.

Eadington, W.R. 1994. 'Casinos in Canada: Policy Challenges in the 1990s.' In C. Campbell, ed., *Gambling in Canada: The Bottom Line*. Criminology Research Centre, Simon Fraser University. 3–16.

– 1996. 'Ethical and Policy Considerations in the Spread of Commercial Gambling.' In Jan McMillen, ed., *Gambling Cultures: Studies in History and Interpretation*. London: Routledge. 243–62.

– 1997. 'Understanding Gambling.' In W.R. Eadington and J.A. Cornelius, eds., *Gambling: Public Policies and the Social Sciences*. Reno: Institute for the Study of Gambling and Commercial Gaming. 3–9.

– 2003. 'Research Challenges around Gambling: What We Need to Know and How to Get There.' Presentation to the Alberta Gaming Research Institute, Edmonton, AB, 24 November.

– 2003b. 'Values and Choices: The Struggle to Find Balance with Permitted Gambling in Modern Society.' In Gerda Reith, ed., *Gambling: Who Wins? Who Loses?* Amherst, NY: Prometheus Books. 31–48.

Eadington, William R., and Cornelius, J.A., eds. 1997. *Gambling: Public Policies and the Social Sciences*. Reno: Institute for the Study of Gambling and Commercial Gaming.

Ewald, Francois. 2002. 'The Return of Descartes's Malicious Demon: An Outline of a Philosophy of Precaution.' In Tom Baker and Jonathan Simon, eds., *Embracing Risk: The Changing Culture of Insurance and Responsibility*. Chicago: University of Chicago Press. 273–301.

Eyerman, Ron. 2006. 'Performing Opposition or, How Social Movements Move.' In J.C. Alexander, B. Giesen, and J. Mast, eds., *Social Performance: Symbolic Action, Cultural Pragmatics, and Ritual*. Cambridge: Cambridge University Press.

Fabian, Anne. 1990. *Card Sharps, Dream Books and Bucket Shops: Gambling in 19th Century America*. Ithaca, NY: Cornell University Press.

Fairbrother, M. 2003. 'The Freedom of the State: Recent NDP Governments and a Reply to the Globalization Sceptics.' *Canadian Review of Sociology and Anthropology* 40(3): 311–29.

Felsher, J., Derevensky, J., and Gupta, R. 2003. 'Parental Influences and Social Modeling of Youth Lottery Participation.' *Journal of Community and Applied Social Psychology* 13: 361–77.

– 2004. 'Lottery Playing amongst Youth: Implications for Prevention and Social Policy.' *Journal of Gambling Studies* 20: 127–54.

Felson, M. 1994. *Crime and Everyday Life*. Thousand Oaks: Pine Forge Press.

Ferguson, R. 2007. 'Liberals Nix Inquiry into "Lottogate": Tory Says McGuinty

Trying to "Cover Up" Background on Troubled Lottery Agency.' *The Toronto Star*, 17 April, A7.

Ferris, J., Wynne, H., and Single, E. 1999. *Measuring Problem Gambling in Canada*. Phase I, Final Report to the Inter-Provincial Task Force on Problem Gambling, April.

Fisher, S. 1992. 'Measuring Pathological Gambling in Children: The Case of Fruit Machines in the U.K.' *Journal of Gambling Studies* 8: 263–85.

– 1993. 'Gambling and Pathological Gambling in Adolescents.' *Journal of Gambling Studies* 9: 277–88.

– 1999. 'A Prevalence Study of Gambling and Problem Gambling Adolescents.' *Addiction Research* 7: 509–38.

Fortin, Ghislain. 1996. 'Les casinos au Québec.' *Canadian Public Administration* 39(1): 62–9.

Foucault, Michel. 1991. 'Governmentality.' In Graham Burchell, Colin Gordon, and Peter Miller, eds., *The Foucault Effect: Studies in Governmentality*. Chicago: University of Chicago Press. 87–104.

Fraser, Brian J. 1988. *The Social Uplifters: Presbyterian Progressives and the Social Gospel in Canada, 1875–1915*. Waterloo: Wilfrid Laurier University Press.

Gambling Review Report (Britain). 2001. London: Stationery Office.

Garmezy, N., Masten, A.S., and Tellegen, A. 1984. 'The Study of Stress and Competence in Children: A Building Block for Developmental Psychopathology.' *Child Development* 55: 97–111.

Gazel, R., Rickman, D., and Thompson, W. 2001. 'Casino Gambling and Crime: A Panel Study of Wisconsin Counties.' *Managerial and Decision Economics* 22: 65–75.

Geisst, C. 2002. *Wheels of Fortune: The History of Speculation from Scandal to Respectability*. Hoboken: John Wiley and Sons.

Gephart, Robert B., Jr. 2001. 'Safe Risk in Las Vegas.' *Management* 4(3): 141–58.

Giddens, Anthony. 1991. *Modernity and Self-Identity*. Stanford: Stanford University Press.

Goffman, Erving. 1967. 'Where the Action Is.' In Erving Goffman, ed., *Interaction Ritual*. Garden City, NY: Anchor Books. 149–270.

Goodman, R. 1995. *The Luck Business*. New York: Martin Kessler Books.

Gottdenier, Mark, Collins, Claudia C., and Dickens, David R. 2000. *Las Vegas: The Social Production of an All-American City*. Malden, MA: Basil Blackwell.

Gottfredson, M., and Hirschi, T. 1990. *A General Theory of Crime*. Palo Alto: Stanford University Press.

Government of New Brunswick. 2007. *Responsible Management, Responsible Play in a Responsible Environment: A Responsible Approach to Gaming in New Brunswick*. Available: www.gnb.ca. Accessed 19 March 2008.

Grant, J.E., Chamber, R.A., and Potenza, M. 2004. 'Adolescent Problem Gambling: Neurodevelopment and Pharmacological Treatment.' In J. Derevensky and R. Gupta, eds., *Gambling Problems in Youth: Theoretical and Applied Perspectives*. New York: Kluwer Academic/Plenum Publishers. 81–98.

Griffiths, M.D. 1990. 'The Acquisition, Development, and Maintenance of Fruit Machine Gambling in Adolescents.' *Journal of Gambling Studies* 6: 193–204.

– 1995. *Adolescent Gambling*. London: Routledge.

– 1999. 'The Psychology of the Near Miss (Revisited): A Comment on Delfabbro and Weinfield 1999.' *British Journal of Psychology* 90: 441–5.

Griffiths, M.D., and Wood, R.T.A. 2000. 'Risk Factors in Adolescence: The Case of Gambling, Videogame Playing, and the Internet.' *Journal of Gambling Studies* 16: 199–225.

– 2004. 'Youth and Technology: The Case of Gambling, Videogame Playing and the Internet.' In J. Derevensky and R. Gupta, eds., *Gambling Problems in Youth: Theoretical and Applied Perspectives*. New York: Kluwer Academic/ Plenum Publishers. 101–20.

Grinols, Earl. 2003. 'Cutting the Cards and Craps: Right Thinking about Gambling Economics.' In G. Reith, ed., *Gambling: Who Wins? Who Loses?* Amherst, NY: Prometheus Books. 67–87.

Gupta, R., and Derevensky, J.L. 1997. 'Familial and Social Influences on Juvenile Gambling Behavior.' *Journal of Gambling Studies* 13: 179–92.

– 1998a. 'Adolescent Gambling Behavior: A Prevalence Study and Examination of the Correlates Associated with Excessive Gambling.' *Journal of Gambling Studies* 14: 319–45.

– 1998b. 'An Empirical Examination of Jacobs' General Theory of Addictions: Do Adolescent Gamblers Fit the Theory?' *Journal of Gambling Studies* 14: 17–49.

– 2000. 'Adolescents with Gambling Problems: From Research to Treatment.' *Journal of Gambling Studies* 16: 315–42.

– 2004. 'A Treatment Approach for Adolescents with Gambling Problems.' In J. Derevensky and R. Gupta, eds., *Gambling Problems in Youth: Theoretical and Applied Perspectives*. New York: Kluwer Academic/Plenum Publishers. 165–88.

– 2008. 'A Treatment Approach for Adolescents with Gambling Problems.' In M. Zangeneh, A. Blaszczynski, and N. Turner, eds., *In the Pursuit of Winning: Problem Gambling Theory, Research and Treatment*. New York: Springer Books. 271–90.

Gupta, R., Derevensky, J., and Marget, N. 2004. 'Coping Strategies Employed by Adolescents with Gambling Problems.' *Child and Adolescent Mental Health* 9(3): 115–20.

Halpern, M. 2001. *And on that Farm He Had a Wife: Ontario Farm Women and Feminism, 1900–1970*. Montreal and Kingston: McGill-Queen's University Press.

Hannigan, John. 1999. 'Gambling on Fantasy: Las Vegas, Casinos and Urban Development.' In *Fantasy City: Pleasure and Profit in the Postmodern Metropolis*. New York: Routledge. 151–72.

– 2007. 'Casino Cities.' *Geography Compass* 1(4): 959–75.

Hardoon, K., and Derevensky, J. 2002. 'Child and Adolescent Gambling Behavior: Our Current Knowledge.' *Clinical Child Psychology and Psychiatry* 7(2): 263–81.

Hardoon, K., Derevensky, J., and Gupta, R. 2001. 'Social Influences Involved in Children's Gambling Behavior.' *Journal of Gambling Studies* 17(3): 191–215.

– 2002. *An Examination of the Influence of Familial, Emotional, Conduct and Cognitive Problems, and Hyperactivity upon Youth Risk-Taking and Adolescent Gambling Problems*. Report prepared for the Ontario Problem Gambling Research Centre, Ontario.

Hardoon, K., Gupta, R., and Derevensky, J. 2004. 'Psychosocial Variables Associated with Adolescent Gambling: A Model for Problem Gambling.' *Psychology of Addictive Behaviors* 18(2): 170–9.

Hayward, D., and Kliger, B. 2002. *Breaking a Nasty Habit: Gaming Policy and Politics in the State of Victoria*. Melbourne: Institute of Social Research, Swinburne University of Technology.

Henrikson, L.E. 1996. 'Hardly a Quick Fix: Casino Gambling in Canada.' *Canadian Public Policy* 22(2): 116–28.

Henry, R.R. 2001. 'Making Modern Citizens: The Construction of Masculine Middle-Class Identity on the Canadian Prairies, 1890–1920.' In R. Wardhaugh, ed., *Toward Defining the Prairies: Region, Culture and History*. Winnipeg: University of Manitoba Press.

High Court of Australia. 2008. *Betfair Pty Ltd and Matthew Edward Erseg vs State of Western Australia*. Canberra: High Court of Australia. Available: http://www.austlii.edu.au/au/cases/cth/HCA/2008/11.html. Accessed 28 March 2008.

Hirschi, T. 1969. *Causes of Delinquency*. Berkeley: University of California Press.

Hodgins, D.C., Currie, S.R., and el-Guebaly, N. 2001. 'Motivational Enhancement and Self-Help Treatments for Problem Gambling.' *Journal of Consulting and Clinical Psychology* 69: 50–7.

Hodgins, D.C., and el-Guebaly, N. 2000. 'Natural and Treatment-Assisted Recovery from Gambling Problems: A Comparison of Resolved and Active Gamblers.' *Addiction* 95: 777–89.

Hofstadter, R. 1960. *The Age of Reform*. New York: Vintage Books.

– 1966. *Anti-intellectualism in American Life.* New York: Vintage Books.

Hutchinson, Brian. 1999. *Betting the House: Winners, Losers, and the Politics of Canada's Gambling Obsession.* Toronto: Viking.

Huxley, J., and Carroll, D. 1992. 'A Survey of Fruit Machine Gambling in Adolescence.' *Journal of Gambling Studies* 8: 167–79.

Independent Gaming Authority. 2004. *Inquiry into the Management of Gaming Machine Numbers.* Independent Gaming Authority. Available: http://www.iga.sa.gov.au/publications.html. Accessed 16 November 2005.

Independent Pricing and Regulatory Tribunal (IPART). 2004. 'Promoting a Culture of Responsibility. Review into Gambling Harm Minimisation Measures.' Sydney: Independent Pricing and Regulatory Tribunal. Available: http://www.dgr.nsw.gov.au/gaming_rcg_ipart.asp.

International Gambling Studies. 2007. 'Forum.' 7(2): 233–52.

Ivison, John. 2008. 'Ottawa Targets Gaming: Native Reserve Hosts Illegal Online Poker Sites.' *National Post,* 5 March. Available: www.nationalpost.com/news. Accessed 5 March 2008.

Jackson, A.C., Thomas, S.A., Ross, L., and Kearney, E. 2000. *Analysis of Clients Presenting to Problem Gambling Counselling Services July 1999 to June 2000, Client and Services Analysis: Report No 6.* Melbourne: Department of Human Services.

Jacobs, D.F. 2004. 'Youth Gambling in North America: An Analysis of Long Term Trends and Future Prospects.' In J. Derevensky and R. Gupta, eds., *Gambling Problems in Youth: Theoretical and Applied Perspectives.* New York: Kluwer Academic/Plenum Publishers. 1–26.

Jacobs, D.R., Marston, A.R., Singer, R.D., Widaman, K., Little, T., and Veizades, J. 1989. 'Children of Problem Gamblers.' *Journal of Gambling Behavior* 5: 261–7.

Jessor, R., ed. 1998. *New Perspectives on Adolescent Risk Behavior.* Cambridge: Cambridge University Press.

Kaufman, F., Derevensky, J., and Gupta, R. 2002. 'The Relationship between Life Stresses, Coping Styles and Gambling Behavior among Adolescents.' Poster presented at the annual meeting of the National Council on Problem Gambling, Dallas, June.

Kelley, R., Todosichuk, P., and Azmier, J. 2001. 'Gambling@Home: Internet Gambling in Canada.' Gambling in Canada Research Report No. 16 (October). Calgary: Canada West Foundation.

Kennedy, L., and Forde, D. 1990. 'Routine Activities and Crime.' *Criminology* 28: 101–15.

Kent, G. 2000. 'Ex-Gaming Boss Charged by RCMP.' *Edmonton Journal,* A, no. 14.

Kiedrowski, J. 2001. *Native Gaming and Gambling in Canada.* A report prepared for the Department of Indian and Northern Affairs, Ottawa, ON.

Kingma, S. 1996. 'A Sign of the Times: The Political Culture of Gaming in the Netherlands.' In Jan McMillen, ed., *Gambling Cultures: Studies in History and Interpretation.* London: Routledge. 199–222.

– 1997. '"Gaming Is Play, It Should Remain Fun!" The Gaming Complex, Pleasure and Addiction.' In P. Sulkunen, J. Holmwood, H. Radner, and G. Schulze, eds., *Constructing the New Consumer Society.* London: Macmillan.

– 2004. 'Gambling and the Risk Society: The Liberalisation and Legitimation Crisis of Gambling in the Netherlands.' *International Gambling Studies* 4(1): 47–67.

Klassen, Thomas R., and Cosgrave, J. 2002. 'Look Who's Addicted to Gambling Now.' *Policy Options* 23(5): 43–6.

KPMG Consulting. 2002. *Problem Gambling. ATM/EFTPOS Functions and Capabilities.* Department of Families and Community Services, Canberra.

KPMG Management Consulting. 1995. *One-year Review of Casino Windsor.* Report prepared for the Ontario Casino Corporation, Toronto, ON.

Labrosse, Michel. 1985. *The Lottery ... From Jacques Cartier's Day to Modern Times.* Montreal: Stanke.

Ladd, G., and Petry, N.M. 2002. 'Disordered Gambling among University-Based Medical and Dental Patients: A Focus on Internet Gambling.' *Psychology of Addictive Behaviors* 16: 76–9.

Ladouceur, R., Boisvert, J-M., Pepin, M., Loranger, M., and Sylvain, C. 1994. 'Social Cost Pathological Gambling.' *Journal of Gambling Studies* 10: 399–409.

Ladouceur, R., Bouchard, C., Rhéaume, N., Jacques, C., Ferland, F., Leblond, J., and Walker, M. 2000. 'Is the SOGS an Accurate Measure of Pathological Gambling among Children, Adolescents and Adults?' *Journal of Gambling Studies* 16(1): 1–21.

Ladouceur, R., Sylvain, C., Letarte, H., Giroux, I., and Jacques, C. 1998. 'Cognitive Treatment of Pathological Gamblers.' *Behaviour Research and Therapy* 36: 1111–20.

Ladouceur, R., and Walker, M. 1998. 'Cognitive Approach to Understanding and Treating Pathological Gambling.' In A.S. Bellack and M. Hersen, eds., *Comprehensive Clinical Psychology.* New York: Pergamon.

Lane, Terry. 2005. 'Beating the Pokies in South Carolina.' *The National Interest,* 7 August. Available: http://www.abc.net.au/rn/talks/natint/stories/s1431069.htm. Accessed 31 March 2008.

Langhinrichsen-Rohling, J., Rhode, P., Seely, J.R., and Rohling, M.L. 2004. 'Individual, Family and Peer Correlates of Adolescent Gambling.' *Journal of Gambling Studies* 20: 23–46.

Laycock, David. 1990. *Populism and Democratic Thought in the Canadian Prairies, 1910 to 1945*. Toronto: University of Toronto Press.

Leiss, William. 2001. *In the Chamber of Risks: Understanding Risk Controversies*. Montreal: McGill-Queen's University Press.

Lesieur, H. 1998. 'Costs and Treatment of Pathological Gambling.' *Annals of the American Academy* 556: 38–47.

Lesieur, H.R., Cross, J., Frank, M., Welch, M., White, C.M., Rubenstein, G., Moseley, K., and Mark, M. 1991. 'Gambling and Pathological Gambling among University Students.' *Addictive Behaviors* 16: 517–27.

Lipton, M. 2003. 'Internet Gaming in Canada.' Presentation to the Global Gaming Exposition, Las Vegas, 1 September. Available: http://www.eljlaw.com/print/pub_internet_gaming.html. Accessed 20 December 2005.

Lipton, M., and Weber, K. 2005. *The Legality of Internet Gaming in Canada*. Proceedings of the 4th Annual Alberta Conference on Gambling Research. Calgary: Alberta Gaming Research Institute.

Livingstone, C. 2001. 'The Social Economy of Poker Machine Gambling in Victoria.' *International Gambling Studies* 1(1): 45–66.

Livingstone, C., and Woolley, R. 2007. 'Risky Business: A Few Provocations on the Regulation of Electronic Gaming Machines.' *International Gambling Studies* 7(3): 361–76.

– 2008. 'The Relevance and Role of Gaming Machine Games and Game Features on the Play of Problem Gamblers.' Adelaide: Independent Gambling Authority. Available: http://www.iga.sa.gov.au.

Loto-Québec. 2006. *Annual Report*. Montreal.

Luckinbill, D. 1977. 'Criminal Homicide as a Situated Transaction.' *Social Problems* 25: 176–86.

Lupton, Deborah. 1995. *The Imperative of Health: Public Health and the Regulated Body*. London: Sage.

– 1999. *Risk*. London: Routledge.

Lupton, Deborah, and Petersen, Alan. 1997. *The New Public Health: Health and Self in the Age of Risk*. London: Sage.

Lussier, I., Derevensky, J., Gupta, R., Bergevin, T., and Ellenbogen, S. 2007. 'Youth Gambling Behaviors: An Examination of the Role of Resilience.' *Psychology of Addictive Behaviors* 21: 165–73.

Lyng, Stephen, ed. 2005. *Edgework: The Sociology of Risk-Taking*. New York: Routledge.

MacPherson, I. 1979. *Each for All: A History of the Co-operative Movement in English Canada, 1900–1945*. Toronto: Macmillan of Canada.

Magoon, M., Gupta, R., and Derevensky, J. (in press). 'Juvenile Delinquency and Adolescent Gambling: Implications for the Juvenile Justice System.' *Criminal Justice and Behavior*.

Mandal, V.P., and Vander Doelen, C. 1999. *Chasing Lightning: Gambling in Canada*. Toronto: United Church Publishing House.

Marin, André. 2007. *A Game of Trust: Ombudsman Report Investigation into the Ontario Lottery and Gaming Corporation's Protection of the Public from Fraud and Theft*. Toronto: Ombudsman of Ontario.

Marshall, D., McMillen, J., Doran, B., and Neimeyer, S. 2004. *Gaming Machine Accessibility and Use in Suburban Canberra: A Detailed Analysis of the Tuggeranong Valley*. Canberra: ACT Gambling and Racing Commission.

Marshall, Katherine. 1998. 'The Gambling Industry: Raising the Stakes.' *Perspectives* (Winter). Cat. no. 75-001-XPE, 7–11. Ottawa: Statistics Canada.

– 2003. *Fact Sheet on Gambling, Perspectives on Labour and Income*. Cat. no. 75-001-XIE, June. Ottawa: Statistics Canada.

Martin's Annual Criminal Code. 2005. Aurora: Canada Law Book.

Mason, J.L., and Nelson, M. 2001. *Governing Gambling*. New York: Century Foundation Press.

Mauss, M. 1985. 'A Category of the Human Mind: The Notion of Person, the Notion of Self.' Trans. W.D. Halls. In M. Carrithers and S. Lukes, eds., *The Category of the Person: Anthropology, Philosophy, History*. Cambridge: Cambridge University Press.

– 1990. *The Gift*. Trans. W.D. Halls. London: Routledge.

– 2001. *A General Theory of Magic*. London: Routledge.

McClung, Nellie. n.d. [1914?]. 'International Peace.' In J.S. Woodsworth, ed., *Studies in Rural Citizenship*. Winnipeg: Canadian Council of Agriculture.

McDonald, R. 1998. 'Legalized Gambling and Its Potential Impact on Police Services.' Paper presented to the 9th annual Canadian Association of Police Boards Conference, August, Edmonton, AB.

McFarlane, S., and Roach, R. 1999. 'Strings Attached: Non-Profits and Their Funding Relationships with Government.' Alternative Service Delivery Project Research Bulletin No. 4 (September). Calgary: Canada West Foundation.

McGowan, R.A. 2001. *Government and the Transformation of the Gaming Industry*. Cheltenham, UK: Edward Elgar.

McGurrin, M. 1991. *Pathological Gambling: Conceptual, Diagnostic, and Treatment Issues*. Sarasota: Professional Resource Press.

McKenna, Peter. 2008. *Terminal Damage: The Politics of VLTs in Atlantic Canada*. Halifax, NS: Fernwood Books.

McLaren, A. 1997. *The Trials of Masculinity: Policing Sexual Boundaries, 1870–1930*. Chicago: University of Chicago Press.

McMillen, J. 1993. *Risky Business: A Political Economy of Australian Casino Development*. Unpublished PhD thesis, University of Queensland, Brisbane, Australia.

– 1996a. 'Gambling as an Industry.' In M. Cathcart and Kate Darian-Smith, eds., *Place Your Bets: Gambling in Victoria*. Australian Centre, University of Melbourne. 49–70.

– 1996b. 'Risky Ventures: Casino Regulation in a Changing Market.' In J. McMillen, M. Walker, and S. Sturevska, eds., *Lady Luck in Australia*. Sydney: Sydney University Printing Press. 73–98.

– ed. 1996c. *Gambling Cultures: Studies in History and Interpretation*. London: Routledge.

– 1996d. 'From Glamour to Grind: The Globalisation of Casinos.' In Jan McMillen, ed., *Gambling Cultures: Studies in History and Interpretation*. London: Routledge. 263–87.

– 1997a. 'Social Priorities in Gaming Policy. Case Studies from Two Australian States.' In W. Eadington and J. Cornelius, eds., *Public Policy, The Social Sciences and Gambling*. Reno: Institute for the Study of Gambling and Commercial Gaming, University of Nevada. 103–26.

– 1997b. 'Market Competition: A Sound Foundation for Gambling Policy?' In G. Coman, ed., *Responsible Gambling: Towards 2000. Proceedings of the 1997 NAGS Conference*. National Association for Gambling Studies, Melbourne, Australia. 247–58.

– 1998. *Study into the Impacts of the Auckland and Christchurch Casinos*. New Zealand Casino Control Authority, Wellington, New Zealand.

– 2000a. *Comparative Study of the Social and Economic Impacts of the Brisbane and Cairns Casinos 1996–98*. Report to the Australian Research Council, Canberra, Australia.

– 2000b. *Gambling Regulatory Regimes: A Review of the Regulatory Structures, Powers and Processes Governing Australia's Gambling Industries*. Australian Institute for Gambling Research, University of Western Sydney, Sydney, Australia.

– 2000c. 'Online Gambling: Challenges to Regulation and National Sovereignty.' *Prometheus* 18(4): 391–401.

– 2003. 'Online Gambling.' In J. Forder and P. Quirk, eds., *E-commerce and Law*. 2nd Ed. Brisbane: Wiley Jacaranda. 406–45.

– 2003b. 'From Local to Global Gambling Cultures.' In Gerda Reith, ed., *Gambling: Who Wins? Who Loses?* Amherst, NY: Prometheus Books. 49–63.

– 2005a. 'Why Study Gambling? Reflections on the Past 20 Years.' In G. Coman, ed., *Proceedings of the 14th Annual National Association for Gambling Studies Conference*. Melbourne: National Association for Gambling Studies.

– 2005b. 'Problem Gambling: Prevalence, Impacts and Prevention.' *Proceedings of the South African Regulators' Symposium*. Livingstone, Zambia.

– 2006. 'Trends in Gambling Regulation: Rationales, Risks and Responses.' In

Law, Regulation and Control Issues of the Asian Gaming Industry. Macau: University of Macau. 14–38.

McMillen, J., and Doran, B. 2006. 'Problem Gambling and Gaming Machine Density: Socio-Spatial Analysis of Three Victorian Localities.' *International Gambling Studies* 6(1): 4–37.

McMillen, J., and Eadington, W.E. 1986. 'The Evolution of Gambling Laws in Australia.' *New York Journal of International and Comparative Law* 8(1): 167–82.

McMillen, J., Marshall, D., Ahmed, E., and Wenzel, M. 2004b. 'Victorian Longitudinal Community Attitudes Survey.' Melbourne: Gambling Research Panel. Available: http://www.justice.vic.gov.au.

McMillen, J., and Masterman-Smith, H. 2000. *The Methodology Report*. Report to the Victorian Local Governance Association. Australian Institute for Gambling Research, University of Western Sydney, Sydney, Australia.

McMillen, J., Murphy, L., and Marshall, D. 2004. *The Use of ATMs in ACT Gaming Venues: An Empirical Study*. Report to the ACT Gambling and Racing Commission. ANU Centre for Gambling Research, Canberra, Australia.

McMillen, J., O'Hara, J., and Woolley, R. 1999. *Australian Gambling: Comparative History and Analysis*. Victorian Casino and Gaming Authority.

McMillen, J., and Pitt, S. 2005. 'Review of the ACT Government's Harm Minimisation Measures.' Canberra: Centre for Gambling Research, Australian National University. Available: http://www.gamblingandracing.act.gov.au/Publications/Research/htm.

McMillen, J., and Wenzel, M. 2006. 'Measuring Problem Gambling: Validation of Three Prevalence Screens.' *International Gambling Studies* 6(2): 147–74.

McMillen, J., and Woolley, R. 2000. 'Money Laundering in Australian Casinos.' *Proceedings of the 3rd Gambling Regulation Conference*, Australian Institute for Criminology, Canberra, Australia.

McMillen, J., and Wright, J. 2008. 'Re-regulating the Gambling Industry: Regulatory Reform in Victoria and New South Wales, 1999–2006.' *Australian Journal of Political Science* 43(2): 277–300.

McMullen, J., and Perrier, D. 2007. 'The Security of Gambling and Gambling with Security: Hacking, Law Enforcement and Public Policy.' *International Gambling Studies* 7(1): 43–58.

Meekison, P.J. 2000. *Relocation of and Changes to Existing Gaming Facilities in British Columbia: Review and Recommendations*. Victoria: Ministry of Labour. 31 January.

Messerlian, C., Derevensky, J., and Gupta, R. 2004. 'A Public Health Perspective for Youth Gambling: A Prevention and Harm Minimization Framework.' *International Gambling Studies* 4(2): 147–60.

Miers, David. 2003. 'A Fair Deal for the Player?: Regulation and Competition

as Guarantors of Consumer Protection in Commercial Gambling.' In G.
Reith, ed., *Gambling: Who Wins? Who Loses?* Amherst, NY: Prometheus
Books. 155–72.

– 2004. *Regulating Commercial Gambling: Past, Present and Future.* London:
Oxford University Press.

Miles, Malcolm, and Miles, Steven. 2004. *Consuming Cities.* Basingstoke: Pal-
grave Macmillan.

Miller, W.R., Brown, J.M., Simpson, T.L., Handmaker, N.S., Bien, T.H., Luckie,
L.F., Montgomery, H.A., Hester, R.K., and Tonigan, J.S. 1995. 'What Works?
A Methodological Analysis of the Alcohol Treatment Outcomes Literature.'
In R.K. Hester and W.R. Miller, eds., *Handbook of Alcohol Treatment
Approaches: Effective Alternatives.* Boston, MA: Allyn and Bacon. 12–44.

Mishra, R. 1999. 'After Globalization: Social Policy in an Open Economy.' *Canadian Review of Social Policy* 43: 13–28.

Moodie, L. 2002. 'Ontario's Organized Crime Section – Illegal Gambling Unit:
Its Evolution and Accomplishments.' Paper presented at the Alberta Gam-
ing Research Institute's Gambling, Law Enforcement and Justice System
Issues conference, March, Edmonton, AB.

Morton, Suzanne. 2003. *At Odds: Gambling and Canadians: 1919–1969.* Toronto:
University of Toronto Press.

Mun, Wing Phil. 2002. *Calculated Risk-Taking: The Governance of Casino Gambling
in Ontario.* PhD thesis, University of Toronto.

Munting, R. 1996. *An Economic and Social History of Gambling in Britain and the
USA.* Manchester: Manchester University Press.

Nathan, P. 2001. 'Best Practices for the Treatment of Gambling Disorders: Too
Soon.' Paper presented at the annual Harvard–National Center for Responsible Gambling conference, Las Vegas, December.

National Gambling Impact Study Commission. 1999. *Final Report.* Washington,
DC: Government Printing Office.

National Research Council. 1999. *Pathological Gambling: A Critical Review.* Washington, DC: National Academy Press.

Neal, P., Delfabbro, P., and O'Neil, M. 2005. 'Problem Gambling and Harm: A
National Definition.' Melbourne: Gambling Research Australia. Available:
http://www.gamblingresearch.org.au/CA256DB1001771FB/page/GRA
+Research+Reports.

Neary, Mike, and Taylor, Graham. 1998. 'From the Law of Insurance to the Law
of Lottery: An Exploration of the Changing Composition of the British State.'
Capital and Class 65: 55–72.

Neville, Gwen Kennedy. 1994. *The Mother Town: Civic Ritual, Symbol, and Experience in the Borders of Scotland.* Oxford: Oxford University Press.

Nibert, David. 2000. *Hitting the Lottery Jackpot: Government and the Taxing of Dreams*. New York: Monthly Review Press.

Noel, S.J.R. 1990. *Patrons, Clients, Brokers: Ontario Society and Politics, 1791–1896*. Toronto: University of Toronto Press.

Norris, A. 2002a. 'VLT Kings Rake in Millions from Addicts: Profits from Lax Quebec Permits Policy.' *The Gazette* (Montreal), 22 September, A1.

– 2002b. 'How the Link Was Made: Gazette Did Analysis Based on Postal Codes.' *The Gazette* (Montreal), 30 September, A15.

Nova Scotia Gaming Corporation Annual Report 2004–05. Halifax, NS: Nova Scotia Gaming Corporation.

Nower, L., and Blaszczynski, A. 2004. 'A Pathways Approach to Treating Youth Gamblers.' In J. Derevensky and R. Gupta, eds., *Gambling Problems in Youth: Theoretical and Applied Perspectives*. New York: Kluwer Academic/Plenum Publishers. 189–210.

Nower, L., Derevensky, J.L., and Gupta, R. 2004. 'The Relationship of Impulsivity, Sensation Seeking, Coping and Substance Use in Youth Gamblers.' *Psychology of Addictive Behaviors* 18: 49–55.

Nower, L., Gupta, R., Blaszczynski, A., and Derevensky, J. 2004. 'Suicidality Ideation and Depression among Youth Gamblers: A Preliminary Examination of Three Studies.' *International Gambling Studies* 4(1): 69–80.

Nye, F. 1958. *Family Relationships and Delinquent Behavior*. New York: Wiley.

O'Hara, J. 1988. *A Mug's Game: The History of Gambling in Australia*. Sydney: University of New South Wales Press.

Ohmae, K. 1991. *The Borderless World*. New York: Harper.

Ontario Attorney General. 1961. *Report of the Attorney General's Committee on Enforcement of the Law Relating to Gambling*. Toronto: Queen's Printer.

Ontario Casino Corporation. 1999. *Annual Report 1998–1999*. Toronto: Queen's Printer.

Ontario Lottery and Gaming Corporation. 2002. *Annual Report 2001–02*. Toronto: Queen's Printer.

– 2007. *Annual Report 2005–6*. Toronto: Queen's Printer.

Orr, S. 1999. 'Exploring Alternatives: Government Social Policy and Non-Profit Organizations.' Alternative Service Delivery Project (August). Calgary: Canada West Foundation.

Osborne, J.A. 1995. 'Canadian Criminal Law.' In M. Jackson and C. Griffiths, eds., *Canadian Criminology: Perspectives on Crime and Criminality*. 2nd Ed. Toronto: Harcourt Brace. 273–306.

Osborne, J., and Campbell, C. 1988. 'Recent Amendments to Canadian Lottery and Gaming Laws: The Transfer of Power between Federal and Provincial Governments.' *Osgoode Hall Law Journal* 26(1): 19–43.

Palmer, B. 1979. *A Culture in Conflict: Skilled Workers and Industrial Capitalism in Hamilton, Ontario, 1860–1914.* Montreal and Kingston: McGill-Queen's University Press.

Palmer, B., and Kealey, G.S. 1982. *Dreaming of What Might Be: The Knights of Labor in Ontario, 1880–1900.* Cambridge: Cambridge University Press.

Patrick, T. 2001. 'No Dice: Violations of the Criminal Code's Gaming Exemptions by Provincial Governments.' *Criminal Law Quarterly* 44: 108–26.

Peele, Stanton. 2003. 'Is Gambling an Addiction like Drug and Alcohol Addiction? Developing Realistic and Useful Conceptions of Compulsive Gambling.' In Gerda Reith, ed., *Gambling: Who Wins? Who Loses?* Amherst, NY: Prometheus Books. 208–18.

Petry, N.M. 2005. *Pathological Gambling: Etiology, Comorbidity, and Treatment.* Washington, DC: American Psychological Association Press.

Pierce, P.A., and Miller, D. 2004. *Gambling Politics: State Government and the Business of Betting.* London: Lynne Rienner Publishing.

– 2007. 'Legalized Gambling: The Diffusion of a Morality Policy.' In Garry Smith, David C. Hodgins, and Robert J. Williams, eds., *Research and Measurement Issues in Gambling Studies.* Burlington, MA: Academic Press. 593–615.

Piscitelli, F., and Albanese, J. 2000. 'Do Casinos Attract Criminals? A Study at the Canadian–US Border.' *Journal of Contemporary Criminal Justice* 16: 445–56.

Polanyi, K. 2001 [1944]. *The Great Transformation: The Political and Economic Origins of Our Time.* Boston: Beacon Press.

Preston, Frederick W., Shapiro, Paul D., and Reid Keene, Jennifer. 2007. 'Successful Aging and Gambling: Predictors of Gambling Risk among Older Adults in Las Vegas.' *American Behavioral Scientist* 51(1): 102–21.

Productivity Commission. 1999. 'Australia's Gambling Industries, Report No. 10.' Canberra: AusInfo. Available: http://www.pc.gov.au/inquiry/gambling/finalreport/index/html. Accessed 21 December 2006.

Proke, L. 1994. 'When Legalized Gambling Comes to Your Community: Legalized Gambling and Its Effects on Law Enforcement.' *The Police Yearbook* 53: 54–61.

Puxley, C. 2008. 'First Nations Get $3B from Gaming Revenue: Ontario Chiefs Sign 25-year Deal for Share of Casino, Lottery Money.' *The Toronto Star*, 8 February, A17.

Queensland Government. 2005. *Australian Gambling Statistics 1973/74–2003/04.* Brisbane: Queensland Government Office of Economic and Statistical Research.

Queensland Government Treasury. 2002. 'Queensland Household Gambling

Survey 2001.' Brisbane: Queensland Government Treasury. Available: http://www.qogr.qld.gov.au.

– 2008. 'Australian Gambling Statistics 1980–81 to 2005–06: 24th Edition 2007.' Brisbane: Queensland Government Treasury.

– n.d. 'Queensland Responsible Gambling Strategy: A Partnership Approach.' Available: http://www.responsiblegambling.qld.gov.au. Accessed 12 December 2006.

Queensland Responsible Gambling Strategy. Available: http://responsiblegambling.org.au. Accessed 16 November 2005.

Raffensperger, Carol, et al. 1998. 'Final Wingspread Precautionary Principle Statement.' *Implementing the Precautionary Principle Conference.* Wisconsin: Johnson Foundation.

Raylu, N., and Oei, T.P.S. 2002. 'Pathological Gambling: A Comprehensive Review.' *Clinical Psychology Review* 22: 1009–61.

Reiss, A. 1951. 'Delinquency as the Failure of Personal and Social Controls.' *American Sociological Review* 16: 196–207.

Reith, Gerda. 1999 [2002]. *The Age of Chance: Gambling in Western Culture.* London: Routledge.

– 2003. 'Pathology and Profit: Controversies in the Expansion of Legal Gambling.' In G. Reith ed., *Gambling: Who Wins? Who Loses?* Amherst, NY: Prometheus Books. 9–28.

– 2005. 'On the Edge: Drugs and the Consumption of Risk in Late Modernity.' In Stephen Lyng, ed., *Edgework: The Sociology of Risk-Taking.* New York: Routledge. 227–45.

Responsible Gambling Council of Ontario (RGCO). 2002a. *It's Only a Game: The Responsible Gambling Handbook.* Toronto: RGCO.

– 2002b. *Responsible Gambling in Canada: A Shared Pursuit.* Toronto: RGCO.

Roach, R. 2000. 'Building Better Partnerships: Improving Relations between Governments and Non-Profits.' Alternative Service Delivery Project Research Bulletin (September). Calgary: Canada West Foundation.

Romei, S. 2005. 'Punters Are Mugs in the Online Betting War.' *The Australian,* October.

Roncek, D., and Maier, P. 1991. 'Bars, Blocks and Crimes Revisited.' *Criminology* 29: 725–53.

Room, R., Turner, N., and Ialomiteanu, A. 1999. 'Community Effects of the Opening of the Niagara Casino.' *Addiction* 94(10): 1449–66.

Rose, I. Nelson. 1988. 'Compulsive Gambling and the Law: From Sin to Vice to Disease.' *Journal of Gambling Behaviour* 4(4): 240–60.

– 1998. 'Final Wingspread Precautionary Principle Statement.' *Implementing the Precautionary Principle Conference.* Wisconsin: Johnson Foundation.

– 2003. 'Gambling and the Law©: The New Millennium.' In G. Reith, ed., *Gambling: Who Wins? Who Loses?* Amherst, NY: Prometheus Books. 113–31.
– 2003a. *Gambling and the Law©: Status of Gambling Laws.* Available: www. gamblingandthelaw.com.
– 2005. *Internet Gaming: U.S. Beats Antigua in WTO.* The Brief Addiction Science Information Source, 14 September. Division of Addictions, Cambridge Health Alliance, Harvard Medical School. Available: http://www.basisonline. org.

Rose, Nikolas. 1993. 'Government, Authority and Expertise in Advanced Liberalism.' *Economy and Society* 22(3): 282–300.
– 1996. 'The Death of the Social? Re-figuring the Territory of Government.' *Economy and Society* 25(3): 327–56.
– 1999. *Powers of Freedom: Reframing Political Thought.* Cambridge: Cambridge University Press.

Rugle, L., Derevensky, J., Gupta, R., Winters, K., and Stinchfield, R. 2001. *The Treatment of Problem and Pathological Gamblers.* Report prepared for the National Council for Problem Gambling, Center for Mental Health Services (CMHS), and the Substance Abuse and Mental Health Services Administration (SAMHSA), Washington, DC.

S.A. (Government of South Australia) Department of Health. 2007. 'Gambling Patterns in South Australia: October to December 2005.' Adelaide: S.A. Department of Health.

Sacco, V., and Kennedy, L. 1994. *The Criminal Event.* Scarborough: Nelson Canada.

Sahlins, M. 1972. *Stone Age Economics.* Chicago: Aldine.

Saskatchewan Provincial Auditor. 2001. *Fall Report,* vol. 2. Regina, SK.

Schaps, E., DiBartolo, R., Moskowitz, J., Palley, C.S., and Churgin, S. 1981. 'A Review of 127 Drug Abuse Prevention Program Evaluations.' *Journal of Drug Issues* 11: 17–43.

Schellinck, T., and Schrans, T. 2000. *2000 Nova Scotia Video Lottery Players Follow-up Survey.* Halifax: Nova Scotia Department of Health.
– 2003. *2003 Nova Scotia Gambling Prevalence Study Highlights.* Halifax: Nova Scotia Department of Health.
– 2005. *A Framework for a Global Gambling Strategy, Responsible Gambling, Public Policy and Research: The Halifax Model.* Proceedings of the 4th Annual Alberta Conference on Gambling Research. Calgary: Alberta Gaming Research Institute.

Schrans, T., Schellinck, T., and Walsh, G. 2000. *Technical Report: 2000 Regular VL Players Follow Up: A Comparative Analysis of Problem Development and Resolu-*

tion. Focal Research Consultants, Ltd. Available: http://www.gov.ns.ca/health/downloads/VLPlayers_Technical_Report.pdf.

Schwartz, David. 2003. *Suburban Xanadu: The Casino Resort on the Las Vegas Strip and Beyond.* New York: Routledge.

– 2006. *Roll the Bones: A History of Gambling.* New York: Gotham Books.

Seelig, M.Y., and Seelig, J.H. 1998. 'Place Your Bets! On Gambling, Government and Society.' *Canadian Public Policy* 24: 91–106.

Shaffer, H.J., and Hall, M.N. 1996. 'Estimating Prevalence of Adolescent Gambling Disorders: A Quantitative Synthesis and Guide toward Standard Gambling Nomenclature.' *Journal of Gambling Studies* 12: 193–214.

Shaffer, Howard. 2004. 'The Extent to which Gambling Is a Recent Area of Study.' www.thewager.org (now defunct).

Skolnick, J. 1979. 'The Dilemmas of Regulating Casino Gambling.' *Journal of Social Issues* 35(3): 129–43.

– 2003. 'Regulating Vice: America's Struggle with Wicked Pleasures.' In G. Reith, ed., *Gambling: Who Wins? Who Loses?* Amherst, NY: Prometheus Books. 311–21.

Slater, Don, and Tonkiss, Fran. 2001. *Market Society: Markets and Modern Social Theory.* Oxford: Polity Press.

Smith, G. 1997. *Gambling and the Public Interest?* (November). Calgary: Canada West Foundation.

Smith, G., Hodgins, D.C., and Williams, R.J. 2007. *Research and Measurement Issues in Gambling Studies.* London: Elsevier.

Smith, G., and Wynne, H. 1999. *Gambling and Crime in Western Canada: Exploring Myth and Reality.* Calgary: Canada West Foundation.

– 2000. *A Review of the Gambling Literature in the Economic and Political Domains.* Prepared for the Alberta Gaming Research Institute, Edmonton, AB.

– 2004. *VLT Gambling in Alberta.* Edmonton: Alberta Gaming Research Institute.

Smith, G., Wynne, H., and Hartnagel, T. 2003. *Examining Police Records to Assess Gambling Impacts: A Study of Gambling-Related Crime in the City of Edmonton.* Report prepared for the Alberta Gaming Research Institute, Edmonton, AB.

Smith, J. 1998. *Gambling Taxation in Australia.* Australian Tax Research Foundation. Research Study No. 32. Sydney, Australia.

South Australian Centre for Economic Studies. 2005. *Study of the Effect of Caps on Electronic Gaming Machines.* Prepared for the Victorian Gambling Research Panel. Available: http://www.justice.vic.gov.au/CA2569020010922A/page/Gaming+and+Racing-Research?OpenDocument&1=0-Gaming+and+Racing~&2=0-Research~&3=~. Accessed 16 November 2005.

Statistics Canada. 2002. 'Taking a Chance?' *Perspectives*. Cat. no. 75–011-XPE. Ottawa: Statistics Canada.

– 2007. 'Perspectives on Labour and Income: Gambling.' Cat. no. 75-001-XIE, May. Available: www.statcan.ca/english/freepub/75–001-XIE/comm/ 01.pdf. Accessed 19 March 2008.

– various years. *Provincial Economic Accounts*. Cat. no. 13-213-PPB. Ottawa: Statistics Canada.

Ste-Marie, C., Gupta, R., and Derevensky, J. 2006. 'Anxiety and Social Stress Related to Adolescent Gambling Behavior and Substance Use.' *Journal of Child and Adolescent Substance Use* 16: 55–74.

Stinchfield, R. 2000. 'Gambling and Correlates of Gambling among Minnesota Public School Students.' *Journal of Gambling Studies* 16: 153–73.

Stinchfield, R., and Winters, K.C. 1998. 'Gambling and Problem Gambling among Youth.' *Annals of the American Academy of Political and Social Sciences*, 556: 172–85.

Stokowski, P. 1996. *Riches and Regrets: Betting on Gambling in Two Colorado Mountain Towns*. Niwor, CO: University Press of Colorado.

St Petersburg Times. 2008. 'Union Calls for Softer Gambling Law.' #1355(19), 11 March. Available: www.times.spb.ru. Accessed 24 March 2008.

Strange, S. 1996. *The Retreat of the State*. Cambridge: Cambridge University Press.

Teeple, G. 1995. *Globalization and the Decline of Social Reform*. Aurora, ON: Garamond Press.

Tesoriero, Heather Won, and Martinez, Barbara. 2005. 'Lone Holdout Forces Mistrial on Vioxx, Forcing Merck to Try the Case Again.' *The Globe and Mail* (Toronto), 13 December, B14.

Thompson, J.H. 1982. '"The Beginning of Our Regeneration": The Great War and Western Canadian Reform Movements.' In R.D. Francis and H. Palmer, eds., *The Prairie West: Historical Readings*. Edmonton: Pica Pica Press.

Thompson, W.N. 1997. *Legalized Gambling*. Santa Barbara, CA: ABC-CLIO.

Thorne, D. 2002. 'Quebec Lawsuit a Warning to Alta. Researcher.' *Newscan* 4(16), 19 April. Available: http://www.responsiblegambling.org/articles/ 041902_16.pdf. Accessed 8 February 2005.

Titmuss, R.M. 1970. *The Gift Relationship: From Human Blood to Social Policy*. London: Allen and Unwin.

Toby, J. 1957. 'Social Disorganization and Stake in Conformity.' *Journal of Criminal Law, Criminology and Police Science* 48: 12–17.

Toneatto, T. 1999. 'Cognitive Psychopathology of Problem Gambling.' *Substance Use and Misuse* 34: 1593–604.

Toneatto, T., and Ladouceur, R. 2003. 'Treatment of Pathological Gambling: A

Critical Review of the Literature.' *Psychology of Addictive Behaviors* 42: 92–9.

Toronto Star. 2004. 'Editorial: Ontario Ignoring Its Gambling Addicts.' 22 December 2004, A26. Available: www.torontostar.com.

Turner, Victor. 1988. *The Anthropology of Performance*. New York: PAJ Publications.

Vaillancourt, F., and Roy, A. 2000. 'Gambling and Governments in Canada, 1969–1998: How Much? Who Pays? What Payoff?' *Canadian Tax Foundation* (Special Studies in Taxation and Public Finance) 2.

Valverde, M. 1991. *The Age of Light, Soap and Water: Moral Reform in English Canada, 1885–1925*. Toronto: McClelland and Stewart.

Verlik, K. 2005. 'The Role of Social Responsibility Management in the Alberta Gaming Policy and Regulatory Framework.' Presented at the conference *Public Policy Implications of Gambling Research*, University of Alberta (Sponsored by Alberta Gaming Research Institute), 22 March. Available: http://www.abgaminginstitute.ualberta.ca/2005_program.cfm. Accessed 26 October 2005.

Victorian Casino and Gaming Authority (Australia). 1996–2000. Available: http://www.vcgr.vic.gov.au/CA256F800017E8D4/Statistics/36AB8 1950861EF0BCA25701C004FF69C.

Victorian Local Governance Association (VLGA). 2002. 'Gambling: Counting the Costs. Research for Local Governments on Assessing the Community Impacts of Gambling.' Melbourne: Victorian Local Governance Association.

Vitaro, F., Ferland, F., Jacques, C., and Ladouceur, R. 1998. 'Gambling, Substance Use, and Impulsivity during Adolescence.' *Psychology of Addictive Behaviors* 12: 185–94.

Vitaro, F., Wanner, B., Ladouceur, R., Brendgen, M., and Tremblay, R.E. 2004. 'Trajectories of Gambling during Adolescence.' *Journal of Gambling Studies* 20: 47–69.

Voisey, P. 1988. *Vulcan: The Making of a Prairie Community*. Toronto: University of Toronto Press.

Volberg, Rachel A. 2001. *When the Chips Are Down*. New York: Century Foundation Press.

– 2003. 'Has There Been a Feminization of Gambling and Problem Gambling in America?' *Electronic Journal of Gambling Issues: eGambling* 8, feature article.

Wacquant, L.D. 1989. 'Toward a Reflexive Sociology: A Workshop with Pierre Bourdieu.' *Sociological Theory* 7: 26–63.

Walden, K. 1997. *Becoming Modern in Toronto: The Industrial Exhibition and the Shaping of a Late Victorian Culture*. Toronto: University of Toronto Press.

Walker, M. 1996. 'The Medicalisation of Gambling as an "Addiction."' In Jan McMillen, ed., *Gambling Cultures: Studies in History and Interpretation*. London: Routledge. 223–42.

– 1997. 'The Impact of Casinos in Urban Centers on Problem Gambling.' In W. Eadington and J. Cornelius, eds., *Gambling: Public Policies and the Social Sciences*. Reno: Institute for the Study of Gambling and Commercial Gaming. 377–82.

– 1998. *Gambling Government: The Economic and Social Impacts*. Sydney: University of New South Wales Press.

Wallisch, L. 1993. *Gambling in Texas: 1992 Texas Survey of Adolescent Gambling Behavior*. Austin: Texas Commission on Drug and Alcohol Abuse.

Wear, Rae. 2000. 'Country Mindedness Revisited.' Paper presented at Australian Political Studies Association 2000 Conference, ANU Canberra, 3–6 October. Available: apsa2000.anu.edu.au/confpapers/wear.rtf. Accessed 15 March 2008.

Weber, Max. 1958. *The Protestant Ethic and the Spirit of Capitalism*. Trans. Talcott Parsons. New York: Charles Scribner's Sons.

Weinstein, D., and Deitch, L. 1974. *The Impact of Legalized Gambling: The Socio-Economic Consequences of Lotteries and Off-Track Betting*. New York: Praeger.

Wenzel, M., McMillen J., Marshall D., and Ahmed, E. 2004. *Validation of the Victorian Gambling Screen*. Gambling Research Panel. Available: http://www.justice.vic.gov.au/CA2569020010922A/page/Gaming+and+Racing-Research?OpenDocument&1=0-Gaming+and+Racing~&2=0-Research~&3=~. Accessed 16 November 2005.

Werner, E. 2005. 'McCain Takes Aim at Off-Reservation Gambling.' Associated Press article in *USA Today,* 29 June. Available: http://www.usatoday.com/news/washington/2005–06–28-mccain-gaming_x.htm?csp=34. Accessed 20 December 2005.

Westhead, R. 2005. 'Lottery Agency Forces CFL to Ban Sponsor.' *The Toronto Star*, 26 November.

Will, George F. 1999. 'Hooked on Gambling: Other Comment.' *Herald Tribune*, 26–7 June.

Williams, Robert, and Wood, Robert. 2004. *Final Report: The Demographic Sources of Ontario Gaming Revenue*. Guelph, ON: Ontario Problem Gambling Research Centre.

– 2005. *Proportion of Gaming Revenue Derived from Problem Gamblers*. Presentation to the Alberta Gaming Research Institute Conference on Public Policy Implications on Gambling Research, Edmonton, AB, 31 March to 1 April.

– 2007. 'The Proportion of Ontario Gambling Revenue Derived from Problem Gamblers.' *Canadian Public Policy* 33(3): 367–87.

Winters, K.C., and Anderson, N. 2000. 'Gambling Involvement and Drug Use among Adolescents.' *Journal of Gambling Studies* 16: 175–98.

Winters, K.C., Stinchfield, R., Botzet, A., and Anderson, N. 2002. 'A Prospective Study of Youth Gambling Behaviors.' *Psychology of Addictive Behaviors* 16: 3–9.

Winters, K.C., Stinchfield, R., and Fulkerson, J. 1993. 'Patterns and Characteristics of Adolescent Gambling.' *Journal of Gambling Studies* 9: 371–86.

Winters, K.C., Stinchfield, R., and Kim, L.G. 1995. 'Monitoring Adolescent Gambling Behavior in Minnesota.' *Journal of Gambling Studies* 11: 165–83.

Woodsworth, James Shaver. 1972 [1911]. *My Neighbour*. Toronto: University of Toronto Press.

– ed. n.d. [1914?]. *Studies in Rural Citizenship*. Winnipeg: Canadian Council of Agriculture.

Wynne, H.J., Smith, G.J., and Jacobs, D.F. 1996. *Adolescent Gambling and Problem Gambling in Alberta*. Edmonton: Alberta Alcohol and Drug Abuse Commission.

Wynne Resources. 1998. *Adult Gambling and Problem Gambling in Alberta, 1998*. Report prepared for the Alberta Alcohol and Drug Abuse Commission, Edmonton, AB.

Yealland, B. 2005. 'Research and the Public Voice: Shedding Light on Gambling Policy.' Presented at the conference *Public Policy Implications of Gambling Research*, University of Alberta (Sponsored by Alberta Gaming Research Institute), 21 March. Available: http://www.abgaminginstitute.ualberta.ca/2005_program.cfm. Accessed 26 October 2005.

York, Geoffrey. 2005. 'Turning Macau into a Temple for Gamblers.' *The Globe and Mail* (Toronto), 15 February, A1, A10.

Zimring, F., and Hawkins, G. 1973. *Deterrence*. Chicago: University of Chicago Press.

Index